Forging Transnational Belonging through Informal Trade

Analyzing informal trading practices and smuggling through the case study of Novi Pazar, this book explores how societies cope when governments no longer assume the responsibility for providing welfare to their citizens.

How do economic transnational practices shape one's sense of belonging in times of crisis/precarity? Specifically, how does the collapse of the Ottoman Empire – and the subsequent migration of the Muslim Slav population to Turkey – relate to the Yugoslav Succession Wars during the 1990s? Using the case study of Novi Pazar, a town in Serbia that straddles the borders of Montenegro, Serbia and Kosovo that became a smuggling hub during the Yugoslav conflict, the book focuses on that informal market economy as a prism through which to analyze the strengthening of existing relations between the émigré community in Turkey and the local Bosniak population in the Sandžak region.

Demonstrating the interactive nature of relations between the state and local and émigré communities, this book will be of interest to scholars and students interested in Southeastern Europe or the Yugoslav Succession Wars of the 1990s, as well as social anthropologists who are working on social relations and deviant behavior.

Sandra King-Savic is a postdoctoral fellow at the Center for Governance and Culture in Europe (GCE) at the University of St. Gallen (HSG). She served as a human rights educator for Amnesty International and conducted research for the Foreign Military Studies Office at the University of Kansas (KU) before receiving a Swiss National Foundation scholarship for her dissertation on the transversal relationship between migration and informal markets.

Southeast European Studies
Series Editor: Florian Bieber

The Balkans are a region of Europe widely associated over the past decades with violence and war. Beyond this violence, the region has experienced rapid change in recent times though, including democratization, economic and social transformation. New scholarship is emerging which seeks to move away from the focus on violence alone to an understanding of the region in a broader context drawing on new empirical research.

The Southeast European Studies Series seeks to provide a forum for this new scholarship. Publishing cutting-edge, original research and contributing to a more profound understanding of Southeastern Europe while focusing on contemporary perspectives the series aims to explain the past and seeks to examine how it shapes the present. Focusing on original empirical research and innovative theoretical perspectives on the region the series includes original monographs and edited collections. It is interdisciplinary in scope, publishing high-level research in political science, history, anthropology, sociology, law and economics and accessible to readers interested in Southeast Europe and beyond.

The Politics of Memory of the Second World War in Contemporary Serbia
Collaboration, Resistance and Retribution
Jelena Đureinović

Social Mobilization Beyond Ethnicity
Civic Activism and Grassroots Movements in Bosnia and Herzegovina
Chiara Milan

Memory Politics and Populism in Southeastern Europe
Edited by Jody Jensen

Forging Transnational Belonging through Informal Trade
Thriving Markets in Times of Crisis
Sandra King-Savic

For more information about this series, please visit: https://www.routledge.com/SoutheastEuropeanStudies/bookseries/ASHSER1390

Forging Transnational Belonging through Informal Trade

Thriving Markets in Times of Crisis

Sandra King-Savic

Routledge
Taylor & Francis Group
LONDON AND NEW YORK

First published 2021
by Routledge
2 Park Square, Milton Park, Abingdon, Oxon OX14 4RN

and by Routledge
52 Vanderbilt Avenue, New York, NY 10017

Routledge is an imprint of the Taylor & Francis Group, an informa business

British Library Cataloguing-in-Publication Data
A catalogue record for this book is available from the British Library

Library of Congress Cataloging-in-Publication Data
Names: King-Savic, Sandra, author.
Title: Forging transnational belonging through informal trade : thriving markets in times of crisis / Sandra King-Savic.
Description: Abingdon, Oxon ; New York, NY : Routledge, 2021. | Series: Southeast European studies | Includes bibliographical references and index.
Identifiers: LCCN 2020051436 (print) | LCCN 2020051437 (ebook) | ISBN 9780367900731 (hardback) | ISBN 9781003022381 (ebook)
Subjects: LCSH: Smuggling—Social aspects—Serbia—Novi Pazar. | Informal sector (Economics)—Serbia—Novi Pazar. | Transnationalism—Economic aspects—Serbia—Novi Pazar. | Muslims—Serbia—Novi Pazar—Social conditions. | Belonging (Social psychology)—Serbia—Novi Pazar. | Novi Pazar (Serbia)—Economic conditions. | Novi Pazar (Serbia)—Social conditions. | Serbia—Foreign economic relations—Turkey. | Turkey—Foreign economic relations—Serbia.
Classification: LCC HJ7015 .K56 2021 (print) | LCC HJ7015 (ebook) | DDC 382—dc23
LC record available at https://lccn.loc.gov/2020051436
LC ebook record available at https://lccn.loc.gov/2020051437

ISBN: 978-0-367-90073-1 (hbk)
ISBN: 978-0-367-75403-7 (pbk)
ISBN: 978-1-003-02238-1 (ebk)

DOI: 10.4324/9781003022381

The Open Access publication of this book has been published with the support of the Swiss National Science Foundation

Contents

Illustrations

Figures

Tables

Acknowledgements

There are a great many people who supported my research project, the result of which is this publication. I am deeply grateful to those individuals who participated in this research in and out of the field. The completion of this study would have been impossible without your willingness to invite me to your homes and into your lives.

The Center for Russian, East European and Eurasian Studies (CREES) at the University of Kansas (KU) initially enabled this research financially and logistically. My research was financed by a joint initiative between KU, the Foreign Military Studies Office (FMSO), and the Foreign Language and Area Studies (FLAS) scholarship. Just as important was the camaraderie among peers, including Austin Charron who supported me in the creation of a proper questionnaire. I received invaluable academic support from Mehrangiz Najafizadeh, who read countless drafts of my MA thesis which ultimately turned into a PhD dissertation and then this book. Eve Levin supported my efforts at securing funding, and Donald Stull introduced me to the art of doing anthropology.

The Department for Russian Culture and Society at the University of St. Gallen (HSG) enabled all subsequent research trips since 2013, including travel, room and board, and the administration of the questionnaires. Ulrich Schmid was not only an academic adviser but also turned into an important collaborator and friend. His advice and critical assessment of my work continues to shape my academic development.

The Basler Working Group on Southeastern Europe (BASO) invited me to present early chapter drafts and provided an invaluable and much-needed forum to discuss my research. Apart from being a friend, Nataša Mišković turned into an important mentor considering all things to do with Southeastern Europe.

I am grateful to Vladan Jovanović, with whom I discussed informal practices in the Western Balkans during a workshop on informality that was graciously hosted by the Centre for Advanced Studies in Sofia, Bulgaria. Our discussions continued together with Srdjan Korac at the Association for Nationalities conference in New York, and I am especially grateful to Christian Axboe Nielsen, whose helpful comments and questions improved the manuscript.

The historical colloquium at the University of St. Gallen, the IMISCOE 3CI PhD Winter School 'Migration and Urban Change', as well as members of the PhD

Peer Group at the University of St. Gallen provided critical insight and thoughts on migration, questions of identification, informal trade practices, memory and social space, and how these phenomena come together in times of precarity. I am indebted to Caspar Hirschi, Marco Martiniello, Sunčana Laketa, and Karen Lambrecht, who supported my thinking about this topic, and to Alice Froidevoix and her critical reading of the entire manuscript.

I am beholden to the Swiss National Foundation (SNF) for endowing me with the freedom to ruminate on questions regarding state failure, socialization processes, and informal markets between 2015 and 2018.

Introduction
Šverceri, people like you and me

It was July 2012,[1] and I was about to return to Novi Pazar, Serbia, illustrated in Figure 0.1.[2] Once on the public bus, I stowed away my luggage, settled into my seat, and awaited the bus ride ahead of me. By now, I was familiar with this route. I knew the bus would take about six hours to get from Belgrade to Novi Pazar and how to time the bathroom breaks according to the drivers' preferred places of rest. No surprises – until Čačak,[3] that is. After we had left the bus station, a burly man ran after the bus and motioned the driver to stop with a plastic bag. I guessed the man was middle-aged. He wore a blue tracksuit, a gray T-shirt, and house shoes. Heavy set, though quick on his feet, he got on the bus in a swoop, trailed by strong body odor. After sitting beside me and behind the bus driver, the man immediately apologized for smelling bad. "Sorry guys, I stink," he said. "I was just released from prison. They don't even let you take a shower there. They locked me up, *čoveče* [man]! Can you believe it?" he said to no one in particular. In all, there were about five other people on the bus, a couple of elderly men, a young woman, an even younger man, and an elderly lady. The heat felt suffocating. I looked around the bus to gauge the reaction among the other passengers; no one batted an eye. Nobody seemed to care, and neither did the man who had just been released from prison. He was not concerned with the other passengers, or if anybody had listened to his vociferous protest about his detention. After apologizing, he explained that *someone* had ratted him out. "I know the man who sold me out to the cops, too!" He then leaned over to the bus driver and asked:

> Do you remember how easy it was during the war? There was no red tape, we stuck together! Nobody sold you out to save their own skin. Now, they would sell their grandmother to save themselves! And I only trade legal goods, unlike the crook who sold me to the police – I only smuggle cigarettes, coffee and other legal stuff, not guns and drugs like that '*stoka*'![4]

After venting, the man borrowed the bus driver's mobile phone. "I need to make a phone call," the man said. He was obviously agitated when he spoke to the person on the other end of the receiver. "What do you mean you are calling a lawyer? Why?" he asked over and over. "It's not as if I murdered someone! *Čoveče božiji*!"[5] He paused and replied, "I am going to see that guy right away as

DOI: 10.4324/9781003022381-1

Figure 0.1 Sandžak region
Source: Map created by Lyubomyr Oliynyk, siteGist.co.

soon as I get back to Raška! That guy owes me some answers!" He repeated the last sentence after hanging up and sunk into silence.

Eventually, the bus ground to a halt. It was one of the bus driver's habitual resting spots. When the driver motioned the end of the break, all of us returned to our seats, except the man who had just been released from jail. "*Gdje je ovaj?*"[6] the bus driver asked. "The guy with the plastic bag and the house shoes? He hitched a ride on some guy's truck," someone in the back answered.

The burly man did not care one bit about who was on the bus, and the people on the bus found nothing strange in this episode either. *Šverc* (smuggling), in other words, was (is) not uncommon in Serbia; the people of Novi Pazar call the business of *šverc a javna tajna* – a public secret.[7]

Context and research setting

Novi Pazar was a hub of smuggling activities between 1991 and 1995. Tucked in between the southern hills of Serbia that border Montenegro and Kosovo, Novi Pazar was a thoroughfare for goods, and attracted shoppers, traders, and workers from nearby villages, as well as the greater area around Macedonia, Kosovo, Serbia, and Montenegro.

Due to the busy market activities, residents of Novi Pazar had at once a commonplace and yet distinct experience of the 1990s war years compared to other citizens of Serbia and those Bosniak and/or Muslim citizens who lived through the siege in Bosnia and Herzegovina (BiH). Like other citizens of Serbia, residents of Novi Pazar endured the internationally imposed sanctions. Living within Serbian state borders, however, spared this population from the hardship that Bosniaks of BiH experienced. At the same time, locals in Novi Pazar became benefactors of Turkish charity and development projects during the conflict and after the Yugoslav Succession Wars had ended, as was the case with citizens of Bosnia. This unique in- and out-of-state experience of the local community in Novi Pazar is at the core of this book. Smuggling – or *šverc*, as the practice is known locally – illustrates this in- and out-of-state experience. Because the informal market connects Novi Pazar to Bosnia, Turkey, and also to Serbia proper, I examine how informal transnational practices between 1991 and 1995 shaped this community's collective sense of belonging and social relations *locally* following the Yugoslav Succession Wars.

Throughout the first half of the 1990s, Novi Pazar experienced an economic boom for two reasons. First, Novi Pazar's state sponsored industry and biggest employer, the *Tekstilni Kombinat Raška* (Raška Textile Factory, TKS), collapsed due to the economic downturn and subsequent war in the Socialist Federal Republic of Yugoslavia (SFRY). Second, in order to safeguard their continued income, Bosniaks traveled between Turkey and Novi Pazar and utilized diaspora family connections to acquire material and fabrics for the production of jeans and other apparel with which they set up makeshift clothing factories in their homes, often hidden from officials. As a result, locals who had been employed by the TKS put their skills to use in the informal production of counterfeited clothing. Locals also sold food items, coffee, and cigarettes on the Novi Pazar market, also known as *buvljak*, to other Yugoslavs who traveled to the city in search of commodities that were in short supply and/or altogether inexistent elsewhere.

The twin processes of existing transnational relations with the local and diaspora community in Turkey, together with the internationally imposed sanctions, created a new class of successful traders in Novi Pazar. At the same time, employment and goods were difficult to come by in other areas of Serbia. Both Serbs and Bosniaks initially profited from this trade. James Lyon noted that "overnight, a new class of wealthy – both Serb and Bosniak – entrepreneurs sprang up, although many Serbs remained in low-paying state sector jobs."[8] In Novi Pazar, factories produced up to 30,000 pairs of counterfeit jeans a day that included brands such as Levi's, Diesel, and Reply.[9] Because of low wages and the relative ease of tax evasion, the cost of textile production dropped considerably. Residents of Sandžak thus started to capitalize on these advantages to set up textile, shoe, and leather manufacturing companies. Because of the general chaos of the war years, however, no reliable figures exist that could illustrate the exact revenue and production output. Be that as it may, analysts and scholars figure that "several hundred thousand pairs of jeans" and other apparel items were produced in the region while annual revenues were "between $50 and $100 million."[10] Sandžak, specifically Novi Pazar, attracted thousands of individuals that sought to work in the sprouting textile industry with its up to 500 factories by the end of the 1990s, according to Lyon.[11] Belgrade, too, capitalized on these relations by sending 'tax collectors' – commonly referred to as racketeers among the local population – to Novi Pazar.

Ironically, the end of the international sanctions regime also heralded the end of the booming market in Novi Pazar. In 2008, there were only some 50 firms left that produced up to 1 million pairs of jeans a year, and revenues dropped sharply, barely reaching 50,000 euros annually.[12] With the exception of the local fish hatchery *Vojin Popov*,[13] Novi Pazar's formative industries of cement, textile, and battery manufacturing have not revitalized markedly at the time of writing. Since then, Novi Pazar has slowly sunk into economic ruin. However, the informal market, meanwhile, continues to this day, albeit on a comparatively small scale. While the end of the Yugoslav conflicts foreshadowed the end of the booming market, existing transnational networks continue to connect Bosniaks in Serbia and present-day Turkey.

Aims and contributions

How do economic transnational practices shape one's sense of belonging in times of crisis/precarity? Specifically, how does the collapse of the Ottoman Empire – and the subsequent migration of the Muslim Slav population to Turkey – relate to the Yugoslav Succession Wars during the 1990s? These questions form the core aim of this book, which examines how the Yugoslav Succession Wars influenced transnational relations between the émigré Bosniak community of Turkey and those Bosniaks who remained in Southeastern Europe. Bereft of acceptance among their co-denizens of different religions at the turn of the century, and again in 1991, some Bosniaks turned to Turkey for refuge and then for material aid. In order to show this mechanism, I analyze the case study of Novi Pazar, Serbia, where informal trading practices flourished between 1991/92 and 1995. This book therefore focuses on Novi Pazar's informal market economy during the Yugoslav Succession Wars as a prism through which to analyze the strengthening of existing relations between the émigré community in Turkey and the local Bosniak population in the Sandžak region, specifically its urban center that is Novi Pazar. The goal of this book is to demonstrate the interactive nature of relations between the state and local and émigré communities.

Researching the Sandžak region of the former SFRY is particularly valuable because this corner of the Balkans has received scant attention, not least because this cross-border region remained largely untouched by the armed conflicts during the Yugoslav Succession Wars.[14] Kenneth Morrison and Elizabeth Roberts published a much-needed and excellent history of the Sandžak region that allowed me to situate my findings in a historic frame,[15] and I was fortunate to meet and discuss my research with James Lyon, who has published an article on the informal market in Novi Pazar.[16] Empirically driven, however, this book is the first longitudinal analysis that examines how the Bosniak community of Novi Pazar in Serbia traded as a means to endure the Yugoslav Succession Wars of the 1990s. The relative peace that characterized the Sandžak during this decade makes it all the more critical that we try to understand how its ethnically and religiously diverse population negotiated this trying period.

The focus on informality and on 'making do' in Sandžak, an ambiguous border region situated between Serbia, Montenegro, and Bosnia and Herzegovina (BiH), is not an isolated case study of an informal market in Novi Pazar. Informal practices are spread across the globe and have been examined in a variety of projects[17] and publications before.[18] By looking closely at smuggling and other informal practices without prejudice and without being judgmental, I hope to contribute a better understanding about the mechanisms behind the establishment of such markets. The question of how communities frame reconnecting with diaspora populations to re-create belonging in light of crisis and/or precarity through the prism of informality that arrives in the form of aid is of specific interest here.

For a migration scholar, the Western Balkans are a fertile ground to examine the movement of people across lands so as to learn about the social, cultural, and political effects thereof. Sandžak epitomizes this transitory and border characteristic of the Balkan region. As such, this book provides an outlook on migration as it spans questions of identification, informal trade practices, memory, and social space and investigates how these phenomena come together in times of precarity. By using a conceptual framework that spans history, sociology, social anthropology, and geography, I hope to go beyond grand narratives of geopolitical alignments between states to uncover a complex web of personal and intimate relationships that suffuse the on-the-ground struggles of 'making do'. In doing so, this book contributes to our understanding of how national and transnational communities are forged in times of uncertainty and crisis. At the same time, this book reshapes preconceived notions of ethnicity, nationality, and the state in the Balkan region. Drawing on the field of human geography was particularly fruitful in my effort to understand the region through the very networks in which people operate as opposed to emphasizing ethnicity. Discarding the ethnic frame, to put it in Tim Hall's words, forced me "to think of space not in Euclidian terms, but rather in networked or relational terms."[19]

Politicians, residents, journalists, pundits, and academics alike considered ethnicity as a lens through which to understand the collapse of social values during the Yugoslav wars, the reconciliation thereafter, and subsequent questions revolving around minority rights in the newly created states. I, too, traveled to Novi

Pazar with the initial intention of researching interethnic relations and upward social mobility in Southern Serbia. Taking to heart Clifford Geertz, and his advice to "see(ing) things from the native's" point of view, I abandoned this approach upon arriving in the field in May 2012.[20] As I moved from a text-based understanding of the region to the field site of Novi Pazar, I realized that the ethnic lens was a mental straitjacket I sought to discard. Moving away from the ethnic-lens approach opened fresh possibilities for my understanding of the social experiences of a *community* as opposed to those of Bosniaks, Serbs, Roma, and so forth. To be sure, I analyze trans*national* relations between the Bosniak diaspora in Turkey and local Bosniaks, and how social relations in Novi Pazar changed in view of the informal market that flourished there in the first half of the 1990s. Important, however, is that the market benefited and affected the social experience of all individuals in Novi Pazar, not merely the Bosniak community. Aspiring to Jerome Kirk and Marc L. Miller, I sought to "represent the natives' way of making sense of their experience in a language that transcends the culture-specific experience of the world of either the natives or the readers."[21] Looking beyond ethnicity, in other words, encouraged me to observe a community that lived under the tutelage of a nationalist *and* an international sanctions regime. Local attitudes do not exist in a vacuum. They are shaped by events from within and outside politically imposed boundaries.

International sanctions did not materialize out of thin air but were a direct result of the proxy war Belgrade had waged in Croatia and Bosnia. As Belgrade engaged in a violent surrogate war to enlarge its political territory, the government in Belgrade alienated the population within its borders. In light of the prewar propaganda barrage against Muslims of SFRY and the mounting violence in BiH, politicians and representatives from the cultural and religious sphere in Novi Pazar, the urban center of the Sandžak region, sought to gain autonomy from Serbia. Organized by Sulejman Ugljanin, head of the Democratic Action Party (SDA),[22] together with the umbrella organization under the name of Bosniak National Council of Sandžak (BNVS), the Muslim enclave of Sandžak adopted a referendum demanding autonomy from SFRY in 1991. The referendum was put to a vote and accepted by 187,473 (70.19 percent) of all 264,156 eligible voters in the Sandžak region. Belgrade, meanwhile, denied the validity of the referendum and charged Ugljanin with an attempt to overthrow the Serbian constitutional order and terrorism.[23] Besides indicting Ugljanin, 25 additional members of the Bosniak community were imprisoned and charged on the grounds of violating the territorial integrity of SRFY.[24] Ugljanin fled to Turkey, while the trial against these individuals has been postponed 108 times.[25]

In short, I argue that the foundation of the once existing social solidarity among the former Yugoslav peoples disintegrated by way of the economic crisis, the Yugoslav Succession Wars, and subsequent sanctions. While the social disintegration affected all citizens of the former state, Bosniaks of Novi Pazar had a valve to relieve this pressure. And yet, trading with the diaspora community in Turkey was not only a means to an economic end but a practice that forged new and renewed social ties with the Muslim Slav diaspora community in Turkey and the Turkish state writ large.

Europe in the head, Turkey in the heart

Turkish involvement in the Western Balkans received much attention since Ahmet Davutoğlu devised the 'Zero Problems with Neighbors' doctrine.[26] According to Davutoğlu, formerly the minister for foreign affairs and member of the Justice and Development Party (AKP), Turkey was prone to assume greater geopolitical responsibilities in world affairs, in part due to its history and geographic location. The Balkans, too, fall into the former category owing to the Western Balkan inclusion in the former Ottoman Empire, especially since the Yugoslav Succession Wars during the 1990s. Since then, a number of Turkish state-sponsored and non-state actors finance a variety of projects in the Western Balkans, including the Cooperation and Coordination Agency (TIKA),[27] the presidency for religious affairs called Diyanet,[28] and the Yunus Emre language institute.[29] Bahar Baser, Erdi Öztürk, Samim Akgönül, and Kerem Ötkem examined these cultural and political institutions and the encroaching authoritarian tendencies under the AKP presidency of Recep Tayyip Erdoğan[30] and its support of cultural and educational institutions in the region extensively.[31] Simon P. Watmough and Öztürk examined the Gulen Movement as a 'transnational network' that utilizes diaspora communities to strengthen its 'parapolitical organization'.[32] These authors provide us with much-needed and critical insight regarding not only the transformation of the Turkish state under the AKP but also a fundamental understanding about how the AKP *utilizes* diaspora communities to proliferate its geopolitical relevance.

Turkish investments in the region loom large, to be sure, but appear trifling compared to the involvement of the European Union. To put it in the words of one interlocutor, "Turkey is in people's hearts while Europe is in their heads." Indeed, financial, cultural, and political investments dwarf those of Turkey when compared with those of the European Union, as illustrated by Matteo Bonomi and Milica Uvalić.[33] Moreover, Turkey is not the sole investor in the Western Balkans. Instead, Florian Bieber and Nikolaos Tzifakis,[34] and Dimitar Bechev[35] examine myriad state and non-state sponsored actors that variously engage with the Western Balkans. Their respective research builds an important frame for the present study in which I situate my question of how transnational practices shape one's sense of belonging in times of crisis/precarity.

John F. Freie makes an intriguing argument regarding the human desire for genuine communities and social relations in *Counterfeit Community – The Exploitation of Our Longing for Connectedness*.[36] Counterfeit communities, according to Freie,

> appeal to real needs and concerns of people and their desires for association, but instead of creating environments and relationships that meaningfully satisfy those desires, they provide only the appearance of community and are, therefore, never fully satisfying.[37]

Freie posed the question of community-building in an American context that he perceived as rampant with selfish individualism and greed. Instead of partaking in a consensus-making, participatory democracy, US citizens gather at shopping malls or other community-like places that are void of communal experiences. As a result, Americans no longer associate the necessity of governance in their everyday lives, with the consequence that "citizens (who) claim to be a part of a community [but] feel no sense of social responsibility other than paying dues."[38] Freie's contemplations on community-building are compelling, with a view toward the social disruption brought about by the Yugoslav Succession wars and local desire for a continued sense of community in all of Serbia, particularly in Novi Pazar. Did the local *buvljak* ('flea market', colloquially understood as a market containing smuggled goods) in Novi Pazar create a renewed sense of community with the émigré community in Turkey in retrospect of the Ottoman Empire? Freie compels us to consider this question regarding this community's real and/or desired connection with the Turkish state.

Local connections with the diaspora, as well as the Turkish state, are undisputed and very real. Interviewees repeatedly asserted that Novi Pazar belonged to a Turkish sphere of influence based on the historically constituted cultural realm of the former Ottoman Empire and filial relations. Yet does a common religion, kin relations, and historic memory suffice the act of forging a common bond across time and space, as is the case of Novi Pazar and Turkey?

Magnus Marsden sheds light on this question and invites us to assess narratives with an overt historic dimension with caution in *Trading Worlds – Afghan Merchants Across Modern Frontiers*.[39] *Trading Worlds* is a supreme examination of Afghan merchants because Marsden analyzes ordinary material encounters and their significance for social encounters in Central Asia, the Black Sea region, and Europe. I build on Marsden's idea, and most of all, I heed his advice on ethnic historic determinism. In Marsden's words:

> Such images of the present's relationship to the past are embedded in and arise out of political economies; they are actively constructed by both local and global actors. It is important, therefore, that scholarship is critical of the ways in which such images of pre-modern forms of trade are deployed in order to understand contemporary realities. By rendering the region's modern history as inauthentic to its historic cultural composition and wider global significance, these images foreclose any attempt to explore the unique ways in which people are forging relations across cold war boundaries.

The present study follows Marsden's cautionary note in its exploration of *how* locals construct and reconstruct the past based on the present in a fixed geographic space. Revisiting Fry's argument on the human desire for community in light of Marsden's advice then directs our attention toward the possibility that locals construct historicized narratives to *cope* with the present.

The question that arises is how locals navigated and experienced this two-tiered pressure of living within a nationalist-dominated government and internationally imposed sanctions. The gray and informal market itself thus serves as a prism that highlights the narrative accounts of locals and their proximity to Turkey.

During my time spent in the field of Novi Pazar, I filtered out two story lines that dominate the narrative sense-making process of locals in retrospect of the 1990s and the second market. As such, locals transpose a two-dimensional tale about *šverc* and transnational family relations onto a historical plane. At the core of the *primary narrative* lies an emphasis on the close-knit connections between Novi Pazar and the diaspora community in Turkey. "Without the diaspora," I heard time and again, "we would not have made it." On the surface of this first narrative is the diaspora community that saved Novi Pazar from descending into the economic chaos that people in other towns of Serbia experienced. Yet this narrative also serves as a 'sense-making tool' that provides locals with a chronological continuity that bypasses the cruel experience of the war years.[40] Trade with the Bosniak diaspora created an atmosphere that allowed locals to make sense of their new situation in economic and social terms by which they were able to "anticipate the future based on retrospection," to frame it in Paul Ricoeur's words.[41]

Repeated probing over the course of four years in and out of the field slowly revealed a *second narrative*, namely a local deterioration of values and a deep-seated feeling of anomie *because* of this market. It is crucial, however, that locals might not have reconnected with the Bosniak diaspora in Turkey, the Turkish state, and their history to the extent they did in the absence of this war. The Yugoslav Succession Wars that enabled this market, one may thus pose, permitted the creation of the primary narrative. Only by illuminating the 1990s in general and the market that created and/or strengthened these links between the local and the diaspora community specifically, in other words, can one understand the process of revitalized relations between the local and diaspora community.

The significance of this question goes far beyond the limited space of Novi Pazar, exactly *because* locals repeatedly associate(d) the gray market with the Bosniak diaspora in Turkey.

It is important to emphasize that I do not examine transnational actors as dangerous, criminal, and/or intentionally malicious traders, even though they enabled the initial practice of *šverc*. I conceptualize transnational networks as a solidarity chain that enabled locals to make a living but also as a system of connections within which locals cohere the transmutation of their existence in the former Yugoslav state.

Methodological considerations and data

Upon arriving in Novi Pazar in 2012, I first took up residence in an informal 'student dorm' that was located in a private residence. I have since chosen to stay at the hotel, each time in the same place. Staying at the hotel allowed for a distance between me and the field to evaluate my daily impressions in private. Both options constituted considerable drawbacks and/or advantages as I preserved my freedom of movement by staying at the hotel. On the contrary, the proximity to residents in the informal student dorms allowed for instant contact with residents and, significantly, the host family. And yet, having established relations with the hosts of the informal dorm during the pilot project in 2012 meant I was able to approach family members whenever I returned to Novi Pazar and surrounding areas. In Istanbul, I talked with merchants in the *Kapalıçarşı* (Grand Bazaar) in 2016, and met with interlocutors in Sarajevo in 2014 and 2016. In 2017, I resided in Belgrade to view newspaper collections and archival material at the National Library and the Yugoslav Archive, respectively.

Much of my time was spent in social and professional areas including cafes, non-governmental organizations (NGOs), beauty parlors, indoor shops, outdoor markets, churches, mosques, downtown streets, and other "third places that host regular, voluntary, and informal gatherings of individuals beyond home and work."[42] "Third places," according to Ramon Oldenburg and Dennis Brissett,

> exist outside the home and beyond the 'work lots' of modern economic production. They are places where people gather *primarily* to enjoy each other's company.[43]

Indoor shops, beauty parlors, and outdoor market stalls to be sure, too, are places of work. Yet, individuals also visit these places to meet and chat with acquaintances.

Beauty parlors are, for instance, a wonderful example of third places that combine work with the voluntary gathering of friends. Tucked away in a back street off the main drag in Novi Pazar, women of all walks of life, age, religion, and/or national affiliation – self-imposed and otherwise – readily shared experiences and gossip with their beauticians and co-patrons, out of earshot from male companionship. Seeing that Serbia is still a patriarchal, male-dominated society, beauty parlors presented a valuable research site in which to gain insight into a female perspective on the informal economy in Novi Pazar and the greater Sandžak region during the 1990s, and often beyond. I further increased female participation by way of questionnaires, as illustrated in Figure 0.6.

Residents also gathered frequently at NGOs to discuss local and national politics. There was often an air of surreptitious camaraderie as staff members and visitors alike – young, old, female, and male of all backgrounds – exchanged views on the current state of affairs in Serbia and the Western Balkans in general. NGOs were an ideal site of entry to the field and practical places to meet further interlocutors. Individuals who frequented these organizations not only had a point of view on informal market activities and the Bosniak diaspora in Turkey, but they also were eager to share their insights.

Downtown streets and cafes were ideal for informal conversations with established as well as potential informants, and strolls during which I was able to observe the goings-on in town through the eyes of locals. Meandering through downtown Novi Pazar with interlocutors taught me about local details of the town, including the projects paid for by the Turkish Cooperation and Coordination Agency (TIKA) that invested in schools, hospital equipment, and the renovation of mosques, for instance. As such, local cafés, NGOs, and beauty parlors *are* places of work. Yet these places are, as Oldenburg and Brissett described them,

> modest business establishments where concern over image has not yet replaced the delights of 'shooting the bull', those merely hanging out will be found, most often, to outnumber the customers.[44]

Life indeed takes place in these third places in Novi Pazar, and I was able to learn about the local code of conduct in these various settings.

Restrictions and limiting conditions

How does one study the practice of *šverc*? Felia Allum and Stan Gilmour provide a practical note as regards data collection on transnational organized crime (TOC):

> Often, there exists very little data which could help from the basis of an in-depth analysis. We must not forget that getting primary data is difficult and dangerous. Some researchers have undertaken participant observation (for example, Ianni and Reuss-Ianni 1972; Ianni 1974; Chambliss 1971) but this is difficult to organize. Therefore, there is often a necessity to rely on police figures and data. . . . Thus, fieldwork is the key to a realistic account of organized crime but also the main stumbling block: "field work depends to a great extent on complicated continuous concerns, the most central of which is how one is seen by others."[45]

Primary data is indeed very difficult to come by considering the volume of *šverc* between 1991 and 1995, who participated, and the quality of goods that were shipped from and through Serbia. Finding specific data to quantify the informal trade in Novi Pazar, moreover, was even more difficult. To be sure, the UN states:

> The links between the state and organized crime were strengthened during the 1990s following the collapse of the socialist regimes and during the violent dissolution of Yugoslavia. After international sanctions were imposed, great fortunes were made smuggling weapons, oil, and other commodities needed by the warring parties. These were paid for, in part, through other forms of trafficking, including the smuggling of drugs and untaxed cigarettes, made possible by the chaos of the war and fledgling democratic institutions. Wars and the new relationship with the West also led to large scale emigration and human trafficking.[46]

One can thus only deduce, together with reports and the oral testimonies, that TOC was present in Novi Pazar, too, though I was unable to quantify the volume thereof.

In my effort to learn about the quantity and exact nature of the market during the 1990s, I arranged an informal conversation with a former police official in

Novi Pazar, though was unable to retrieve primary documentation thereof. As such, I rely on the secondary sources. Primary sources from the UN, Europol, and Eulex, for instance, figure especially relevant about the legacy of the informal market.

Due to the difficulty of finding primary documentation, participant observation and the collection of semi-structured interviews became a necessary choice to learn about the smuggling activities of the 1990s. Doing so, however, inevitably shifted my focus toward the question of how locals coped with this situation of living under a nationalist regime and international sanctions. The focus, in other words, shifted from studying organized crime to that of researching how locals experienced the war years within Serbian state borders, and how social relations transformed as a result of this transnational trade.

And yet, participant observation bears its own problem, as I chose not to cross borders with anyone who alleged to smuggle or indeed *did* smuggle goods. This created a strange dynamic at times, as I asked personal questions and yet purported to show no interest in traveling with a person as they went about their business. In a late stage of my fieldwork in 2015, for instance, I received a WhatsApp message with a request to drive a car from Germany to Serbia, which I denied. The conversation went as follows

SALIM: We got this car in Germany, and it needs to be driven here to Serbia, aren't you coming to Serbia, soon? You could drive the car here?
ME: I'm not doing that. What kind of car anyway, and why? I thought your brother lives in Germany, why doesn't he drive the car there?
SALIM: He does not want to do it.

My contact with this informant broke off shortly thereafter. Because I did not participate in cross-border trading myself and did not sell any goods on the market together with interlocutors, I do not have an empirical account of how wares are traded.

Another difficulty inherent to participant observation and semi-structured interviews stems from the personal situation of the informant and his or her inclination to divulge personal information. I enjoyed excellent rapport with Asem, for instance, with whom I had regular contact in the field between 2012 and 2016 and beyond. At the beginning of our meetings, he was good-natured and an excellent source of reliable information as regarded his personal family history and his expert opinion on the 1990s. In due course of these four years, however, I detected an increased detachment that went hand in hand with his worsening socioeconomic condition, to the point where he once asked me to turn off the recorder during an interview. Though my contact to Asem stayed intact, it was necessary that I realize how personal circumstances influence the data informants provide.

These brief insights highlight that participant observation and the collection of oral data depend on people, most of whom may or may not carry a personal burden. Shifting circumstances in an individual's life will thus influence the rapport with informants. Given these restrictions and limiting conditions, it was paramount to triangulate my data with additional situational interviews, questionnaires, and newspaper articles.

Who speaks

The completion of this study would have been impossible without the collaboration of individuals in the Sandžak region. The following table describes the individuals who agreed to sit with me for a recorded interview. It is important to iterate here that casual conversations, participant observation, and field notes are not quantified and included in this list, though they nevertheless contribute significantly to the data set.

Amer (25–30, M)	Amer visited Bosnia and Herzegovina as a tourist at the time of our first meeting, during which we spent the day by walking through the streets of a city in BiH before settling into a quiet restaurant for our recorded, semi-structured interview in 2016. Amer and I have kept in touch since then via social media channels.
Asem (55–60, M)	Asem was one of the key informants, especially during the early phase of this research. Asem had worked for an international not-for-profit organization and is deeply rooted in the greater Sandžak region. A wealth of information, Asem's first recorded interview with me took place in 2012. Two follow-up interviews took place in 2014 and 2015. We continue to have sporadic interactions via social media channels. All interviews took place in the greater Sandžak region.
Bojana (60–65, F)	Bojana, a native of the greater Sandžak region, worked for an international organization when we first met to record a semi-structured interview in her office in 2012. Several in-person, unrecorded meetings followed between then and 2015.
Burhan (55–60, M)	Burhan and I met for our first and only interview in 2012. Burhan invited me to his office in the greater Sandžak region. The building seemed modern, though abandoned, and looked like it had once been a shopping mall.
Chip (45–50, M)	Chip was a gatekeeper concerning my access and introduction to individuals of the local and international non-governmental community who worked on questions related to the greater Sandžak region. Our e-mail contact started as early as 2011. Our first in-person meeting took place in 2015. The e-mail contact continued thereafter.
Daud (35–40, M)	Daud, a merchant in the greater Sandžak region, agreed to a semi-structured interview in 2012. We had two follow-up interviews in 2014 and 2015. Daud and I met for various in-person and unrecorded meetings between 2012 and 2015. Most of our meetings took place in his store in the market.
Dragan (60–65, M)	Dragan served as a public official and was an individual with a great wealth of information about informal activities in the greater Sandžak region. We met in May 2012 when he agreed to sit with me for an interview.
Dubravko (35–40, M)	Dubravko works for a local aid agency. He invited me to his office in the greater Sandžak region to record a semi-structured interview in 2012.

(*Continued*)

Ekrem (40–45, M)	Ekrem and I met in 2012 when he invited me to his office in the greater Sandžak region for our scheduled, semi-structured interview. Unhappy with how the sociopolitical situation developed in the aftermath of the Succession Wars, he signaled his desire to leave the greater Sandžak region early on. A professional in the international not-for-profit sector, he left the greater Sandžak region soon after our interview. After our first interview, we met up occasionally until he left the greater Sandžak region.
Emela (35–40, F)	Emela is employed in the public sector. We first met in 2012 and have since met in person on a regular basis upon my arrival in the greater Sandžak region. In 2015, we conducted a semi-structured interview in the presence of her sister and scheduled a follow-up interview in 2016.
Erol (25–30, M)	Like many in his age group, Erol was unemployed when I first met him in May 2012. While being unemployed, however, a great majority of young people in the greater Sandžak region work odd jobs here and there, as was the case with Erol. Our first interview on record took place in 2012. We conducted two follow-up interviews in 2014 and 2016. Erol and I met regularly whenever I returned to the greater Sandžak region, and we continue to talk via social media channels.
James (M)	James is a civil servant. James and I were in contact before our first in-person meeting in Serbia 2012, where he provided me with important background information on the Sandžak region.
Jim (40–45, M)	Jim used to work as a civil servant, and he introduced me to the Sandžak region as I traveled through Serbia, Macedonia, and Montenegro during February and March 2011. By way of numerous discussions about the Yugoslav Succession Wars, the drawing and redrawing of borders, and ethnic entrepreneurs, questions of belonging crystallized, as examined in this book. Our conversation continues into the present.
Jon (50–55, M)	Jon works in higher education and is also active in the not-for-profit sector. A wealth of information regarding the historiography of political events in the Sandžak region, Jon and I first met in Bosnia and Hercegovina in 2014 where we recorded one interview.
Leijla (93–98, F)	I met Leijla by way of having lived in the informal student dormitory in 2012. I conducted the semi-structured interview with Leijla in the presence of her two daughters in June 2014, and I saw her daughters, as well as other family members, whenever I returned to the greater Sandžak region between 2012 and 2016.
Mirijam (50–55, F)	An acquaintance introduced me to Mirijam before we recorded a semi-structured interview in the presence of a daughter and one of Mirijam's friends in 2014. Mirijam provided me with important background reading. She collects and records oral histories related to the Muslim migration to interior Ottoman lands.
Omar (60–65, M)	Omar was just about to be retired from the public sector when we met in Bosnia and Herzegovina in 2014. Like Mirijam, he has been interested in and researches the Muslim migration to interior Ottoman lands.
Saleh (25–30, M)	Saleh is a self-described trader. We first met in the greater Sandžak region in 2014 and recorded our semi-structured interview in 2015. We met at various times in person and talked via social network channels between 2014 and 2016 and beyond.

Salim (40–45, M)	Salim is a self-described *švercer*, a smuggler. I met Salim in the *Kapalıçarşı* in Istanbul in 2015. We stayed in touch via social media and set up a semi-structured interview in 2016 in Serbia.
Semina (F)	Semina is active in the non-governmental sector in the greater Sandžak region. I was introduced to Semina in 2015 before we recorded a semi-structured interview, which took place in the presence of one male and two female bystanders.
Senad (45–50, M)	Senad is a local gatekeeper who introduced me to residents of all walks of life. He works at an NGO and invited me to his office for our first semi-structured interview in the greater Sandžak region in 2012. Two follow-up interviews took place in 2015 and 2016. Many unrecorded meetings, in person and online, took place between 2012 and 2016 and beyond.
Siniša 35–40, M)	Siniša works at a not-for-profit organization and spent much of his life in the greater Sandžak region. We first met in Serbia for a semi-structured interview in 2012. The interview was followed by many unrecorded in-person meetings and conversations via social media channels until 2016 and beyond. Another recorded follow-up interview took place in 2015.
Zarifa (F)	Zarifa is an ardent supporter of the AKP and a young woman who had just taken up the practice of wearing a hijab when we met in the greater Sandžak region. We recorded one semi-structured interview in 2012.

Semi-structured interviews as narratives

Over the course of the four years I spent in and out of the field, I came to interpret the informal trade as a narrative sense-making tool – a prism – that highlighted the social transformation locals experienced as a result of the Yugoslav crisis. Seen from this perspective, then, narrating is an activity, as highlighted by Elinor Ochs and Lisa Capps, that emphasizes the "sense-making *process*" as opposed to "a finished product in which loose ends knot together into a single story-line."[47] There is, in other words, no unifying, chronological historiography. "Instead, the stories that people tell about themselves are about many selves, each situated in particular contexts, and working strategically to resist those contexts," as Corinne Squire noted.[48]

Building on Bakhtin's paradigm of heteroglossia, Andrea Smith interpreted the multiplicity of voices by distinguishing those situations according to which informants convey stories to a general audience from contexts in which individuals narrate personal experiences.[49] Interlocutors in Novi Pazar, too, replicated official histories in their narration of 'the general history', though they tended to use singular first-person pronouns 'when speaking of personal experiences'. This approach fits the two-tiered narrative because interlocutors often used the plural 'we' (*nas, mi smo, naše*, etc.) when speaking about the Bosniak communities' being connected to the greater historical processes in view of the Porte, the Ottoman Empire's collapse, and the subsequent migration processes. Individuals, concurrently, often used the singular pronoun 'I' (*ja, moj/a, mene*, etc.) when relating personal opinions about and accounts of the market in the 1990s. It is interesting to note here that 'I' narratives most often concurred between Serbian, Roma, and Bosniak informants, whereas 'we' narratives conveyed a Bosniak-centered interpretation of events. This two-tiered narrative approach illustrates the at once historic perception among locals in the greater Sandžak region and individualized accounts of living in a nationalist and mafia-like state under international sanctions.

Understanding life stories as narratives means that I concede the claim to represent one true version of the world as I saw it. To be sure, I adjusted my initial research upon repeated entry to the field to more closely reflect local circumstances as seen by locals, as noted earlier. And yet, *I* am the author of this text, and thus *created* a narrative by having *chosen* interview partners. History and the narration of life events, as previously argued by Hayden White, does not illustrate an innocent reconstruction of the truth that is free of ideology.[50] John Van Maanen, too, advises that institutions and academic traditions shape ethnographers as much as the "narrative and rhetorical conventions" a writer assumes.[51] I thus not only selected characters but also specific narrative representations. I chose a topic – in this case the informal market as a prism – encoded facets of the interview, and selected an angle – in this case the social relations – by which I approached the narratives *and* informants. Acknowledging this fact is necessary because doing so allows for a critical assessment of the multiplicity of voices in the field – including my own.

Questionnaire

Questionnaires substantiate claims about the extent of the informal market, correlations between individual tradesman, and the nature of their connection to Turkey, family relations, or otherwise. The first round of questionnaires was conceptualized as a pilot study that I administered in 2012. Upon evaluating the first round of interviews, casual conversations, and participant observation, I adjusted the questionnaires thereafter. In 2015, I arranged for a local NGO to administer the 500 questionnaires.

The $N = 500$ of participants were set to reflect the census data as illustrated in Figure 0.2, and a rough parity between male and female participants. For reasons outlined earlier, however, more males than females participated in the questionnaire.

Participants were free to choose between having the questionnaire read to them or completing their questionnaire independently in the company of the interviewer. This was important, in case participants had questions about specific sections of the questionnaire.

More than half of the participants (55 percent) were between the ages of 36 and 65 at the time of filling out the questionnaire (Figure 0.7). Participants who were older than 36 at the time are more like to remember the market. Conversely, participants younger than 36 have a presumably obscure memory of the market. And yet, participants who were 36 and younger at the time of filling out the

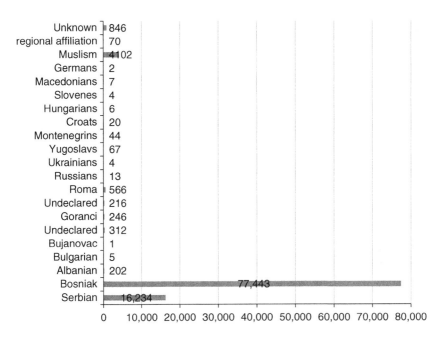

Figure 0.2 National affiliation

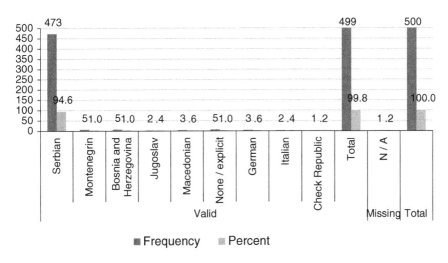

Figure 0.3 Citizenship

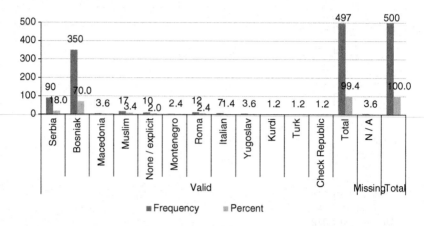

Figure 0.4 National identification

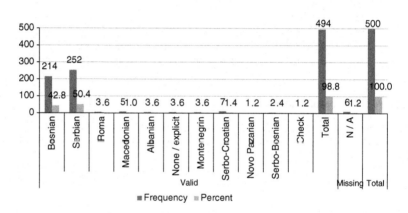

Figure 0.5 Native language

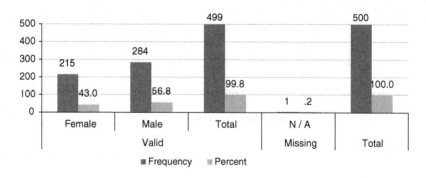

Figure 0.6 Gender

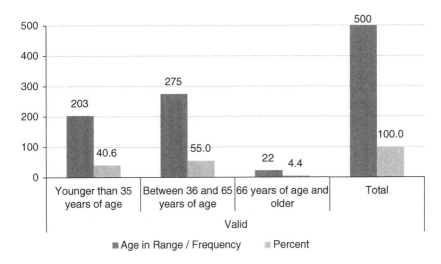

Figure 0.7 Age in range

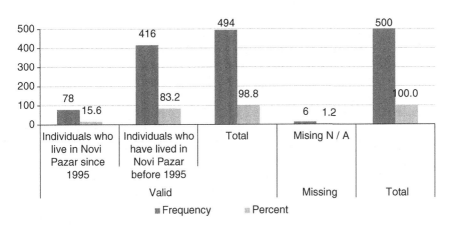

Figure 0.8 How long a resident in Novi Pazar

questionnaire were brought up during the sanctions and thus socialized in a system during which *šverc* was a mundane activity.

Most of the participants (83.2 percent) in this study have lived in Novi Pazar since before 1995 (Figure 0.8). This is important, because these participants experienced social rupture brought about the Yugoslav Succession Wars and the subsequent sanctions as examined in this book.

Newspaper articles

The local population in Serbia was virtually and quite literally isolated between 1991 and 1995, which also pertains to the news that Serbian citizens variously read in the print media, viewed on television, and listened to through the radio waves. Determinations to silence dissenting voices within the media began as early as 1990. In their effort to quash anticipated dissent among journalists, the Serbian regime purged the media staff following the electoral victory of the Socialist Party in 1993. The *Independent* (London) reported the sacking of 1,500 journalists in January 1993, calling it the "single biggest purge of political opponents in Serbia."[52] By 1994, *Borba* (resistance) was the only reliably independent newspaper, which too was purged by regime-loyal individuals in December 1994.[53]

Instead of starving the local population of news, however, the regime obscured fact and fiction to render Serbian citizens pliable. Inga Saffron, staff writer at The *Philadelphia Inquirer*, for instance, stated "the rule of Serbian President Slobodan Milosevic, propaganda is a subtle art form. People aren't so much denied information as confused by too much of it. Fact, fiction and rumor are intermingled."[54] To be sure, Milošević's stranglehold over the television and radio media was much stronger compared to the print media, though the information flow in the papers was far from free. Protest and dissent, too, were difficult given the heavy police presence in Serbia – a "one policemen per every seventh individual" ratio by 1993.[55] Besides, the internationally imposed sanctions increased the power of the regime. Susan Woodward said it best when she explained:

> But the imposition of economic sanctions against Serbia, beginning with the EC and the United States in November 1991 and then the UN (Security Council Resolution 757) on May 30, 1992, worked to restore (his) [Milošević's] control by cutting alternative sources of information and communication with the outside world and making subscriptions to print media prohibitively expensive. The sanctions also prevented his opposition from obtaining the foreign financial support and imported equipment (such as a transmitter with enough power to beam the one truly independent television station, Studio B, beyond Belgrade) that was necessary to compete with Milošević's domestic control through police and customs officials.[56]

Due to this virtual and literal isolation of the Serbian population within Serbia proper, it is not only necessary to deconstruct the overarching narrative of a purportedly homogenous Serbian nation-state during the war years; it is vital to *re*construct a version of a 'reality' that governed this state between 1991 and 1995.

To reconstruct a version of events as they transpired between 1991 and 1995, I viewed the daily *Večernje Novosti* newspaper issues at the National Library in Belgrade, Serbia, that were published between 1993 and 1995. In a first viewing, I selected articles pertaining to *šverc* in all its forms, including the various *buvljaci*, the black-market currency exchange, and topics connected to the establishment of *fri šopovi* (a version of duty-free shops set up in the wake of international sanctions). Building on my interviews and casual conversations with locals in Novi Pazar, I also selected articles that portrayed the financial insecurity as well as the loss of safety as seen through the increasingly habitual crime and violence that transpired on the streets of Serbia.

The *Večernje Novosti* newspaper is an ideal daily paper by which to reconstruct a version of the reality as it existed in Serbia between 1991 and 1995. *Večernje Novosti* served governing forces to shape the nationalizing discourse during the 1990s, and it continues to do so at present.[57] *Večerne Novosti* was, at the same time, less overtly political compared to *Politika*, seeing that *Večerne Novosti* included gossip sections, nude pictures, and the television guide, for instance. *Večerne Novosti* may, in other words, be characterized as a tabloid, and thus it reached a broader audience.

Following Ruth Wodak, I analyzed the newspaper articles through the lens of a discourse historical approach (DHA). As such, I am not examining the *Večerne Novosti* articles as a 'linguistic unit'. Instead, to put it in Wodak's words, I "study(ing) social phenomena which are necessarily complex and thus require a multidisciplinary and multi-methodological approach."[58] I thus view the paper as an additional tool by which to understand how the public discourse as generated and shaped by the government in turn shaped the social practice of citizens in Serbia.

Structure

Novi Pazar lends itself as a geographic location from which to study transnational practices because doing so allows for the examination of relations across time and space. Not only was Novi Pazar an integral part of the Ottoman Empire, but the town also served as a transitory space for migrants who left alongside the retreating empire and again for goods in the 1990s. During interviews and casual conversations, locals often referred to their history as integral to their economic and to an extent social persistence during the 1990s and beyond. The practice of transnational trade relations in Novi Pazar illustrates this community's physically entrenched (in-state) experience in this mafia-like state structure that engulfed all areas of the Serbian state. Transnational *šverc* practices simultaneously produced an alternative connotation for the local population – one in which Bosniaks invigorated communal bonds with Turkey by way of material encounters. Performative acts illustrate how locals view the present in terms of the past. The 1990s thus serve as an emotive bridge that connects local *Novo Pazarci* with the three protracted migratory waves that left Southeastern Europe since the collapse of the Ottoman Empire.

My approach toward the question of how social relations changed in Novi Pazar during the Yugoslav Succession Wars is characterized by the assumption that the Bosniak diaspora in Turkey supported local Bosniaks in Novi Pazar during the international sanctions regime on Serbia between 1991 and 1995. Because informal trading practices materialized by way of cross-border trade between Turkey and Serbia, I apply the philosophical underpinnings of practice to the theoretical frame of transnationalism to analyze how locals experienced the international sanctions on an everyday basis. The informal market itself serves as an interpretive tool that carries the narratives of locals and their experience with transnational diaspora-come-trade practices.

In what follows, I address in three parts the overarching question of how material encounters influence social relations in detached spaces. Part I introduces the reader to a historical context as well as philosophical and theoretical considerations that underpin this book. Parts II and III are based on empirical data, and each part is further divided into two chapters.

In Part II, I examine the catalysts that induced anticipatory properties in the Bosniak community in Novi Pazar to analyze how locals narrate the past. The question of how informants identify with the past must be examined to gauge if and how material encounters carry anticipatory properties concerning the manifestation of transnational figurations. This part of the book is based on mnemonics, as I identify the medium through which locals remember the past to explore how autobiographical narratives differ from historic ones. What are the vehicles by which interlocutors transmit memory in Novi Pazar? Does the town of Novi Pazar serve as a mnemonic nucleus, and to what extent is family the primary carrier of memory? Important in this segment are characteristics by which locals collapse the time-space continuum when narrating the past.

In Part III, I move away from the mnemonic functions to explore the practice of *šverc*. In Chapter 4, I reconstruct the socioeconomic and political ambience that prevailed in Serbia as presented by *Večerne Novosti* to 'recontextualize' the narratives told by locals in Novi Pazar. In Chapter 5, I demonstrate the inherent ambiguity of *šverc* as both a legitimate and inappropriate practice. Locals sanctioned *šverc* as legitimate by way of narrating the past as a symbolic anchor while simultaneously deeming *šverc* inappropriate due to the connecting of informal practices with the Milošević regime. By probing into the actual *practice* of smuggling goods, I filter out how the practice of *šverc* cut(s) across ethnic, religious, and political boundaries. I end this segment with a discussion on anomie.

Notes

1 Field notes, capital city, and greater Sandžak region in Serbia, 2012.
2 Parts of this introduction were published as field notes in September 2012 in Sandra King-Savic, "Impressions from the Field III," *Transitions Online Next in Line*, September 3, 2012, http://nextinline.eu/impressions-from-the-field-iii/.
3 A town in south-central Serbia, some two and a half hours from Novi Pazar.
4 Literal translation 'livestock or beast'; an insult.
5 Literally meaning 'man of God', meaning similar to the expression of 'Jesus Christ!'
6 "Where is that guy?"
7 A public secret.
8 James Lyon, "Serbia's Sandžak under Milošević: Identity, Nationalism and Survival," *Human Rights Review*, no. 9 (2008): 71–92.
9 Denisa Kostovicova, "Fake Levis, Real Threat," *Balkan Reconstruction Report*, no. 08/18 (2003).
10 Lyon, "Serbia's Sandžak under Milošević: Identity, Nationalism and Survival," 85.

11 Ibid.
12 Christian and Bisera Šećeragić Pfeifer, *Percepcija privatnog biznis sektora Sandžaka o političkom i ekonomskom ambijentu* (Evropski Pokret U Srbiji, Novi Pazar: Forum ZDF, 2009), 14.
13 The fish hatchery is reported to produce fish as of 2018. For more information, see A/N., "Novopazarski ribnjak 'Vojin Popović' ponovo u funkciji," in *Sandžakpress* (Novi Pazar, Serbia, 2010), https://sandzakpress.net/novopazarski-ribnjak-vojin-popovic-ponovo-u-funkciji.
14 Note that Novi Pazar was one of the locations that was to be paid 'special attention' by the Territorial Defense unit (paramilitary organization) and the Jugoslav National Army during the Yugoslav Succession Wars. For more information, see Christian Axboe Nielsen, "The State Security Service of the Republic of Serbia and Its Interaction with Ministries of Internal Affairs in Serb-Controlled Entities, 1990–1995," Research Report Prepared for the Case of Stanišić and Simatović (IT-03-69) (2016): 280.
15 Kenneth Morrison and Elizabeth Roberts, *The Sandzak: A History* (London: Hurst, 2013), 3; see also James Ron, "Boundaries and Violence: Repertoires of State Action along the Bosnia /Yugoslavia Divide," *Theory and Society* 29, no. 5 (2000); *Serbia's Sandžak Still Forgotten*, The International Crisis Group (2005), www.files.ethz.ch/.
16 Lyon, "Serbia's Sandžak under Milošević: Identity, Nationalism and Survival," 71–92.
17 See, for instance, "In/Form: 'Exploring Tactical Maneuvering between Formal and Informal Institutions in Balkan Societies'," https://www.ucl.ac.uk/ssees/research/funded-research-projects/inform/home.html or "The Global Informality Project," http://www.in-formality.com/wiki/index.php?title=Global_Informality_Project.
18 See, for instance, T.A. Thieme, "The Hustle Economy: Informality, Uncertainty and the Geographies of Getting By," *Progress in Human Geography* 42, no. 4 (2017): 529–548; József Böröcz, "Informality Rules," *East European Politics and Societies* 14, no. 2 (2000): 348–380; Abel Polese, Alessan Russo, and Francesco Strazzari, *Governance beyond the Law: The Immoral, the Illegal, the Criminal* (Palgrave Macmillan, 2019); Alena V. Ledeneva, *The Global Encyclopaedia of Informality. Volume I* (London: UCL Press, 2018), 1; Basudeb Guha-Khasnobis and Ravi Kanbur, *Linking the Formal and Informal Economy: Concepts and Policies* (Oxford: Oxford University Press, 2006); Aadne Aasland, Åse Berit Grødeland, and Heiko Pleines, "Trust and Informal Practice among Elites in East Central Europe, South East Europe and the West Balkans," *Europe-Asia Studies* 64, no. 1 (2012): 115–143; János Kornai, *Economics of Shortage* (Amsterdam: North-Holland, 1980); Mark Granovetter, "Economic Action and Social Structure: The Problem of Embeddedness," *American Journal of Sociology* 91, no. 3 (1985): 481–510; Endre Sik and Claire Wallace, "The Development of Open-Air Markets in East-Central Europe," *International Journal of Urban and Regional Research* 23, no. 4 (1999): 697–714; Galia Valtchinova, "Kinship and Transborder Exchange at the Bulgarian-Serbian Border in the Second Half of the 20th Century," *European Journal of Turkish Studies. Social Sciences on Contemporary Turkey*, no. 4 (2006); Anna Danielsson, "Reforming and Performing the Informal Economy: Constitutive Effects of the World Bank's Anti-informality Practices in Kosovo," *Journal of Intervention and Statebuilding* 10, no. 2 (2016).
19 Tim Hall, "The Geography of Transnational Organized Crime," in *The Geography of Transnational Organized Crime – Spaces Networks and Flows, Routledge Handbook of Transnational Organized Crime*, ed. Felia Allum, and Stan Gilmour (New York: Routledge, 2001), 173.
20 Clifford Geertz, "From the Native's Point of View: On the Nature of Anthropological Understanding," *Bulletin of the American Academy of Arts and Sciences*, no. 28 (1974): 1.
21 Jerome and Marc L. Miller Kirk, "Reliability and Validity in Qualitative Research," in *Qualitative Research Methods Volume 1* (Newbury Park, CA: Sage, 1986), 38.

24 *Introduction*

22 An offshoot of President Alija Izetbegović's SDA of Bosnia, and the party with the greatest number of supporters among the Bosniak population in the 1990s.
23 "Bošnjačko nacional novijeće Sandžaka 1991–2011," *Sandzak News.com*, December 24, 2011, http://www.sandzaknews.com/kolumna/73-bosnjacko-nacionalno-vijece-sandzaka-1991-2011.html.
24 Almir Mehonjić, "Teror se nastavlja a mi šutimo," February 15, 2012, http://www.bicent.com/kolumne/teror-se-nastavlja-a-mi-sutimo.
25 "Suđenje 'sandžačkoj grupi' ponovo odloženo," *Sandžačke Novine*. sandzacke.rs, January 12, 2012, http://www.sandzacke.rs/vijesti/drustvo/sudenje-sandzackoj-grupi-ponovo-odlozeno/.
26 Ahmet Davutoğlu, "Turkey's Foreign Policy Vision: An Assessment of 2007," *Insight Turkey* 10, no. 1 (2008).
27 See Turkish Cooperation and Coordination Agency (TIKA), https://www.tika.gov.tr/en.
28 See Presidency of the Republic of Turkey/Presidency of Religious Affairs, https://www.diyanet.gov.tr/en-US/.
29 See Yunus Emre Enstitusu, https://turkce.yee.org.tr.
30 Bahar Başer and Ahmet Erdi Öztürk, *Authoritarian Politics in Turkey: Elections, Resistance and the AKP* (London, New York: I.B. Tauris, 2017).
31 See Ahmet Erdi Öztürk, "Turkey's Diyanet under AKP Rule: From Protector to Imposer of State Ideology?" *Southeast European and Black Sea Studies* 16, no. 4 (2016): 619–635; Ahmet Erdi Öztürk and Samim Akgönül, "Turkey-Forced Marriage or Marriage of Convenience with the Western Balkans," in *The Western Balkans in the World: Linkages and Relations with Non-western Countries*, ed. Florian Bieber and Nikolaos Tzifakis (New York: Routledge, 2020); Kerem Öktem, "Global Diyanet and Multiple Networks: Turkey's New Presence in the Balkans," *Journal of Muslims in Europe* 1, no. 1 (2012): 27–58.
32 See Gulen Movement, http://www.gulenmovement.com; Simon P. Watmough and Ahmet Erdi Öztürk, "From 'Diaspora by Design' to Transnational Political Exile: The Gülen Movement in Transition," *Politics, Religion & Ideology* 19, no. 1 (2018): 33–52.
33 "The Economic Development of the Western Balkans, The Importance of Non-EU Actors," in *The Western Balkans in the World: Linkages and Relations with Non-western Countries*, ed. Florian Bieber and Nikolaos Tzifakis (New York: Routledge, 2019).
34 Florian Bieber and Nikolaos Tzifakis, *The Western Balkans in the World: Linkages and Relations with Non-western Countries* (New York: Routledge, 2019).
35 Dimitar Bechev, *Rival Power: Russia's Influence in Southeast Europe* (New Haven, CT: Yale University Press, 2017).
36 John F. Freie, *Counterfeit Community – The Exploitation of Our Longings for Connectedness* (Lanham, MD: Rowman & Littlefield, 1998).
37 Ibid., 5.
38 Ibid., 35.
39 Magnus Marsden, *Trading Worlds – Afghan Merchants Across Modern Frontiers* (London: Hurst, 2016), 29.
40 Niklas Luhmann, *Die Wirtschaft der Gesellschaft* (Berlin: Suhrkamp, 1994).
41 Paul Ricoeur, *Time and Narrative – Volume 3*, trans. Kathleen Blamey and David Pellauer (Chicago: University of Chicago Press, 1990), 259–261.
42 Ray Oldenburg, *The Great Good Place: Café, Coffee Shops, Community Centers, Beauty Parlors, General Stores, Bars, Hangouts, and How They Get You through the Day* (New York: Paragon House, 1989).
43 Ramon Oldenburg and Dennis Brissett, "The Third Place," *Qualitative Sociology* 5, no. 4 (1982): 9.
44 Ibid., 269.

45 Felia Allum and Stan Gilmour, "Introduction," in *Routledge Handbook of Transnational Organized Crime*, ed. Felia Allum and Stan Gilmour (London: Routledge, 2015), 10.
46 *Crime and its Impact on the Balkans*, United Nations Office on Drugs and Crime (March 2008), https://www.unodc.org/documents/data-and-analysis/Balkan_study.pdf.
47 Elinor Ochs, Lisa Capps, and Press Harvard University, quoted in *Living Narrative: Creating Lives in Everyday Storytelling* (Cambridge, MA: Harvard University Press, 2002), quoted by Matti Hyvärinen, "Analyzing Narratives and Story-Telling," in *The Sage Handbook of Social Research Methods*, ed. Pertti Alasuutari, Leonard Bickman, and Julia Brannen (Los Angeles: Sage, 2008), 452.
48 Corinne Squire, "Narrative Genres," in *Qualitative Research Practice*, ed. Clive Seale et al. (London: Sage, 2004), quoted by Hyvärinen, "Analyzing Narratives and Story-Telling," 451.
49 Andrea L. Smith, "Heteroglossia, 'Common Sense', and Social Memory," *American Ethnologist* 31, no. 2 (2004): 254.
50 Hayden White, "The Politics of Historical Interpretation: Discipline and De-sublimation," *Critical Inquiry* 9, no. 1 (1982): 137.
51 John Van Maanen, *Tales of the Field: On Writing Ethnography* (Chicago: University of Chicago Press, 1988), 5.
52 Marcus Tanner, "Belgrade Sacks Anti-Milosevic Journalists," *Independent* (1993).
53 "Scooping the Dictator; Serbia's Last Independent Newspaper Fights for Its Life," *Washington Post* (1995).
54 Inga Saffron, "In Serbia, the News is an Art Form," *Philadelphia Inquirer* (1993).
55 Susan L. Woodward, *Balkan Tragedy: Chaos and Dissolution after the Cold War* (Washington, DC: Brookings Institution Press, 1995), 293.
56 Ibid., 232; see also Milan Milošević, "The Media Wars," in *Burn This House: The Making and Unmaking of Yugoslavia*, ed. Jasminka Udovicki and James Ridgeway (Durham, NC: Duke University Press, 2000), 109–130.
57 Karmen Erjavec and Zala Volčič, "Rehabilitating Milošević: Posthumous Coverage of the Milošević Regime in Serbian Newspapers," *Social Semiotics* 19, no. 2 (2009).
58 Ruth Wodak and Michael Meyer, "Critical Discourse Analysis: History, Agenda, Theory and Methodology," in *Methods of Critical Discourse Analysis*, ed. Ruth Wodak and Michael Meyer (London: Sage, 2009), 9.

Part I

1 Narrating history through the prism of *šverc*

According to the 2011 census data, there are 100,410 residents in the municipality of Novi Pazar, illustrated in Figure 1.1, of which 77,443 (77.2 percent) identify as Bosniak (or 81,545 if those who identify as Muslim are included; 81.2 percent), 566 identify as Roma (0.5 percent), and 16,234 as Serbian (16.2 percent).[1] This corresponds roughly with the questionnaire data as illustrated in Figures 0.3 and 0.4. Official unemployment numbers in Serbia hover around 11 percent, and youth unemployment accounts for 29.1 percent.[2] However, during my time in the field, I learned that these numbers are inaccurate. According to casual conversations and unofficial documents retrieved from the local employment agency, the unemployment numbers are lower. A number of locals work in unrecorded occupations, including personal care services, the housing and rental sector, and at the local market. Due to the international sanctions regime, informal employment and the market grew exponentially during the first half of the 1990s, when Novi Pazar was a hub of smuggling activities. Novi Pazar, as an urban center, served as a thoroughfare for goods and attracted shoppers, traders, and workers from nearby villages as well as the greater area around Macedonia, Kosovo, Serbia, and Montenegro.

Due to the busy market activities, residents of Novi Pazar had at once a commonplace and yet distinct experience of the 1990s war years compared to other citizens of Serbia and those Bosniak and/or Muslim citizens who lived through the siege in Bosnia and Herzegovina (BiH). Like other citizens of Serbia, residents of Novi Pazar endured the internationally imposed sanctions. Living within Serbian state borders, however, spared this population from the hardship that Bosniaks of BiH experienced. And yet, locals in Novi Pazar became benefactors of Turkish charity and development projects during the conflict and after the Yugoslav Succession Wars ended, as was the case with citizens of Bosnia. This unique in- and out-of-state experience of the local community in Novi Pazar is at the core of this book. Smuggling – or *šverc*, as the practice is known locally – illustrates this in- and out-of-state experience. Because the informal market connects Novi Pazar to Bosnia, Turkey, and also to Serbia proper, I examine how informal transnational practices between 1991 and 1995 shaped these communities' collective sense of belonging and social relations *locally* following the Yugoslav Succession Wars.

DOI: 10.4324/9781003022381-3

Figure 1.1 Sandžak region including municipalities
Source: Map created by Lyubomyr Olinyk, siteGist.com.

Cultivating belonging across time and space

Though Montenegro split from Serbia in 2006, locals refer to their region as the *Sandžak* – an Ottoman-Turkish language loanword that translates into 'banner'. For the duration of the Ottoman Empire, the term 'Sandžak' denoted an administrative district that symbolizes a common foundation among local Bosniaks today. The region is, in other words, not a legal entity but rather a mental map that reflects a common history as understood by a segment of the local Bosniak population.[3] "While it was referred to as Raška within the medieval empire, as it is by Serbs even today," according to Kenneth Morrison and Elizabeth Roberts, "the region became known as Sandžak (or Sanjak of Novi Pazar) only during the latter part of the nineteenth century as the Ottoman Empire's authority over the Balkans began to erode."[4] At present, many locals identify as *Sandžaklije* (i.e., as inhabitants of the Sandžak region).

Novi Pazar, once a far-reaching merchant town, connected locals (especially merchants) with the Porte – also known as the Ottoman High Porte or the central government of the Ottoman Empire – as well as Florence. With the inclusion of present-day Bosnia and Herzegovina into the former Ottoman Empire in 1463, Ottoman trade routes expanded to Italy. Thenceforth, the seaport in Ragusa gained increasing prominence as a connecting hub between the Ottoman realm and beyond. Because merchants transported valuable goods such as silks, Chinese porcelain, spices, European wool, drugs, and textiles as well as gold and silver coins, Ottoman officials maintained a strict security regime along these trade routes.[5] To be sure, robberies did occur. Halil Inalcik, reflecting on Gertrude Richards,[6] relates an episode of stolen silk wear near Foça in present-day Bosnia. Ottoman officials apparently arrested the thief, recaptured the remnant silks, and forced locals to atone for the difference.[7] Inalcik's reflection on Richards illustrates that merchants traveled under the protection of Ottoman officials.

Towns along these routes, too, acquiesced relevance as places where travelers could rest in caravanserais, feed their horses, and/or pray at local mosques. These towns, unsurprisingly perhaps, turned into "typical Ottoman cites," as stated by Inalcik. Novibazar – or Novi Pazar as the city is called today – was along this route. Morrison and Roberts affirm: "the Sandžak became part of the *paşalık* of Bosnia, and one of the key Balkan trading centres; a land bridge linking Ottoman lands"[8] with the present-day Western Balkans. In Inalcik's words, "as trade with Florence expanded, the route between Ragusa and Bursa or Istanbul, through Foça, Novibazar, Edirne, and thence to Istanbul, or Bursa by way of Gallipoli, gradually gained importance."[9] Locals know this and repeatedly emphasized Novi Pazar's character as a historic merchant town during casual conversations and interviews.

Ottoman officials did not eradicate pre-existing cultural traditions on the peninsula. Instead, the Sublime Porte adopted cultural and religious aspects and incorporated them into the overarching social fabric. Mark Mazower sets forth, however, "the truth is that while for many centuries coexistence was undoubtedly more accepted under the Ottomans than almost anywhere in Christendom, there was certainly no sense of equality."[10] One must therefore acknowledge the existence of socioeconomic inequalities between Muslim and non-Muslim subjects. Non-Muslims held a second-class status throughout the empire. According to Mazower, non-Muslims were taxed for the assumed opting out of military services, disallowed to ride horses, or wear the color green, while authorities at court valued testimony of a non-Muslim less compared to that of a Muslim.[11] Conflicts were thus not of ethnic or theistic nature but had perhaps more to do with socioeconomic grievances. These rules, moreover, were not intractable. Inalcik suggested that rigid conditions prevailed when the sultan "sought to fulfill the provisions of the *Şeriat*" (Islamic law).[12] The full enforcement of such decrees was, in other words, likely not effective at all times and did not correspond with the everyday socioeconomic situation on the ground.[13] As such, Muslims and non-Muslims often belonged to the same class, says Inalcik, while "Jewish, Greek and Armenian merchant(s) dressed and acted like Muslims."[14] The distinction between Muslims and non-Muslims then, while undoubtedly existent, was prone to be more fluid as opposed to acutely present.

Seen from this perspective, various reasons contributed to the local populations' embrace of the Mohammedan faith, including upward social mobility. Conversion, however, took place gradually and in a nonviolent fashion.[15] Inalcik explains this process by stating that local *Vlach knezovi* (local Slavic noblemen) were able to retain their *baštine* – land they could levy taxes on (*not* private land) – and enjoyed the same privileges as Muslims did.[16] Some noblemen, according to Inalcik, retained their religious conviction while their sons adopted Islam. Nenad Maočanin found that some of these noblemen embraced the faith later to thereby increase the plot of land they could levy taxes on, thus officially becoming *sipahis* (landholders, cavalry men).[17] Mazower further asserts that "Greek and Serbian notable families converted to Islam to enjoy upward social mobility; a few, for a time, held on to their estates without converting."[18] Either way, conversions to Islam were not carried out forcefully, though connections with and adaptation to the dominant Ottoman power structure led to greater economic security.

In explaining general conversation mechanisms, Salim Ćerić, too, found that locals were influenced by the ruling regime, "as is the case in all class-systems."[19] Some were impressed by the power of the feudal forces and convinced of Ottoman longevity in the region. Banac echoes this notion and stated, "the progress of Islam in Bosnia and the notion – encouraged by the Bosnians themselves – of being the vaumure of the Ottoman fortress assured this region a special status in the Ottoman state."[20] Others, especially traders who held a privileged position, adopted Islam to elicit the liberty of traveling safely and to obtain and sell goods freely across the Ottoman Empire. Merchants, like craftsmen and servants, for instance, were tied to the feudal class as the primary consumers of material goods at the time. It was in part the acquired privilege, argued Ćerić, that tied these people to the Porte.[21]

Overall, Ćerić presents his reader with a historiographic interpretation of BiH within the Ottoman Empire from a socialist perspective. This is most obvious in his choice of words, and his repeated description of the Ottoman Empire as a *feudalni klasni sistem* (a feudal class system). And yet, it is interesting to point toward the resembling debate between Ćerić and Nina Glick-Schiller here. Like Glick-Schiller,[22] who analyzed social agents within a 'dialectics of place concept', so too does Ćerić – implicitly – who considered how respective classes related to the ruling Ottoman regime within the capacity of their profession:

> It is certain that the governing system was of military nature, though the Turkish army certainly came in tandem with a team of civilian officials and

servants. All their suits as well as the pottery, carpets and the like, might have initially been ordered from the homeland, but soon the material needs of officers and other state officials demanded these goods be produced on the spot. Transport routes were long and the communication along these routes was poor. Underdeveloped domestic craftsmanship and weak links with the West meant that goods were purchased in the East. Conquerors, who came with their specific cultural traditions, were considered superior, and had no reason to assume Christian customs, manner of dress, food, and housing. It should be added that the local people, who embraced Islam, automatically assimilated to the customs enacted by the conqueror, to prove their sincere acceptance of the new faith, and all attributes of the new ideology.[23]

Ćerić, in continuance of his argument, maintains that these customs were not exclusive to the Muslim population. Instead, Christians, too, adopted Ottoman manners of speech, diet, style of clothing, and means of housing.[24] As such, one might argue that Ćerić articulates a version of the networked nature between the Porte, their officials, and traders who sustained representatives with goods that ultimately influenced the everyday lives of local communities.

During this time, cultural influences traveled from Central Asia and Turkey to the Balkans, though ideas and folk customs certainly also traveled the other way, not least because of the Janissary Corps – the Ottoman Empire's elite guard – that comprised a sizable Slavic population with an equally sizable number of women that resided in the sultan's harem. While local non-Muslims often portray the *devşirme,* or so-called blood-tax, for instance, as cruel and damaging to the Slavic population, Inalcik found that "although some families especially in poor, mountain districts, gave their children of their own accord, sources indicate that people usually sought to avoid the *devşirme.*"[25] Considering that one received an education in the capital, which included the possibility to rise through the Ottoman Empire's ranks, Inalcik's argument illustrates that Slavs were not simply 'under the yoke' of the Porte. Instead, Inalcik demonstrates that Slavs possessed agency and were able to *become* participants in the empire's bureaucratic apparatus. This is significant, because one comes to understand that 'ethnic' identification did not factor in during the Ottoman Empire's existence. Perhaps Mazower said it best when he stated, "if there was no ethnic conflict, it was not because of tolerance but because there was no concept of nationality among the Sultan's subjects, and because Christianity stressed the 'community of believers' rather than ethnic solidarity."[26] Inalcik's reflection on the *devşirme* further indicates that the Ottoman Empire's culture was considered a *Leitkultur* of which one aspired to become a member, as previously indicated by Ćerić. Slavs thus emulated the ways of dressing, speech, and various Ottoman traits because doing so reflected an individual's socialization processes.

With the onset of the declining Ottoman Empire in the 19th century, traders who were tied to the Porte lost their privileged position gradually and were superseded by the Orthodox merchants.

The Orthodox merchant class rose to prominence in the 19th century, as documented by Traian Stojanović.[27] Espoused to the advancing Austro-Hungarian Empire, Orthodox merchants passed through five successive stages of professional affiliation before reaching the stage of politician, magnate, or intellectual, according to Stojanović. Aspiring statesmen often started as muleteers, peddlers, or sailors that practiced brigandage or piracy on the side during that first stage. When they moved up the social ladder, they evolved into commission agents or forwarders with moneylending on the side in a second stage. Next, they became merchants in a third step before moving into the business of banking. Merchants, according to Stojanović, often held political office on the side, in a fifth step, before assuming the position of statesmen, at which point most of them continued the practice of holding businesses.[28]

Toward the close of the 17th century, Orthodox merchants fell largely into the first two categories, while many remained in the third, fourth, and even fifth bracket in the 18th century.[29] Merchants were, significantly, among the few people who could read and write, beside teachers and several priests. They collected political experiences and ideas in Austro-Hungary and then related these ideas to the local population, as argued by Stojanović. Merchant activities were initially limited to subsidizing Orthodox Churches and schools. Soon, however, merchants emerged as carriers of a distinct Serbian national movement.[30] The Serbian Orthodox church thus rose to power in tandem with the Orthodox merchant-cum-political/intellectual entrepreneur class sometime in the 19th century.

This new merchant class was, however, not ethnically and/or theistically uniform. In describing the town of Novi Pazar at an unspecified time between 1911 and 1941, Miodrag Radović depicts the *dućan* (store) of one Samuel Konforti, whom locals called Sumbuliko.[31] Konforti, according to one online source,[32] belonged to an influential Jewish family with relatives in present-day Bulgaria, BiH, Italy, and Turkey, and owned a store in downtown Novi Pazar that served as what one might contemporarily call a *mjenjačnica* (exchange office). Exchanging gold, first Turkish lira (1923–2005), silver, and other valuables, Konforti maintained connections with traders in Thessaloniki in present-day Greece and issued checks to merchants who traveled there in pursuit of trading goods and/or livestock. Upon returning from their business trips to Novi Pazar, traders collected their valuables from Konforti who soon turned into a local magnate after combining his exchange business with that of selling foodstuffs. Radović, reflecting on Omar Efendi's memoires, believed Konforti paid some 50 assistants to buy livestock from surrounding villagers in support of his business. Konforti was allegedly an extraordinarily successful entrepreneur who grew his commercial power after the agrarian land reform of 1918.

With the proclamation of the land reform, land grants passed to those individuals who tilled the fields. In the process, *çiftliks* (landowners) lost their livelihood, and were forced to pawn their possessions, which frequently consisted of gold jewelry. "An absolute majority," according to Radović, pawned these valuables at Sumbuliko's store; Sumbiliko grew wealthier in the process.[33] Most of the individuals that were forced to forfeit their land, meanwhile, were unable to retrieve their valuables from him thereafter. Though Radović's reflections on Sumbuliko end here, one learns from the aforementioned online source that Sumbuliko died prior to WWII. His family members, save his daughter Sarina and her daughters, perished in the Holocaust.[34]

Besides illustrating the transnational character of Novi Pazar as a far-reaching merchant town, the preceding episode further exemplifies that merchants were connected to specific regimes in some way. Čerić highlighted, for instance, that merchants sought to increase and maintain the purchasing power of their respective 'commercial bourgeoisie' – their customers – even by political means. Merchants were thus variously tied to the Habsburg Monarchy and the Ottoman Empire.

A number of related incidents led to the rise of the Orthodox merchants, including domestic political decay in the Ottoman Empire, imperial overstretch, conflicts with Russia and the Austro-Hungarian Empire, respectively, and a series of economically crippling concessions that led to the decline and final collapse of the Ottoman Empire in 1918.[35] Within this context, the Porte capitulated to the Serbian twin demands of economic and national(ist) emancipation by decreeing the two *Hatišerifs* of 1830 and 1833 during the *Tanzimat* period. Ljubinka Ćirić-Bogetić and Miroslav Djordjević explained that Serbs were now free to define their borders and internal affairs:[36] "Serbs, Turks, and foreign subjects" were now able to trade without restrictions.[37] Ćirić-Bogetić and Djordjević's words are particularly noteworthy in this context as they state: "*posebne odredbe odnose se na slobodu trgovine Srba, Turaka i stranih podanika.*"[38] Both Serbs and Turkish people were, according to Ćirić-Bogetić and Djordjević, considered local because the authors differentiate between Serbs and Turks on the one hand and *foreigners* on the other. And yet, between the decree and subsequent autonomy in 1878, Orthodox subjects secured the right to own land, while Muslims and/or Turks were forced to move either into the city or away.

Nationalization and migration processes: a shrinking world for the Muslim population of Novi Pazar

With the preceding historical sketch in mind, the *Tanzimat* period not only brought about the socioeconomic emancipation of the Serbian nation and/or those individuals who identified as Orthodox but also heralded the expulsion and/or forced emigration of the Muslim and/or Turkish population from the Balkans, specifically from present-day Serbia. It is instructive, however, to point toward the initially fledgling and/or potentially absent sense of national identification among the Orthodox population here. Ćirić-Bogetić and Djordjević cite Jevrem Gruić, who described the Serbian population of the 19th century as

> a bare agent who can belong to one entity, and to yet another at any given time. . . . Our nation has no will of its own, but not because he is unable. . . . For internal liberation to take place, our people must understand who they are as a nation, the kind of rights this nation should have, why,

and given by whom, [our people] must know their borders; It means telling people what it means for a nation to live in a state, and to invite people to live as such.[39]

Gruić describes an essentially inexistent Serbian national consciousness that yet had to be instilled from above – from the top down. As such, economic disputes might have contributed to the social unrest in the region as opposed to sheer 'ethnic hatred'. In this context, retaliations against Muslims in the wake of the First and Second Balkan Wars and thereafter may be interpreted as a rivalry among classes. Though the ensuing violence accompanying the two Balkan and two World Wars is too extensive to cover in this book,[40] it is imperative to understand that the Muslim population was driven to leave Southeastern Europe for Turkey by violence and fear – fear that was compounded by their loss of land.

Following the first Serbian uprising, according to Ćirić-Bogetić and Djordjević, Turkish and Muslim-Slavic families were stipulated to leave Serbia within five years following the ratification of the *Hatišerifs* in 1830 and 1833, and made to yield their rights to property.[41] Šaban Hodžić states that Muslims moved and/or fled to those territories that were yet considered Ottoman protectorates, including the Sandžak of Novi Pazar.[42] Homogenization processes were thus underway before the Austro-Hungarian occupation of BiH in 1878, though they sped up markedly after the Treaties of San Stefano and Berlin.

Safet Bandžović provides his readers with vivid picture of the nationalization processes during the late 19th century. Reflecting on Slobodan Jovanović,[43] Bandžović relates a discussion about the strategic location of the *Novopazarski* Sandžak that separated Serbia from Montenegro prior to the signing of the San Stefano treaty: "the Russians initially pressured Serbia to grant Niš to Bulgaria; the Serbs, in turn, would get Novi Pazar from where they would expel the Turks, if they refused to leave on their own."[44] The Sandžak was not only strategically important as regarded the unification of Montenegro and Serbia as well as Serbian access to warm-water ports, but it also served as a migratory corridor to and through which Muslim Slavs and/or Turks traveled during the protracted collapse of the Ottoman Empire. According to Vladan Jovanović, following the Austro-Hungarian occupation in 1878 and subsequent annexation of BiH in 1909, the number of Muslim inhabitants in the Novo Pazarian Sandžak rose from 45 to 60 percent.[45] Bandžović illustrates this inherent fluidity of borders and population movement between 1876 and 1919, all the way up to WWI and beyond.[46]

The Sandžak region became a center for immigration as well as a place of transit from which Muslims immigrated to Turkey. Migrants – or *muhadžiri*, as they are called locally – migrated through Novi Pazar and on to present-day Macedonia, Albania, and Turkey. Novi Pazar thus developed into an ephemeral space for the out-migrating group yet localized the membership for those who stayed behind. These families became the 'vehicle by which locals remember'[47] and/or engage with the past.

Diaspora as a "category of practice":[48] a precondition for the creation of transnational trade practices

Though in-depth research about migration and diaspora mechanisms far exceeds the limit of the present book, the very concept of transnational diaspora practices necessitates a clarification in terms. Building on Rogers Brubaker's three categories of dispersion, homeland orientation, and boundary maintenance, I conceptualize diaspora and migrant experiences as a category of practice.

Brubaker's first criterion regards dispersion. Bosniaks who relocated to Turkey were not strictly forced, though they *were* dispersed traumatically across space and time. The first migratory wave of Bosniaks leaving Southeastern Europe for Turkey followed Austro-Hungarian occupation and the subsequent collapse of the Ottoman Empire after 1876/78. A combination of factors drove the first wave of outmigration, including the introduction of compulsory military duty on the side of the Habsburgs. Austria-Hungary subordinated formerly autonomous properties, including *vakifs* (religious endowments), to the imperial bureaucracy and abolished the *timariot* ('feudal' Ottoman land laws). Austria-Hungary finally transmogrified the Bosnian system from a subsistence into a monetary economy, which impoverished previously landowning *beys*.

Based on the preceding first criterion, the Bosniak community of Novi Pazar, too, falls within the category of diaspora since this community was severed from Bosnia proper by the Austro-Hungarian Empire and subsequently KSHS/SFRY. As such, Novi Pazar indeed consists of a "settled population . . . that lives as a minority outside its ethnonational homeland,"[49] which is Bosnia and Herzegovina. This situation became tangible again during the Yugoslav Succession Wars.

The largest wave of Muslims left Southeastern Europe following WWII.[50] Though Turkey and Yugoslavia had by now signed the Turkish-Yugoslav convention in 1938 and arranged further population exchanges in the form of the so-called Gentlemen's Agreement in 1953, Edvin Pezo states that it was Turkey's open-door policy that facilitated emigration from Yugoslavia and immigration to Turkey, respectively. Turkey's Settlement Law 2510, according to Pezo, was especially instrumental regarding this open-door policy, seeing that this law facilitated the emigration of Muslim Slavs to Turkey, provided they spoke the Turkish language or else ascribed to republican values. Bosniaks, Torbeši, and Pomaks were particularly welcome in Turkey as these groups were thought to assimilate to Turkish values and norms with ease.[51] Jovanović adds another reason for the large-scale emigration to Turkey, namely that of an information campaign by which authorities promised 'rich prospects' upon moving to Turkey.[52] Though documentary proof of the Gentleman's Agreement is missing,[53] academics generally agree that Muslim Slavs were 'free' to leave Yugoslavia upon giving up their citizenship.[54] The agreement further allowed for, or rather stipulated, that Muslim Slavs could leave for reasons of family reunification in the Turkish republic.

Brubaker reflects on William Safran in considering his second point on 'homeland orientation'.[55] According to Safran, diasporas ought to (1) "maintain(ing) a collective memory or myth about the homeland"; (2) "regard(ing) the ancestral homeland as the true, ideal home, and as the place to which one . . . will eventually return home to"; (3) be "collectively 'committed to the maintenance or restoration of the homeland and to its safety and prosperity'"; and (4) "'continu[ing] to relate, personally or vicariously', to the homeland, in a way that significantly shapes one's identity and solidarity."[56] Brubaker and Safran's insightful analyses force us to differentiate between successive migratory waves and one's resulting identification with the new and/or old homeland, respectively.

The first and second migratory waves differ from the third in that emigrants of the former migrated to a state in the making. One might argue they *became* citizens of Turkey in the process because they helped to build the Turkish Republic. Though individuals were surely aware of their confessional, gender, and class belonging and so forth, the national experience was not as mature compared to the national label attached to emigrants of the third wave. Émigrés, to be sure, presumably harbored sentimental attachments to their ancestral homeland. And yet, these people generally relocated to Turkey for good. Reasons for the finality of this move were of a structural and personal nature, as interviewees in Novi Pazar and Sarajevo explained. Structural conditions included a non-return stipulation on the part of Turkey that left people stranded on both sides of the border from where they decided to leave, for instance.[57] Individuals were also left without property rights upon leaving their place of origin. Both interlocutors as well as archival research at the *Arhiv Jugoslavije* in Belgrade confirmed this information. One interviewee, for instance, explained she had not seen or spoken to her sister in 30 years after she left Novi Pazar for Turkey in the late 1930s. "She was unable to return," the elderly lady explained, "because they constantly closed the borders. She did not want to be stuck somewhere in between."[58]

Structural conditions hampered family reunification efforts following the 1934 'law of last names'. Reflecting on a paper written by Meltem Türköz,[59] Esra Özyürek stated, "Republican officials were actively involved in the naming process when emigrants arrived in Turkey. They vetoed many names on the basis that they were not Turkish or appropriate last names, and they simply recorded other names in their books."[60] As a result, Bosniaks of Southeastern Europe might have been unable to locate family members who emigrated from the constituting monarchy to Turkey during the first and second waves and vice versa.

Maintaining personal relations with family members who left for Turkey was thus complicated, and this continues to shape transnational relations into the present. Amer, a young interlocutor from Turkey, investigated the origins of his family in Novi Pazar and Macedonia, for instance, without knowing their last names or exact location of their erstwhile residence. He nevertheless kept up the search, hoping to reunite with his lost family in Southeastern Europe. He explained:

> My grandparents' names were changed when they migrated to Turkey in the 1930. When I came here the first time, I could not reconnect, but I brought home some soil because my mother wanted to put it on her mom's grave.[61]

Significant is, however, that Amer does not speak Bosnian/Croatian/Serbian/Montenegrin. The same is true for Leijla's descendants who visited her in Novi Pazar after the Yugoslav Succession Wars had ended. Leijla and her nuclear family members, meanwhile, do not speak Turkish even though her son-in-law smuggled goods from Turkey to Southeastern Europe during the Yugoslav Succession Wars.

Though the Turkish nation-building process lasted well into the 1960s, individuals who joined the third wave may not have perceived themselves as immigrants. And yet, the third migratory wave might come closest to our current understanding of the term 'immigrant', as these people moved to a foreign, established state. This group, perhaps consequently, maintained a stronger link to those Bosniaks of the 'homeland'. Lejla Voloder, for instance, explains the Turkish population perceived Muslim Slavs as Bosniaks, not as co-Turks when they arrived in the Republic.[62] Muslims who left Yugoslavia behind as Turks in the third and last wave thus arrived in Turkey as Bosniaks.

Thomas Schad offers valuable insight on this point. He cites the Bayrampaşa governors' website to illustrate the integral character of the Bosniak-Turkish community in this district[63] that houses "immigrants from the Balkans, and their valued(ing) (of) family networks, (have) that contributed to the development of Bayrampaşa as one of Istanbul's most beautiful cities."[64] Significantly, the Bayrampaşa district is home to the *Bosna Sancak Kültür ve Yardımlaşma Derneği* (Bosnia Sandžak Culture and Solidarity Association) that opened in 1989. Further down, Schad analyzes an autobiographical novel written by Bekir Bayraktar.[65] The author grew up in Rožaje on the Montenegrin side of the Sandžak territory and migrated to Turkey in 1968. Bayraktar may thus be considered an ideal type that characterizes the third migratory wave, a notion that is compounded by the fact that he wrote his text in Bosnian. His audience was in Southeastern Europe, and perhaps also Bosniaks in Turkey who share Bayraktar's experience. In other words, he retained an emotive connection to the territory of Sandžak and his language, unlike those migrants who had come to Turkey with the first and second migratory waves. Bayraktar had not emigrated to a state in the making but had arrived in Turkey as a Bosniak.

Hometown associations in Turkey add further critical insight on the question of diaspora groups and migrants that act as agents of transnational practices. It is interesting to note that the *Bosna Sancak Kültür ve Yardımlaşma Derneği* opened as late as 1989 because it coincides directly with the initial collapse of SFRY. The Yugoslav Succession Wars were indeed a catalyst by which émigrés related personally with the homeland to the extent that this identification shaped their solidarity with Muslims of Southeastern Europe – a place their ancestors had migrated from. Reflecting on Jeanne Hersant and Alexandre Toumarkine, Bulut also identifies the conflicts as "a factor of communal mobilization . . . with long established migrants at the forefront of the mobilization."[66] Yet, early émigrés identify decidedly as citizens of Turkey and not as Bosniaks, as illustrated by the following announcement of the Bosnia-Sandžak Foundations and Associations:

FROM THE BOSNIA-SANDZAK FOUNDATIONS AND ASSOCIATIONS TO THE GREAT TURKISH NATION. We see that when TRT was making a decision to broadcast in different languages, Bosnian was included among these languages. This decision and practice was a surprise for us. We are a community that have mixed like 'SKIN AND NAIL' for centuries with all the people of the Turkish Republic, the greatest legacy left to us by the Great Leader ATATURK. We support with all our heart the spirit and understanding of ATATURK'S expression "HOW HAPPY IS HE WHO CALLS HIMSELF A TURK" and carry our TURKISH identity with pride [original emphasis].[67]

Safran's fourth point seems thus confirmed, though only partially. The local diaspora community evidently relates personally with the homeland to the extent that the Yugoslav Succession Wars shaped their solidarity significantly. Émigrés, however, no longer identify as Bosniaks, as illustrated earlier, but as integral citizens of the Turkish Republic.

With the preceding examples in mind, one may confirm the existence of a collective memory maintenance, as suggested by Safran. The Yugoslav Succession Wars clearly serve as a crucial point of rupture here, because the family unit served as the primary vehicle that harbored these memories in this initial phase. With the outbreak of the war, the practice of collective memory maintenance moved into the public sphere of Bosnia-Sandžak hometown associations. Safran's second point is more difficult to confirm, though one might point to the structural difficulties that prevented people from returning to Southeastern Europe even if they wanted to. Time is a crucial factor here, as individuals, including Amer's family and Leijla's relatives, became settled in their new 'homeland'. The desire to return may have shifted further into the distance and made way for Safran's third and fourth point, namely, a collective commitment for the maintenance and restoration of a *distant* homeland.

Brubaker's third and final criterion involves the question of boundary maintenance that involves "the preservation of a distinctive identity vis-à-vis a host society."[68] To be sure, Bosniak émigrés often settled in the Istanbulite *mahalles* (city districts) of Pendik and Bayrampaşa. Bosniaks also initiated the construction of hometown associations and collected aid for Bosnia. Yet, these people did not wish to be instrumentalized, as illustrated in the preceding quote. Instead, they demonstrated their identification with the Turkish state. And yet, Bosniak émigrés are dispersed across time and space since the border of the Ottoman Empire moved beyond the territories they currently inhabit.

Locals in Novi Pazar are twice removed: once from BiH and once from the former Ottoman Empire and present-day Turkey. There was, however, no collective desire to return to the homeland or any vigorous homeland orientation that altered and/or influenced the collective identification mechanisms of this émigré group. While attitudes shifted to active commemoration of the 'homeland' since the 1990s, this group does not collectively aspire repatriation to one of the former Yugoslav republics or to Bosnia specifically. I thus agree with and build on Brubaker, who argues for a "category of practice" instead of defining émigré groups as bounded entities.[69]

Categories of practice allow for a diachronic analysis of transnationalism without assuming that post-Ottoman communities share one unified culture. Joseph Rouse states:

> Instead of positing such a unified conception of culture, practice theories recognize the co-existence of alternative practices within the same cultural milieu, differing conceptions of or perspectives on the same practices, and ongoing contestation and struggle over the maintenance and reproduction of cultural norms. . . . Instead of treating cultural interaction as a matter of translation between whole cultural systems, practice theorists can recognize more localized practices and meanings that function within each of the interacting fields of cultural practice.[70]

Rouse's argument about disparate cultural milieus is imperative here for the very understanding of the diachronic narrative structure presented in this book. The practice of *šverc* reveals ongoing contestations over the maintenance of cultural values among Bosniak citizens. It is thus commonplace to learn about *šverc* as a pragmatic practice that subsided with the end of the sanctions. Sanja Kljajić, for instance, declared the "talk of brotherly relations" between the Turkish émigré population and local Bosniaks a myth.[71] Others argue that *švercerci* of all backgrounds embraced Milošević because traders got rich in the process. Again, others emphasize the personal links that connect Bosniaks of Novi Pazar with the diaspora community in Turkey. It is this very emphasis on the "dynamics of social structures and their governance or constraint of individual actions [that] gives a strongly historical dimension to" the present examination of *šverc* in Novi Pazar.[72]

Diaspora connections and neo-Ottomanism: a Turkish perspective

Every successful narrative necessitates a responsive sender and receiver. Transnational relations between émigrés and local Bosniaks, in other words, did not transpire in a vacuum but fell on fertile ground in Turkey. At the inception of this project in 2012, the Zero Problems with Neighbors policy served as a focal point for the analysis of Balkan-Turkish connections, transnational and otherwise. Prof. Dr. Ahmet Davutoğlu, Turkey's former minister of foreign affairs, developed this strategy in response to cope with and influence regional political developments following the seismic shifts of the post–Cold War era. Turkey was, according to Davutoğlu, not simply a bridge between East and West but *central*, based on its historical heritage.[73] Interlocutors gravitated toward this heritage and never tired of emphasizing their historic connection with Turkey.

Turkish citizens, too, mined "through the remnants of their past in order to find clues to help them understand or control the present," according to Esra Özyürek.[74] Turgut Özal, Turkey's prime minister from 1983 to 1989 and acting president of Turkey between 1989 and 1993, was instrumental regarding this shift from Turkish isolationism to one of expansion. In his tenure as prime minister and acting president, Özal importantly sanctioned the reinterpretation of *Kemalism*. Former president Özal thus not only invited the government to reconsider the past but also allowed for a public discourse about and reconciliation with the history of the former Ottoman Empire. Turkish repositioning within the geopolitical context based on its past coincided directly with the Yugoslav Succession Wars.

Most astute in this context is perhaps Joshua Walker's dissertation on "How Post-Imperial Successor States Shape Memories."[75] In identifying Özal as the original architect behind the neo-Ottoman turn, Walker points toward Özal's ruminations on the post–Cold War constellation of states. Özal was not, according to Walker, interested in a network of Islamic states, but guided by pragmatism. In Walker's words:

> It was instead a pragmatic political agenda – based on real, historically-guided identity networks and political culture legacies – aimed at capitalizing on the new regional dynamics of the 1990s in a manner impossible within the nation-state structure that had held sway since World War I in Turkey.[76]

Walker's analysis rings familiar, especially when considering the above quote by which the Turkish cultural office in Novi Pazar seeks to "promote Turkey's cultural heritage in all its different expressions, and to offer the possibility of meeting and dialogue between the cultural reality locally, and the Turkish cultural heritage."[77] Southeastern Europe presents an ideal territory that unites both historic and cultural aspects of Ankara's pragmatic foreign policy.

Some Serbian scholars, meanwhile, perceived the Zero Problems with Neighbors policy with a hefty dose of suspicion. In his book *Neoosmanizam*, Darko Tanasković summed the policy up as follows:

> Neo-Ottomanism streamlines the nostalgia of a great historical nation that is dissatisfied with her current position in the world. As such, this policy serves as a beacon that guides Turkey's foreign policy despite all the real and transparent ideas, including Atatürk's radical secular revolution. Neo-Ottomanism runs as an undercurrent [to official policies].[78]

Tanasković, an Orientalist by training and former ambassador to Turkey, distrusted the Neo-Ottoman discourse of the early 2000s. He understood the actions of Recep Tayyip Erdoğan as a ploy by which the *Adalet ve Kalkınma Partisi* (Justice and Development Party, AKP) sought to dismantle the secular state in favor of a cross-border ideology based on Islamic values. I disagree with Tanasković in much of his analysis, most notably that Islam serves as a legitimating factor in Turkish politics. With the benefit of hindsight, one must, however unfortunately, agree with Tanasković that the AKP dismantled the secular state of Turkey, as analyzed by Bahar Baser and Ahmet Erdi Öztürk.[79] At the time, however, participating in and having perhaps even a sense of admiration for those who organized the trade was normal.

In part, Turkish rumination on the past fueled and perhaps legitimized the cross-border connections that materialized in the form of aid and trade. Significantly, the Bosniak émigré community welcomed Bosniak refugees during the Yugoslav Succession Wars. Kemal Kirişci, senior fellow at the Brookings Institution, stated: "many of their relatives and friends (came to Turkey) as refugees, bringing them into direct contact with first-hand disturbing news about the conflict. . . . the conflict affected directly a large number of people because of their personal ties to Bosnia."[80] Extending material aid in any form and shape thus seemed not only legitimate but crucial, albeit informal and to some extent illegal from the perspective of international lawmakers. Turkey supported the implementation of sanctions against Belgrade and even proposed a 'Gulf-like' military operation against Serbia.[81]

Sandžak, the predominantly Muslim enclave between Montenegro and Serbia, thus reveals two important aspects, one relating to the supposedly "unified conception of culture" and the second about pragmatism in international politics. I will return to the former further later. The latter aspect, however, is instructive in our understanding of Turkish positioning in the post–Cold War world and Ankara's own understanding of the inviolability of sovereignty. Meddling in the Sandžak region, in other words, might have lent credibility to the Kurdish question in Turkey and was therefore unacceptable. Material aid to the Sandžak region, consequently, transpired covertly by way of informal relations between émigré Bosniaks and locals in Novi Pazar. This feeling of perceived normalcy legitimized transnational trade practices, a notion that radiated all the way into the 2000s, also because of the local perception of Turkey as a stable state, especially in comparison to the crumbling Yugoslav state.

Transnationalism as a constituent component of trading practices, and the formation of social relations

This book reflects transnational theories as discussed by Thomas Faist, Rainer Bauböck, and Nina Glick-Schiller's particularly astute discussion about the 'good versus bad' migration narrative.[82] Heeding Glick-Schiller's criticism on the conflation of state and society, the present study of transnational diaspora relations addresses historical processes that go beyond the narrow confines of the nation-state to include how international developments affect and influence local experiences with migration. Serbia is not, to put it in Glick-Schiller's words, a "historically discrete sovereign state" but is connected to the greater post-Ottoman realm by way of shared "experiences, norms and values. . . [that are] embedded in social, economic and political processes, networks, movements and institutions that exist both within and across state borders."[83] Examining transnational kin-*com*-trade-networks illustrates that international organizations (IOs) do not possess the power to isolate a state economically. Neither does the state have the sole authority to shape the behavior of people *within* its boundaries socially. Instead, it is a dynamic interplay between IOs, the state in question, and the legitimacy locals confer upon the former. Sandžak, particularly Novi Pazar, is a favorably situated space in which to analyze this process empirically. Novi Pazar is, to put it in Pierre Bourdieu's words, a "vast social laboratory"[84] in which one is able to examine the *longue durée* of transnational diaspora connections.

Cross-border practices are embodied, as opposed to virtual cross-border assignations. Procuring goods, contacts, and trading with commodities involves physical motion across borders and engagement with material goods coming from abroad. As such, the theoretical underpinnings of this study in part diverge from transnationalism as defined by Eva Østergaard-Nielsen.[85] Crossing the border physically, she states, is not a precondition when examining political practices among migrants and refugees. Political links, according to Østergaard-Nielsen, contrast with "economic and social practices" in that political engagement does not require "actual travel."[86]

Schad introduced a similarly disembodied approach in his working paper "The Rediscovery of the Balkans? A Bosniak-Turkish Figuration in the Third Space Between Istanbul and Sarajevo."[87] Schad dismisses transnationalism because the paradigm

> assumes the existence of the nation as a category in the first place. . . . Violent expulsions of Muslims form the Balkans and Christians from Anatolia, population exchanges, resettlement agreements, pogroms killings, and genocide in the name of the nation can absolutely not be ignored.[88]

Transnational relations, to be sure, insinuate a national coefficient, as suggested by Schad. Yet, 'trans' as a prefix delimits a transformation of "having changed from one thing to another,"[89] Transnationalization thus defines exactly the process of looking *beyond* the nation to describe cross-border practices. Utilizing the analytic tool of transnationalism does not obviate that one dismisses nationalism, or worse, condones atrocities committed in the name of a nation as suggested by Schad. Transnationalism is not "simply about migration and development, but also transnationalization"; it is about the *process* of looking how internal and external events influence individuals within artificially created borders.[90] Perhaps Faist said it best when he explained:

> Transnational syncretism [is] not located on a magic carpet of a deterritorialized space of flows. It only makes sense when firmly tied to specific spaces in different nation states. It is not a notion above nation-states but a combination of both the inside and the between.[91]

The practice of transnationalism must be, in other words, situated within nation-states because this is the reality of the international system. The task then, is to tangibly filter out these social connections across state borders.

Speaking of embodied cross-border mobility bears analytical consequences. First, physical border crossings indicate the presence of a manned border, however dysfunctional the state in question may be. The Yugoslav rump state was not only an internationally recognized state and thus policed from within, but it was also regulated from without due to the international sanctions regime. Second (and related) is the fact that *Novo Pazarci* did not travel to Turkey en masse. How, in other words, does one extrapolate from and apply the embodied experience of mobile traders to the sedentary experience of those who did not travel to Turkey? Esra Bulut, too, examines this conundrum in her research on transnational links between Turkey and the Balkans.[92]

For Bulut, the state is central in her analysis of transnational relations. She thus proposed a paradigm shift from transnational to trans-state relations. Considering the case of the SFRY, Bulut suggested that

> physical and virtual trans-state interaction between individuals, groups and organizations in Turkey and the rest of the Balkans has been altered by changes in the means and conditions of communication and movement, framed by the opening up of the region with the demise of the Eastern bloc.[93]

Her insight is valuable, though raises some analytic questions. Yugoslavia belonged to the Eastern Bloc only until 1948 and was in fact a founding member of the Non-Aligned Movement (NAM). Yugoslav citizens were thus relatively free to travel and enjoyed much greater freedoms until the end of the Cold War. Following the Yugoslav Succession Wars, Bosniaks, Serbs, Montenegrins, and Kosovo-Albanians were barred from traveling visa free until 2009. Statements about the virtual sphere, too, must be qualified. International sanctions, coupled with the Milošević regime's information propaganda, impeded access to the Internet until 1996.[94] The analysis put forward by Bulut, to be sure, is vital to our understanding about how the Turkish *state* utilized 'migrants', and diaspora relations.

Transnational practices highlight how agents shape narratives from below – histories that rarely fit neatly within the narrow confines of nation-states. I thus agree with Bulut in her assessment that states remain to be the main *unit* of analysis, though I diverge from her conclusion that transnationalism results from contrived ideas "academics [found in their] search(ing) for an alternative to the destructive statism and nationalism in the region."[95] This analysis is deceptive for three reasons. First, finding solutions to the persistent problems with nationalism ought not be an intellectual riddle. I therefore agree with Bulut that individuals in the Western Balkans need applicable solutions for the economic and social vows the Yugoslav Succession Wars created back in the 1990s, and not an academic 'search for alternatives' to describe real problems people face on a daily basis. Second, such assumptions further play into the hands of nationalist leaders and narratives about the dangers of cross-border connections that are not sanctified by the state. Third, and perhaps more important, is the fact that states are not the primary problem, but political actors are; a faceless state does not nationalism make, but political actors do.

To understand the discord of the term 'nation' within the conceptual frame of transnationalism, we must return shortly to the preceding point about the nation within the transnational paradigm. In *Homeland Calling*, Paul Hockenos asserts, "the primordial pull of Balkan ancestry forges a timeless bond, indubitably stronger than the acquired legal credentials of foreign citizenship."[96] Expatriate kin, Hockenos argues, thus remain to be part of the nation "eternally." Though I disagree with the former analysis, his argument about the heterogeneity of migrant and diaspora experiences is instructive. Hockenos differentiates Albanian, Croatian, and Serbian exile patriots and nationalists from the *Gastarbeiteri* (guest workers), the latter of which mainly migrated to work in Germany and Switzerland. Notably, he states the former "vigilantly nursed dreams of a return triumphant" while the latter migrated to earn money.[97] As reflected by the difference between the Albanian, Croatian, and Serbian expatriate and *Gastarbeiter* diaspora, one must differentiate between the various experiences of exile and reasons as to why people left their home following the dissolution of the Ottoman Empire.

The road to hell is paved with good intentions: illicit trade practices and sanctions-busting in Serbia during the 1990s

Nekome rat, nekome brat.[98]

During the 1990s, the 'international community' imposed the most comprehensive set of sanctions to date against the Yugoslav rump state.[99] Considering the gruesome war in the former Yugoslav state with the benefit of hindsight, it is clear that the sanctions against Serbia and Montenegro backfired. Local 'patriots' despised the international community for their meddling in Yugoslav (i.e., Serbian and Montenegrin) affairs, and those victimized by the war lost their faith in the United Nations (UN) and the North Atlantic Treaty Organization (NATO), as convincingly argued by Thomas G. Weiss in *The United Nations and Changing World Politics*.[100]

Measures taken by the international community allowed for, and replicated, the very nationalism these IOs sought to extinguish. Boutros Boutros Ghali, who served as UN secretary-general between 1992 and 1995, conceded that sanctions, instead of achieving the sought-after modification in behavior of the state in question, often provoked nationalist backlash domestically,[101] as was the case in Serbia.

> Sanctions, as is generally recognized, are a blunt instrument. They raise the ethical question of whether suffering inflicted on vulnerable groups in the target country is a legitimate means of exerting pressure on political leaders whose behavior is unlikely to be affected by the plight of their subjects. Sanctions also always have unintended or unwanted effects.[102]

By 1995, it was painfully clear that the sanctions against Serbia were not only futile but strengthened Slobodan Milošević's position in social and military terms. In fact, Belgrade benefited from the international arms embargo because most of the military equipment was stationed within Serbian territory.[103] Also, the Yugoslav National Army (JNA) was designed on the premise of self-sufficiency. The international arms embargo, in other words, created a strategic advantage for the

Belgrade-sponsored paramilitary unit *Jedinica za specijalne operacije* (Unit for Special Operations, JSO). R.T. Naylor examined the repercussions of the embargo in *Economic Warfare – Sanctions, Embargo Busting and Their Human Cost*.[104] Serbia was well equipped in military terms, and continued to produce and then ship equipment to, for instance, Rwanda – yet another state under international sanctions.[105] Serbian arms dealers even provided Bosniak combatants with artillery shells during the Croat-Bosniak hostilities[106] and sold arms to Libya[107] and Croatia[108] in exchange for oil. These examples illustrate the shallow depth of the supposedly deep-seated nationalism that separated ordinary Serbs, Croats, and Bosniaks. One indeed wonders if, as Peters Andreas argued, the international communities' inadequate involvement in the Yugoslav Succession Wars prolonged the war in the former Yugoslavia, especially the Bosnian war.[109]

Serbian officials were further involved in massive financial pyramid schemes. Dafina Milanović and Jezdimir Vasiljević, managers of the infamous Dafiment and the Jugoskandik Savings Bank, respectively, collaborated with the authorities in their money-laundering arrangements and to ship oil and food to Serbian rebel armies in Bosnia and Croatia.[110] The Dafiment and Jugoskandik Bank also served as tools by which Belgrade deprived the Serbian population of their savings. Vasiljević's Jugoskandik Bank, according to Naylor, amassed "more than $2 billion dollars in savings from more than 2 million people."[111] Others, including Robert M. Hayden and Mladen Dinkić, likened this massive fraud to the failed transition from socialism, a transition in which those who engineered the destruction of the state profited from the war.[112]

Given the dimension of this large-scale fraud, one must consider Donald Cressey's groundbreaking study on organized crime networks in the United States.[113] Cressey examined the organizational structure that swept the Cosa Nostra to the top of the criminal underworld during the 1960s. Paying special attention to the nexus between the cultural background, family ties, the code of conduct, the division of labor among Sicilian migrants, and the organizational strength of the mafia structure forged in the United States, Cressey confirmed the initial connection between family ties and criminal activities among individuals of the Sicilian migrant community. The relevance of cultural attachment, however, atrophied when the organization grew. Instead, trust among allies and, decisively, professionalization befitted the Cosa Nostra's growth and ultimate endurance, much as previously illustrated by Klaus von Lampe on transnational crime networks.[114]

One might be tempted to relate Cressey's work to the present study on the social connections between the local Bosniak and diaspora community in Turkey in view of illicit trade practices. Yet, *Theft of the Nation* correlates with activities performed by the Serbian state, considering the consolidation between Belgrade and the criminal netherworld. Misha Glenny explored the connection between criminals and Belgrade between 1991 and 1995, and stated:

As a consequence of war, sanctions and corruption in the Balkans during the first half of the 1990s, the states of the former Yugoslavia turned to and nurtured mafias to run the logistics of their military effort, and it was not long before the criminals were in control of the economy, the government and the war. Anyone with any serious political ambition had no choice but to get mobbed up.[115]

By 1995, Serbia turned into an archetype for Cressey's *Theft of the Nation*, seeing that one was no longer able to discern the mafia from the state.[116] Belgrade broke the social contract that not only shattered Yugoslavia but also the integrity, the social fabric, and the moral compass among the citizens of Serbia. Entrepreneurship, according to Naylor, became synonymous with "smuggling and war profiteering," while ordinary people turned to the informal market to procure and sell goods.

'Making do'

The designation of 'relations' is too descriptive in terms and thus inadequate when seeking to analyze how social interactions between Novo Pazarian and émigré Bosniaks and/or Turkish people inform local narratives about transnational ties between the Western Balkans and Turkey. Instead, practice, as defined by Joseph Rouse, offers a cogent roadmap to examine *how* the creation of this second market informed habits that transformed local values from within empirically.[117] According to Rouse:

> Practices are sometimes regarded as tacit propositional attitudes, and sometimes as inarticulable competences or performances. In either case, however, the concept of practices is typically invoked to explain continuities or commonalities among the activities of social groups.[118]

Locals absorbed the practice of trading because they tolerated the market as a necessary means of survival and security. Narrative accounts indicate that *Novo Pazarci* not simply condoned the market but welcomed its existence with enthusiasm.

The Yugoslav Succession Wars and subsequent international sanctions on Serbia created a niche market for elastic goods, including textiles, cigarettes and coffee – goods locals sought and knew how to procure elsewhere. Trading was thus an acquired practice that individuals professionalized over time. At one point during my fieldwork, for instance, I had this exchange with an interlocutor:

ME: So, how did this work? How did you guys get the goods, and how did this whole thing start?

SENAD: What do you mean by how did it start!? We just picked up the phone and called someone we knew there. Easy. We asked, "Hey, we don't have window-frames, clothes, concrete, coffee, whatever. Do you know someone who can get us this stuff?" You know, that's how it worked. We knew someone, who knew someone, who knew someone.

ME: Aha, OK. And what about the sanctions, how did you get it here?
SENAD: What sanctions? . . . There were no sanctions against us from Turkey.[119]

This short example illustrates that private connections facilitated the trade between Novi Pazar and Istanbul, though it sheds light on the fact that kin relations served as crucial *intermediary* connections. As such, family connections expedited the procurement of necessary contacts for other traders, Bosniaks and otherwise. The concept of practice thus offers empirical insight to examine transnational practices without the fallacy of studying Turkish-Bosniak relations from a homogenous perspective. Addressing this point is significant in that it liberates analyses of transnational relations from what Nina Glick-Schiller calls "methodological nationalism."[120] Conceptualizing *šverc* as a transnational practice then highlights that all parties involved benefited from this trade – Bosniaks, Serbs, Roma, Albanians, and even the Milošević regime, not to mention the people who worked in the *Kapalıçarşı* (the Grand Bazar in Istanbul, Turkey).

It is crucial to emphasize the complexity of the preceding point. A large number of Bosniaks *and* Serbs believe that Novi Pazar's second economy supplied Novi Pazar, Serbia, and Montenegro with otherwise inaccessible goods during the first half of the 1990s. Additional research in the news stacks at the National Library of Serbia, documentaries, newspaper articles, and a substantial body of local and international academic and non-academic literature illustrates that *šverc* was common in all of Serbia at the time. *Šverc* thus situates local modes of existence at the intersection of a quintessentially Serbian in-state experience and cross-border/transnational practice that fostered connections between Turkey and Southeastern Europe.

Still, the question of extrapolating from individual actors to society en masse remains unanswered. The practice of 'small-scale entrepreneurship' – or *šverc* across porous borders – offers a salient clarification on how to reconcile embodied with sedentary experiences. Individual traders crossed borders to procure elastic goods. Yet these material goods were not simply a means to quench the local population's thirst for coffee or desire for a new pair of jeans. Instead, one must understand these goods as a "shared event of practice"; marketable goods became "enacted objects."[121] Traders did not simply distribute goods from Turkey in Novi Pazar; they also "re-transfer[red] cultural customs" across the border.[122] Traders were thus salient social agents that not only fulfilled material but also emotive needs people cherished. Traders assumed, in other words, affective functions that individuals replicated locally. Rouse positions the learning and emulation of habits at the intersection of individual agency and maintenance of cultural values:

Such learning is not merely a matter of imitating the movements of others or being trained or disciplined into correct performance by straightforwardly casual means, but instead requires appropriate uptake, which involves some *understanding* of the performance to which one responds. The capacity for such 'proto-interpretative' uptake is presumably acquired gradually, as one's responses to earlier performances are assessed in light of a more extensive background of experience, including one's interpretation of others' responses to one's previous performances.[123]

Rouse thus offers a roadmap on how to examine the evolution of the second economy, directing our guise to recognize the culturally relevant context that allowed this market to flourish.

In the present case, the context contained an increasingly self-serving, mafia-like state structure that was policed by armed thugs from within and international sanctions that policed the borders from without. It is in this context that one must understand the growing distrust toward the political establishment in Belgrade, the widening gap between Western/Central European states and the former Yugoslavia, isolation from the international community, and the resulting solidarity networks that crystallized during the war years. Individuals in two or more states thus established cross-border practices that allowed for the import of consumer goods to ensure self-sufficiency and to make do.

Frontier economy

The practice of *šverc* was deemed (and remains) necessary in this system that perpetually fails to satisfy a citizens' basic needs. Because Belgrade has continuously failed to fulfill its social contract, it comes as no surprise that *šverc* was assumed as morally acceptable in Serbia. It is in this context that we must understand the strong cultivation of transnational ties between émigrés in Turkey and Southeastern Europe.

Understanding the discourse about *šverc* as a set of emulated practices allows for a nuanced understanding about transnational trade as a habituated custom that normalized the existence of the informal market. Alejandro Portes and William Haller's research on informal markets is instructive regarding solidarity among networked communities in economically weak states.[124] Building on Yochanan Altman and his research on the second economy in Georgia,[125] Portes and Haller stated "little enforcement capacity may . . . leave civil society to its own devices. This leads to a 'frontier' economy where observance of commodities and regulation of economic exchanges depend on private force or traditional normative structures."[126] Portes and Haller's analysis is especially pertinent because Serbia was militarily strong and able to rely on an extensive web of thugs that also patrolled the Sandžak region. Serbia and Montenegro were at the same time economically weak due to the international sanctions that lasted between 1992 and 1996.[127] The Yugoslav rump state was thus a strong-weak hybrid state[128] that was unable to curb either the massive unemployment or exponential inflation rate.

In view of the economic situation in the Yugoslav rump state, it may come as no surprise that "networked communities accustomed to relying on their own devices for survival . . . view(ed) the organization of informal enterprise as a normal part of life and involvement in the underground economy as a justifiable form of resistance."[129] This statement, however, must be qualified. Different communities within Serbia resisted diverse organizations. Bosniaks, one may generally argue, resisted the Serbian regime, while those who perceived themselves as 'patriots' of the rump state opposed the international community's imposed sanctions regime. Informal trading was thus a badge of honor for those who spited the United Nations and a medium that imbued local experiences in Novi Pazar with anticipatory properties.

As different as the reasons and perceptions of the informal economy were, most people were involved in the second economy one way or another. Smugglers traded illicit and licit goods across the borders, consumers bought the goods on the various *buvljaci*, government officials allowed for and/or partook in the second economy, and neighboring states were implicitly or explicitly letting smuggled goods pass their borders. The necessary cross-border mobility that served as a precondition for the subsequent transnational informal practice was thus multifarious and allowed for what von Lampe termed "criminal foraging."[130]

Von Lampe connects criminal foraging with the creation of criminal network links and dispels claims about ethnicity and family ties as strong sources for such links. Indirect contacts, trustworthiness, and reliability often trump ethnic homogeneity while evidence suggests that criminal networks often form "in the absence of pre-existing ties," according to von Lampe.[131] Seen from this perspective, transnational agents are firmly rooted in but affected by the policies pursued by their states and the international community, as illustrated by the very case of Novi Pazar. What emerges in the case of Serbia is an intersection between transnational practice and opportunistic crime, as defined by von Lampe:

> Transnational crime, as understood here, involves the cross-border movement of one or more of the following: people, goods and information. It has been argued that much of 'TOC', and in fact much of 'organized crime', boils down to international smuggling activities.[132] For the most part this means the cross-border transportation of prohibited, controlled or highly taxed goods such as child pornography, stolen motor vehicles, pirated textiles, drugs, protected animals, illegally logged timber, protected cultural goods, arms, embargoed technology, human organs, hazardous waste, gasoline or cigarettes.[133]

Mobile traders indeed smuggled stolen motor vehicles and entire cars to and from Serbia in addition to controlled goods, pirated textiles, drugs, arms embargoed technology, human organs, gasoline, and cigarettes as variously documented by the Council of Europe, Eulex, the United Nations Office on Drugs and Crime, and local and international scholars and journalists.

Taken together, von Lampe's and Portes and William-Haller's concepts on informal economies and the practice of transnational crime, respectively, illustrate the situation on the ground. Belgrade's aggression toward its own Yugoslav citizens elicited an international trade embargo that allowed for the informal economy to flourish. Sanctions-busting was thus not only necessary to make do but was increasingly perceived as normal. The case of Novi Pazar, further, illustrates von Lampe's findings that informal and criminal networks rarely find their origin in ethnic and/or national homogeneity. As such, examining transnational practices from the perspective of *šverc*, the narrative of diaspora, and local Bosniak relations reveals a much more nuanced depiction that goes beyond the discourse of ethnic hatred and/or ties.

For the aforementioned reasons, one must not conceptualize transnationalism as a tool that subverts state boundaries. Doing so creates a binary discourse about the supposed dangers of migration and resulting diaspora connections, as previously highlighted by Glick-Schiller:

> In these discourses, migrants, are attacked for their supposed lack of loyalty to their new homeland. Politicians, demagogic leaders, and media personalities blame migrants for national economic problems, including the growing disparity between rich and poor, the shrinking of the middle class, the reduction in the quality and availability of public services and education, and the rising costs of health care and housing.[134]

The dangers inherent in a binary view are palpable in the present study of *šverc*, and transnational family relations between the diaspora and local Bosniak community. Considering the Bosniak community that was not a migrant population, but connected to one in Turkey by way of the bygone Ottoman Empire, transnational practices ought to be viewed as a set of mechanisms actors may resort to lest the state fails to assume responsibility for the society it governs.

The nation per se, as suggested by Schad, is equally secondary within the concept of the *trans*national. Understanding the nation as the driving factor in transnational movements implies that all Bosniaks are the same regardless where they live and/or grew up. Such a frame not only insinuates the nation as innate but gives credence to political actors who insist on the protection of 'co-nationals' across borders. Instead, what emerges as the sine qua non is the performance that allowed for the enactment of transnational relations, or in this case, the objects that brought it into existence.

Small-scale trading and *šverc* among common citizens

Rory Archer and Krisztina Rácz explored local experiences about illicit trade practices and small-scale smuggling, or *šverc*, on the Vojvodinian-Hungarian and Vojvodinian-Romanian borders. The authors ask if and how narratives about the socially and economically challenging 1990s differ in relation to the previous period during which Yugoslavs experienced a comparatively high degree of civil liberties. The authors examine their question in light of the expanding European Union in order to glean a better understanding about local interactions and the fluid borders created by states, the nation, social groups, and legal systems. Archer and Rácz seek to demonstrate that small-scale smuggling channels shaped further opportunities for illegal business transactions while existing networks served the purpose of facilitating *šverc*. Archer and Rácz's findings are especially insightful regarding their conclusion that locals in Serbia perceived and still perceive the practice of *šverc* as valuable and morally acceptable, and they define the morally acceptable practice of *šverc* as "subsistence smuggling."[135]

Archer and Rácz's terminology of "imagined hierarchies," however, must be examined. The authors state that imagined hierarchies between the states involved in smuggling were inverted at different points in recent decades – since the 1980s, ever-changing visa requirements and divergent economic conditions prompted various flows of informal and cultural activity across state borders.[136] Yet, were those hierarchies indeed imagined, or were those conditions real and experienced as such by locals? I maintain the latter, especially in light of Archer and Rácz's own explanation that hierarchic changes included "visa requirements" and "divergent economic conditions." The shifting conditions described here seem very real seeing that former Yugoslavs had to cope with issues such as the 'ever-changing' visa requirements. The Yugoslav passport was a prized possession before the Succession Wars,[137] and citizens traveled freely across state borders. With the onset of the war, however, citizens from newly emerging states – including Serbia, Montenegro, Bosnia and Herzegovina, and Macedonia – faced harsh visa restrictions until 2010. In addition, citizens of the states in question indeed encountered diverging financial situations. Inflation in the Yugoslav rump state (Serbia and Montenegro) reached record highs, growing from 3.3 percent in 1993 to 313 million percent per month in 1994.[138] These hierarchies are thus all but imagined; they were/are very real.

Be that as it may, *šverc* is deemed necessary in this system that perpetually fails to satisfy a citizens' basic needs. Because Belgrade has continuously failed to fulfill its social contract, it comes as no surprise that *šverc* is deemed morally acceptable in Vojvodina as well as Novi Pazar and beyond.

Novi Pazar was, as was also the case with a Vojvodinian town, firmly entrenched in the mafia-like state structure that engulfed all areas of the Serbian state during the Yugoslav Succession Wars. The distinctly in-state practice of *šverc*, however, produced an alternative, transnational connotation for the local population of Novi Pazar – one in which Bosniaks invigorated communal bonds with Turkey by way of trade relations.

Small-scale trading and *šverc* among common citizens: looking beyond the Western Balkans

Madeleine Reeves analyzed the continuity of trade relations in the aftermath of the Soviet Union's dissolution in the Ferghana Valley in *Travels in the Margins of the State: Everyday Geography in the Ferghana Valley Borderlands*, and *Border Work – Spatial Lives of the State in Rural Central Asia*.[139] She illustrates that performative acts and material encounters produce state-like spaces notwithstanding governmental efforts to depress trade relations that continue to connect communities across adjoining state boundaries.[140] She encourages us to think of transnational spaces as diagnostic frames in which individual tradesmen and customers produce state-like structures as opposed to mere border areas. Social relations and material encounters are central in forging a sense of community, even when governments criminalize trading practices to legitimize their existence. Reeves states:

> What initially appear as violations of a preexisting boundary between 'state' and 'society', 'legal' and 'illegal', can be understood as constitutive acts. It is precisely through the struggle to define certain activities as falling within the domain of 'state law' or particular encounters of being subject to the norms of 'official' interaction (rather than those of friendship and kinship) that the state is made at its limits coming to figure in daily life and political imaginaries as an autonomous structure.[141]

Reeves's understanding of formal versus informal trade relations is astute – notwithstanding whether they are sanctified and/or barred by the state – and particularly relevant for the present study because she illustrates trade relations as a *tangible* instrument that both generates and sustains social relations.

Geography, the production of state-structures, and the creation of economic interdependencies across (non-)governed borders are also the focus in Janet Roitman's *Fiscal Disobedience*.[142] Roitman examines how licit and illicit transnational trade relations reconstitute citizenship through economic practices in the Chad Basin. Contrary to Reeves who identified how post-Soviet governments in Central Asia criminalize transborder trade relations to solidify the newly created state, Roitman discerns how government officials partake in ill/licit trade practices across the Chad Basin. Her argument is essential because she demonstrates that individuals consider ill/licit trade practices legitimate when officials partake in and thus sanctify the trade.

Fiscal Disobedience highlights the question, which has been overlooked to date, of how state actors foster and thus legitimize illicit trading practices. Seen from this perspective, paramilitary and commercial smuggling networks do not corrode but stabilize the state by offering "the only conceivable frontier of wealth creation in a region that has no viable industrial base and is not even an industrial periphery."[143] Both Roitman and Reeves provide critical insight on the correlation between criminalized practices and government comportment by going beyond the assumption that poverty and unemployment cause misconduct.[144]

Looking beyond the immediate cause-effect argument about poverty and 'criminal' behavior invites questions about the legitimacy of the state and/or governing actors, as previously noted by Daniel M. Goldstein. In *Owners of the Sidewalk: Security and Survival in the Informal City*,[145] Goldstein examines the inability and/or unwillingness of Bolivian authorities to integrate illicit merchants of Cochabamba – the so-called *ambulantes* – into official economic state structures for two reasons. First, ambulantes generate economic resources for the state and wages for themselves and their families. Thus, second, dismantling the sidewalk market would deprive the state, as is the case with the vendors, of economic stability. Ambulantes are, consequently, suspended in a perpetuate state of informality, as Goldstein argues:

> Rather than a fixed position inhabited by permanently 'informal' actors, then, informality is a condition, a pervasive and fluctuating status that may characterize the operations of any given actor or institution at any given moment. State authorities selectively adopt informal behavior when it suits their needs, and at other times they rail against the informal activities of the criminal underclass.[146]

While Goldstein does not explicitly engage Victor Turner's argument of the "liminal *personae* ['threshold people'],"[147] one is nonetheless able to grasp the liminal space these ambulantes inhibit. Ambulantes are indeed "neither here nor there,"[148] or as Goldstein argued, "neither fully included nor entirely excluded . . . always on the fringes but never fully recognized as belonging."[149] Turner's concept of the liminal is highly fruitful when contemplating state security and informal traders, because traders are not simply criminal but often criminalized by governing authorities who seek to emphasize the legitimacy and/or stability of the state, as previously illustrated by Reeves.

Building on Reeves and Roitman, the present study conceptualizes socialization processes through performative acts and material encounters. Roitman's analysis of state-sanctioned ill/licit trade practices and the nexus between citizenship and trade is especially valuable. Because the Sandžak region is not adjacent to Turkey, however, the present study diverges conceptually from both Reeves and Roitman, who examined cohesive spaces that are nonetheless separated by borders. To be sure, the Sandžak region itself, too, is a cohesive transborder region. Yet, the present study aims to answer how individuals in non-cohesive spaces relate by way of informal trade practices locally. More specifically, how do material encounters influence social relations in detached spaces, and how do locals in Novi Pazar, specifically, make sense of these connections in view of the informal economy during the war years?

Because Belgrade used illicit channels to procure products, including oil, weapons, and food, for instance, traders such as those in Novi Pazar, too, were initially not persecuted by the state between 1991 and 1995. Instead, Belgrade fostered transnational trade relations so long as the state benefited from these small-scale, sanctions-busting enterprises. Goldstein and Roitman's work on merchants in Cochabamba and the Chad Basin are instructive here because they corroborate the link between a state's inability and/or unwillingness to dismantle illicit trade practices for the sake of state stability. Belgrade not only approved of but fostered small-scale *šverc* to penetrate the internationally imposed trade sanctions on Serbia during the first half of the 1990s.

Notes

1 "Попис у Србији 2011, Преузимање пописних књига, Књига 1: Национална припадност," accessed July 26, 2017, http://popis2011.stat.rs/?page_id=1103.
2 *Labor Force Survey*, Statistical Office of the Republic of Serbi, https://www.stat.gov.rs.
3 Sandra King-Savic, "Serbia's Sandžak: Caught Between Two Islamic Communities," *Euxeinos: Online Journal of the Center for Governance and Culture in Europe* 23 (2017): 32–37.
4 Kenneth Morrison and Elizabeth Roberts, *The Sandzak: A History* (London: Hurst, 2013), 3.
5 Halil Inalcik, *The Ottoman Empire the Classical Age 1300–1600* (London: Phoenix Press, 1973), 135.
6 Gertrude Randolph Bramlette Richards, *Florentine Merchants in the Age of the Medici. Letters and Documents from the Selfridge Collection of Medici Manuscripts. [With Facsimiles.]* (Cambridge, MA: Harvard University Press, 1932), cited in Inalcik, *The Ottoman Empire the Classical Age 1300–1600*, 135.
7 Ibid.
8 Morrison and Roberts, *The Sandzak: A History*, 3.
9 Inalcik, *The Ottoman Empire the Classical Age 1300–1600*, 135.
10 Mark Mazower, *The Balkans – A Short History* (New York: Modern Library, 2002).
11 Ibid., 47. See also Halil Inalcik, *The Ottoman Empire, the Classical Age 1300–1600* (Great Britain: Orion Publishing Group, 2000), 150.
12 Ibid., 150–151.
13 Ibid.
14 Ibid.
15 Francine Friedman, "The Muslim Slavs of Bosnia and Herzegovina (with reference to the Sandzak of Novi Pazar): Islam as National Identity," *Nationalities Papers* 28, no. 1 (2000): 166; reflecting on Colin Heywood, "Bosnia under Ottoman Rule, 1463–1800," in *The Muslims of Bosnia-Herzegovina: Their Historic Development from the Middle Ages to the Dissolution of Yugoslavia*, ed. Mark Pinson (Cambridge, MA: Distributed for the Center for Middle Eastern Studies of Harvard University by Harvard University Press, 1993), 22–53.
16 Halil Inalcik, "Od Stefana Dušana do Osmanskog Carstva – Hrišćanske spahije u Rumeliji u XV veijeku i njihovo porijeklo," in *Prilozi za orijentalnu filologiju i istoriju jugoslovenskih naroda pod turskom vladavinom iii–iv* (Orijentalni Institut u Sarajevu, no 3–4 (1952): 41.
17 Nenad Maočanin, *Town and Country on the Middle Danube 1526–1690* (Leiden: Koninklijke Brill Academic, 2006), 132.
18 Mazower, *The Balkans – A Short History*, 17.
19 Salim Čerić, *Muslimani Srpskog Hrvatskok Jezika* (Sarajevo: Svijetlost, 1968), 48.
20 Ivo Banac, *The National Question in Yugoslavia – Origins, History, Politics* (Ithaca, NY: Cornell University Press, 1994), 41.
21 Čerić, *Muslimani Srpskog Hrvatskok Jezika*, 118–119.
22 Nina Glick-Schiller, "Transnationality, Migrants and Cities: A Comparative Approach," in *Beyond Methodological Nationalism: Research Methodologies for Cross-Border Studies* (New York: Routledge, 2012).
23 Čerić, *Muslimani Srpskog Hrvatskok Jezika*, 127.
24 Ibid., 135.
25 Inalcik, *The Ottoman Empire, the Classical Age 1300–1600*, 78.
26 Mazower, *The Balkans – A Short History*.
27 Traian Stojanovich, "The Conquering Balkan-Orthodox Merchant," *Journal of Economic History* 20, no. 2 (1960).
28 Ibid., 312.
29 Ibid.

30 Karl Kaser, *Orthodoxe Konfession und Serbische Nation in Bosnien und der Herzegovina im Übergang von der Türkishen zur Österreichisch-Ungarischen Herrschaft,* Süddeutsches Archiv (1983).
31 Миодраг Радовић, *Ефендијина Сећања и Казивања* (Нови Пазар, Историјски Архив Рас – Музеј Рас (Novi Pazar, Istorijski Arhiv Ras – Muzej Ras), 2007), 54–55.
32 "El Mundo Sefarad," updated September 23, 2014, accessed April 17, 2017, http://elmundosefarad.wikidot.com/porodice-konforti.
33 Радовић, *Ефендијина Сећања и Казивања,* 55.
34 Konforti, "El Mundo Sefarad."
35 On the Russo-Turkish war see, for instance, Caroline Finkel, *The History of the Ottoman Empire – Osman's Dream* (New York: Basic Books, 2005), 483–487; on concessions see, for instance, James Gelvin, *The Modern Middle East – A History* (New York: Oxford University Press, 2008), 81, 84–86, 88, 143, 154, 165, 195, 248–249, 283.
36 Ljubinka and Miroslav Djordjević Ćirić-Bogetić, "Iz Političke Istorije Jugoslovenskih Naroda – XIX i XX vek," *Privredni Pregled Beograd* (1980): 97–99; see also Stevan K. Pavlovitch, *A History of the Balkans 1804–1945* (London: Longman, 1999), 23–40.
37 Ćirić-Bogetić, "Iz Političke Istorije Jugoslovenskih Naroda – XIX i XX vek," 98.
38 Ibid.
39 Ibid., 107.
40 On the Balkans Wars of 1912/13 see, for instance, Safet Bandžović, *Iseljavanje Bošnjaka u Tursku* (Sarajevo: Institut za istraživanje zločina protiv čovječnosti I medjunarodnog prava, 2006); George F. Kennan and International Commission to Inquire into the Causes and Conduct of the Balkan Wars, *The Other Balkan Wars: A 1913 Carnegie Endowment Inquiry in Retrospect* (Washington, DC: Brookings Institution Press, 1993); "Balkan Wars (1912–1913)," in *The Encyclopedia of War* (Oxford: Wiley-Blackwell, 2011); Eyal Ginio, "Mobilizing the Ottoman Nation during the Balkan Wars (1912–1913): Awakening from the Ottoman Dream," *War in History* 12, no. 2 (2005); on WWI and WWII see, for instance, Ramet, *The Three Yugoslavias State-building and Legitimation, 1918–2005*; *Утицај Првог светског рата на официрског Минд-сет у балканским пословима: међуратном, Другог светског рата и после (Хуманитарни аспект)* Institut za noviju istoriju Srbije (Washington, DC: Woodrow Wilson Center Press; Bloomington: Indiana University Press, 2016); Wolfgang Höpken, " 'Blockierte Zivilisierung'? Staatsbildung, Modernisierung und ethnische Gewalt auf dem Balkan (19./20. Jahrhundert)," *Leviathan* 25, no. 4 (1997): 518–538. Please note, this list is not exhaustive.
41 Ćirić-Bogetić, "Iz Političke Istorije Jugoslovenskih Naroda – XIX I XX vek," 97–99.
42 Šaban Hodžić, "Migracije muslimanskog stanovništva iz Srbije u sjevernoistočnu Bosnu izmedju 1788–1862 godine," in *Članci i gradja za kulturnu istoriju istočne Bosne* (knj II Tuzla, 1958), 65–143.
43 Slobodan Jovanović, *Sabrana Dela, prvi deo* (Belgrade: Geca Kon, 1932–1940).
44 Bandžović, *Iseljavanje Bošnjaka u Tursku,* 69.
45 Vladan Jovanović, "Iseljavanje Muslimana iz Vardarske Banovine – Izmedju Stijihe I Drzavne Akcije," in *Pisati Istoriju Jugoslavije – Vidjenje Srpskog Faktora* (Belgrade: Altera, 2007), 81.
46 Bandžović, *Iseljavanje Bošnjaka u Tursku.*
47 Maurice Halbwachs, *On Collective Memory*, ed. Lewis A. Coser (Chicago: University of Chicago Press, 1992), 62.
48 Rogers Brubaker, "The 'Diaspora' Diaspora," *Ethnic and Racial Studies* 28, no. 1 (2005): 5.
49 Ibid.
50 Edvin Pezo, "Komparativna analiza jugoslovensko-turske Konvencije iz 1938. i 'džentelmenskog sporazuma' iz 1953. Pregovori oko iseljavanja muslimana iz Jugoslavije," *Tokovi Istorije* 2 (2012): 116.

51 Ibid., 115.
52 Vladan Jovanović, "Land Reform and Serbian Colonization: Belgrade's Problems in Interwar Kosovo and Macedonia," *East Central Europe* 42, no. 1 (2015): 90.
53 Pezo, "Komparativna analiza jugoslovensko-turske Konvencije iz 1938. i 'džentelmenskog sporazuma' iz 1953. Pregovori oko iseljavanja muslimana iz Jugoslavije," 117.
54 Ibid.
55 William Safran, "Diasporas in Modern Societies: Myths of Homeland and Return," *Diaspora: A Journal of Transnational Studies* 1, no. 1 (1991): 83.
56 Ibid., quoted by Brubaker, "The 'Diaspora' Diaspora," 5.
57 Jovanović, "Iseljavanje Muslimana iz Vardarske Banovine – Izmedju Stijihe I Drzavne Akcije," 81, 88.
58 Leijla, May 2014, interviewed by Sandra King-Savic in Novi Pazar.
59 Meltem Türköz, "The Social Life of the State's Fantasy: Turkish Family Names in 1934" (Middle East Studies Association Meeting, San Francisco, 2010).
60 Esra Ozyurek, *The Politics of Public Memory in Turkey: Modern Intellectual & Political History of the Middle East* (New York: Syracuse University Press, 2007), 5–6.
61 Amer Balcan, interviewed by Sandra King-Savic in Sarajevo, Bosnia and Herzegovina in January 2016.
62 Lejla Voloder, "Secular Citizenship and Muslim Belonging in Turkey: Migrant Perspectives," *Ethnic and Racial Studies* 36, no. 5 (2013).
63 Thomas Schad, "The Rediscovery of the Balkans? A Bosniak-Turkish Figuration in the Third Space Between Istanbul and Sarajevo" (Istanbul Bilgi University, Istanbul, 2015).
64 The cited link is broken as of March 26, 2017: Official homepage of the İstanbul governorate, last updated March 26, 2017, http://harika.istanbul.gov.tr/Default.aspx?pid=219.
65 Schad, "The Rediscovery of the Balkans? A Bosniak-Turkish Figuration in the Third Space Between Istanbul and Sarajevo," 17.
66 Jeanne Hersant and Alexandre Toumarkine, "Hometown Organisations in Turkey: An Overview," *European Journal of Turkish Studies. Social Sciences on Contemporary Turkey*, no. 2 (2005). as reflected in Esra Bulut, " 'Friends, Balkans, Statesmen Lend Us Your Ears': The Trans-state and State in Links between Turkey and the Balkans," *Ethnopolitics* 5, no. 3 (2006): 315.
67 Bosnia-Sandžak Foundations and Associations, "Bosna Sancak Vakıf ve Derneklerinden Yüce Türk Milletine (From the Bosnia-Sandžak Foundations and Associations to the Great Turkish Nation)," advertisement in Hürriyet (June 17, 2004). In Bulut, " 'Friends, Balkans, Statesmen Lend Us Your Ears': The Trans-state and State in Links between Turkey and the Balkans," 319.
68 Brubaker, "The 'Diaspora' Diaspora."
69 Ibid., 12.
70 Joseph Rouse, "Practice Theory. Division 1 Faculty Publications, 43" (2007), http://wesscholar.wesleyan.edu/div1facpubs/43.
71 "Sandžak: The Balkans Region Where Turkey is the Big Brother," *Deutsche Welle* (2017), accessed October 21, 2017, http://dw.com/p/2RXJO.
72 Rouse, "Practice Theory. Division 1 Faculty Publications, 43."
73 Ahmet Davutoğlu, "Turkey's Foreign Policy Vision: An Assessment of 2007," *Insight Turkey* 10, no. 1 (2008).
74 Ozyurek, *The Politics of Public Memory in Turkey: Modern Intellectual & Political History of the Middle East*, 2.
75 Joshua W. Walker, "Shadows of Empire: How Post-imperial Successor States Shape Memories" (Princeton University, 2012), https://dataspace.princeton.edu/jspui/handle/88435/dsp01v405s9415.

76 Ibid., 213.
77 "Turski Kulturni Centar," accessed February 5, 2017, http://www.kcnovipazar.com/prostori/turski-kulturni-centar/.
78 дарко танасковић, *неоосманизам – повратак турске на балкан* (Београд: службени гласник републике србије, 2010), 105.
79 Bahar Başer and Ahmet Erdi Öztürk, *Authoritarian Politics in Turkey: Elections, Resistance and the AKP* (London, New York: I.B. Tauris, 2017).
80 Kemal Kirişci, "New Patterns of Turkish Foreign Policy Behavior," in *Turkey – Political, Social, and Economic Challenges in the 1990s* (Leiden: E. J. Brill, 1995), 7.
81 Ibid., 7–8.
82 Nina Glick-Schiller, "A Global Perspective on Transnational Migration: Theorizing Migration without Methodological Nationalism," in *Diaspora and Transnationalism – Concepts, Theories and Methods*, ed. R. Bauböck and T. Faist (Amsterdam: Amsterdam University Press, 2010), 110.
83 Ibid., 111.
84 Pierre Bourdieu, *Picturing Algeria* (New York: Columbia University Press, 2003), 4.
85 Eva Østergaard-Nielsen, "The Politics of Migrants' Transnational Political Practices," *International Migration Review* 37, no. 3 (2003).
86 Ibid., 762.
87 Schad, "The Rediscovery of the Balkans? A Bosniak-Turkish Figuration in the Third Space Between Istanbul and Sarajevo."
88 Ibid., 11.
89 Trans-, as defined by the Cambridge English Dictionary, accessed March 9, 2017, http://dictionary.cambridge.org/dictionary/english/trans.
90 Thomas Faist, "Transnationalization and Development," in *Migration, Development, and Transnationalization: A Critical Stance*, ed. Nina Glick-Schiller and Thomas Faist (New York: Berghahn Books, 2013), 218.
91 Ibid.
92 Bulut, " 'Friends, Balkans, Statesmen Lend Us Your Ears': The Trans-state and State in Links between Turkey and the Balkans."
93 Ibid., 314.
94 D. Pantic, "Internet in Serbia: From Dark Side of the Moon to the Internet Revolution," *First Monday* 2, no. 4 (1997), https://doi.org/10.5210/fm.v2i4.520.
95 Bulut, " 'Friends, Balkans, Statesmen Lend Us Your Ears': The Trans-state and State in Links between Turkey and the Balkans," 323.
96 Paul Hockenos, *Homeland Calling: Exile Patriotism and the Balkan Wars* (Ithaca, NY: Cornell University Press, 2003), 1.
97 Ibid.
98 'For some war, for some a brother': proverb often heard in connection with the Yugoslav Succession Wars.
99 "United Nations Resolution 757," ed. United Nations (1992), https://digitallibrary.un.org/record/142881?ln=en; "Resolution 713: Socialist Federal Rep. of Yugoslavia (September 25)," ed. United Nations (1992); "Resolution 721: Socialist Federal Rep. of Yugoslavia (November 27)," ed. United Nations (1992); "Resolution 724: Socialist Federal Rep. of Yugoslavia (December 15)," ed. United Nations (1992), http://unscr.com/en/resolutions/doc/724; "Socialist Federal Republic of Yugoslavia; S/RES/727; S/RES/740 (1992) Socialist Federal Republic of Yugoslavia; S/RES/743 (1992) Socialist Federal Republic of Yugoslavia; S/RES/749 (1992) Socialist Federal Republic of Yugoslavia; S/RES/752 (1992) Socialist Federal Republic of Yugoslavia," ed. Security Council (1992), https://www.nato.int/ifor/un/u920515a.htm.
100 Thomas George Weiss, *The United Nations and Changing World Politics* (Boulder, CO: Westview Press, 2007), 69.

101 "A/50/60-S/1995/1, Supplement to an Agenda for Peace: Position Paper of the Secretary-General on the Occasion of the Fiftieth Anniversary of the United Nations par. 70" (1995). https://www.securitycouncilreport.org/atf/cf/%7B65BFCF9B-6D27-4E9C-8CD3-CF6E4FF96FF9%7D/UNRO%20S1995%201.pdf.
102 Ibid., quoted in Weiss, *The United Nations and Changing World Politics*, 75.
103 Weiss, *The United Nations and Changing World Politics*, 67.
104 Robin Thomas Naylor, *Economic Warfare – Sanctions, Embargo Busting, and Their Human Cost* (Boston: Northeastern University Press, 1999), 333–361.
105 Ibid., 338.
106 Ibid., 347–348.
107 Ibid., 337–338.
108 Ibid., 357.
109 Peter Andreas, *Blue Helmets and Black Markets: The Business of Survival in the Siege of Sarajevo* (Ithaca, NY: Cornell University Press, 2008).
110 R. T. Naylor, *Patriots and Profiteers: On Economic Warfare, Embargo Busting, and State-sponsored Crime* (Toronto: M&S, 1999), 360.
111 Ibid., 361; see also Miša Brkić, "Pipci i konci svemoćnog gazde," *Vreme* (2001), http://www.vreme.com/cms/view.php?id=96130.
112 Robert M. Hayden, "Reply," *Slavic Review* 4, n.5 (1996).
      See also Mladen Dinkić, *Ekonomija Destrukcije: Velika Pljačka Naroda* (Beograd: Stubovi Kulture, 1996).
113 Donald R. Cressey, *Theft of the Nation: The Structure and Operations of Organized Crime in America* (New Brunswick, NJ: Transaction, 2008).
114 Klaus von Lampe, "The Practice of Transnational Organized Crime," in *Routledge Handbook of Transnational Organized Crime*, ed. Felia Allum and Stan Gilmour (London: Taylor and Francis Group, 2015).
115 Misha Glenny, *McMafia: Seriously Organised Crime* (London: Vintage, 2009), 39.
116 For a track record of involved organizations and individuals during this period, see *Institutions Abused – Who Was Who in Serbia between 1987–2000* by Dušan Bogdanović and Biljana Kovačević-Vučo (Belgrade: Biljana Kovačević-Vučo Fund, 2011).
117 Rouse, "Practice Theory. Division 1 Faculty Publications, 43."
118 Joseph Rouse, "Two Concepts of Practices," in *The Practice Turn in Contemporary Theory*, ed. R. Theodore Schatzki, Karin Knorr Cetina, and Eike Von Savigny (London: Routledge, 2001), 190.
119 Novi Pazar, field notes, Sandra King-Savic 2016; note that Turkey, too, joined the UN sanctions on the rump state.
120 Glick-Schiller, "A Global Perspective on Transnational Migration: Theorizing Migration without Methodological Nationalism," 110–129.
121 John Law, *After Method – Mess in Social Science Research* (New York: Routledge, 2010), 56.
122 Thomas Faist, "Diaspora and Transnationalism: What Kind of Dance Partners?" in *Diaspora and Transnationalism – Concepts, Theories and Methods*, ed. Rainer Bauböck and Thomas Faist (Amsterdam: Amsterdam University Press, 2010), 11.
123 Rouse, "Practice Theory. Division 1 Faculty Publications, 43."
124 Alejandro Portes and William Haller, "The Informal Economy," in *The Handbook of Economic Sociology*, ed. Neil J. Smesler and Richard Swedberg (Princeton, NJ: Princeton University Press, 2005), 403–425.
125 Yochanan Altman, "A Reconstruction, Using Anthropological Methods, of the Second Economy of Soviet Georgia" (PhD dissertation, Centre of Occupational and Community Research, Middlesex Polytechnic, June 1983).
126 Haller, "The Informal Economy," 410.

127 "United Nations Resolution 757"; "Resolution 713: Socialist Federal Rep. of Yugoslavia (25 September)"; "Resolution 721: Socialist Federal Rep. of Yugoslavia (November 27)"; "Resolution 724: Socialist Federal Rep. of Yugoslavia (15 December)"; "Socialist Federal Republic of Yugoslavia; S/RES/727; S/RES/740 (1992) Socialist Federal Republic of Yugoslavia; S/RES/743 (1992) Socialist Federal Republic of Yugoslavia; S/RES/749 (1992) Socialist Federal Republic of Yugoslavia; S/RES/752 (1992) Socialist Federal Republic of Yugoslavia."
128 Madeline Reeves conceptualized a version of the strong-weak state in Madeline Reeves, *Border Work – Spatial Lives of the State in Rural Central Asia* (Ithaca, NY: Cornell University Press, 2014). Based on Scott Radniz, "Informal Politics and the State," *Comparative Politics* 43, no. 3 (2011).
129 Haller, "The Informal Economy," 411.
130 Von Lampe, "The Practice of Transnational Organized Crime," 188–189.
131 Ibid., 193.
132 E. R. van de Bunt Kleemans, H. G., "The Social Embeddedness of Organized Crime," *Transnational Organized Crime* 5, no. 1 (2002): 19–36, cited by von Lampe, "The Practice of Transnational Organized Crime," 193.
133 Von Lampe, "The Practice of Transnational Organized Crime," 187.
134 Glick-Schiller, "A Global Perspective on Transnational Migration: Theorizing Migration without Methodological Nationalism," 23.
135 Rory Archer and Krisztina Rácz, "*Šverc* and the *Šinobus*: Small-Scale Smuggling in Vojvodina," in *Subverting Borders* (New York: Springer, 2012), 74.
136 Ibid., 60.
137 This is especially the case for those individuals who lived within the Soviet sphere; see, for instance, Stef Jansen, "After the Red Passport: Toward an Anthropology of the Everyday Geopolitics of Entrapment in the 'Immediate Outside'," *Journal of the Royal Anthropology Institute* 15 (2009): 815–832.
138 David A. Dyker, "Economic Overview: Serbia," *Europaworld*, accessed March 8, 2012, http://www.europaworld.com/entry/rs.ec.
139 Madeleine Reeves, "18. Travels in the Margins of the State: Everyday Geography in the Ferghana Valley Borderlands," *Everyday Life in Central Asia: Past and Present* (2007): 281–297.
140 Reeves, *Border Work – Spatial Lives of the State in Rural Central Asia*, 10.
141 Ibid., 15.
142 Janet Roitman, *Fiscal Disobedience: An Anthropology of Economic Regulation in Central Africa* (Princeton, NJ: Princeton University Press, 2005).
143 Ibid., 155.
144 Syed Yasir Mahmood Gillani, Hafeez Ur Rehman, and Abid Rasheed Gill, "Unemployment, Poverty, Inflation and Crime Nexus: Cointegration and Causality Analysis of Pakistan," *Pakistan Economic and Social Review* (2009): 79–98.
145 Daniel M. Goldstein, *Owners of the Sidewalk: Security and Survival in the Informal City* (Durham, NC: Duke University Press, 2016).
146 Ibid., 79.
147 Victor Turner, "Liminality and Communitas," *The Ritual Process: Structure and Anti-structure* 94 (1969): 359. See also Bjørn Thomassen, "Anthropology and Social Theory: Renewing Dialogue," *European Journal of Social Theory* 16 (2013): 188–207.
148 Ibid.
149 Goldstein, *Owners of the Sidewalk: Security and Survival in the Informal City*, 79.

Part II

2 The 'inner logic' of transnational relations

Thus, all having the same wishes, it turns out that private interest becomes the general interest: when we express our hopes for ourselves we are expressing them for the republic.

Voltaire[1]

How do material encounters influence social relations in detached spaces, and how do locals in Novi Pazar, specifically, make sense of these connections in view of the constituting informal economy between 1991 and 1995? In other words, how do locals narrate these transnational 'societal configurations' in light of the informal economy? Within the context of this first narrative, I posit that locals understand trading with the émigré Bosniak community in Turkey as a system of connections within which performative acts supersede the loss of belonging to a Yugoslav community. This approach relates to what Faist called "the inner logic of social action"[2] and demonstrates transnationalization processes.

According to popular belief in Novi Pazar, Serbia, there are 3–4 million Bosniaks who live in Turkey. Conventional wisdom there holds that it is this very community of émigrés in Turkey that provided Sandžak Bosniaks with the necessary tools to run and upkeep the textile production that, in part, sustained the informal market during the international communities' economic sanctions on Serbia between 1992 and 1995. "Without the diaspora," I heard time and again, "we would not have made it." This narrative, I contend, provided locals with anticipatory properties. Because Serbia is not a "historically discrete sovereign state,"[3] by reconnecting with the Bosniak émigré community in Turkey locals reconceptualized their associative space as post-Ottoman and Turkish, respectively.[4] As such, material encounters shaped social relations that forged a sense of community between local and émigré Bosniaks in Turkey. Understanding these connections as meaningful transnational solidarity chains illustrates that "experiences, norms and values . . . [that are] embedded in social, economic and political processes, networks, movements and institutions exist both within and across state borders," as previously stated by Glick-Schiller.[5]

In order to answer the overarching question of how material encounters influence social relations in detached spaces, I examine the catalysts that

DOI: 10.4324/9781003022381-5

induced anticipatory properties among the Bosniak community in Novi Pazar and how locals narrate these expectations locally in this chapter. I was especially interested in exploring if material encounters serve as salient carriers of anticipatory properties concerning the manifestation of transnational configurations.

This chapter is based on ethnographic research and open-ended, semi-structured interviews with locals in Novi Pazar, as well as questionnaires with $N = 500$. Following Smith's interpretation of heteroglossia/multivocality, I illustrate that narratives are contingent on the audience, which in turn reveals how interviewees imbue recollections with meaning. In-text interview quotes are in quotation marks, and direct interview excerpts are indicated as such by way of stand-alone passages henceforth.

Belonging through the prism of *šverc*: making sense of the Yugoslav Succession Wars

The TKS is to some extent emblematic for the town of Novi Pazar, where the factory is located. Once a regional giant for the production of textiles, the factory collapsed in the 1980s. Since its establishment in 1956, the Kombinat was a major source of employment up until the economic recession of the 1980s when the company gradually let go of its employees. However, it is instructive to remember here that the Yugoslav system did not allow for laid-off employees. This was particularly the case during the international sanctions and subsequent NATO bombings of Serbia. Factories, for instance, were responsible for the social welfare of their employees as opposed to the state.[6] As a result, companies seldom let their workforce go officially, because doing so incurred higher costs on manufacturing plants. This was also the case for the TKS in 1992, when the factory failed to formally discontinue the contract of its workforce. Instead of laying their workers off, the TKS forced its employees to take an open-ended, unpaid leave of absence.[7]

"All these people were suddenly unemployed," Asem recalls. "But doing so burdened employees especially after the war, because the people of Novi Pazar momentarily utilized their craftsmanship instated of waiting for handouts from the state."[8] Asem is a dashing, tall, middle-aged, very well-educated (Bosniak) man who grew up in Novi Pazar, and one of the interviewees I shadowed between 2012 and 2016. After picking me up in a sleek vehicle that suggested affluence, Asem steered his automobile to a location of his choosing for our first interview in May 2012. We drove up and into the hills that surround Novi Pazar and came to a stop in front of a charming *vikendica* (weekend house). His family inherited this cottage as well as the plot of land on which the small house stands. Once in the yard that surrounded the chalet, Asem made sure to exhibit the roses that nearly covered the entire yard (Figure 2.1). He pointed toward a bunch of plastic jars, filled with what appeared to be water, mixed with those same roses (Figure 2.2). Before returning to his recollection of the 1990s, Asem offered me

Figure 2.1 Starinska ruža (antique rose)
Source: Picture taken by author.

a glass of the syrupy drink. "The Ottomans introduced this beverage to the Balkans," he explained:

> Now . . . why did the government do such things that led me to believe that they do not want me here. Why was there such a mess here, and why did they make us feel as though we are second-class citizens in this country. And so,

Figure 2.2 Starinske ruže (antique roses) in jars
Source: Picture taken by author.

slowly, after being out of work for three, five years . . . there is no work, there is no work, I start to have problems. I can't cover my elementary needs for survival. I don't have a job, so, I have to steal, or do any sort of work that can sustain me. I no longer feel the government provides me with opportunities. Then, what happens, our people, during the 1990s, because our factories here collapsed, lost their jobs. Those were big systems that employed up to 5000 people back then. They all lost their jobs because the system failed. First, the system decays in such places as this one, smaller places, before collapsing in Belgrade. Up there, the government gives, gives, gives, gives, until it is no longer able to give a thing. They seized to support us immediately, and the collapse was instant. Then what happened, our people had to find work. These people were only skilled in the textile and furniture manufacturing business, to work in those state-owned factories.[9]

Asem describes the deteriorating economic situation as it was felt across the entire former SFRY.

By 1989, the hyperinflation rate was 1,256 percent annually.[10] To curb the inflationary rate, Ante Marković – then Prime Minister of Yugoslavia – initiated a fiscal stabilization plan led by the International Monetary Fund (IMF) that prompted a six-month pay freeze, which culminated in the introduction of a new currency.

In Serbia, the inflation kept soaring. By 1992, the annual inflation rate stood at 9,237 percent and rose to "a quite literally astronomical 116.5 to the power of 10 to the power of 12 percent in 1993."[11] Vesna Pešić, a sociologist, politician, and human rights activist, stated this hyperinflation resulted from the Milošević era initiated *narodnjačke revolucije* (populist revolution).[12] According to Pešić, the gross domestic product fell by 20 percent during the four consecutive years since 1990 and up to 1993. The same was true, she states, for the hyperinflation in the Yugoslav rump state that is considered the longest in history.[13]

As a result of the socioeconomic and political crisis, Yugoslavs turned to what Susan Woodward called the established *modus vivendi* in communist regimes: "cultural identities, alternative social networks, and organizations that are already present in society."[14] Bosniaks in Novi Pazar, such as it was, turned to their relatives in Turkey, as explained by Asem:

Now . . . our people (*naši ljudi*) had to do business privately. There was no capital investment with which we could have started this business. We (*mi*) could not expect anything from the state, and the state was disappearing. There was this . . . war, sanctions, all that . . . all that was happening, and our people went to their relatives in Turkey, those who had migrated there. They were fortunate, because they had gained some economic strength. Turkey strengthened economically sometime between 1985 and the 1990s, which is why our people were able to help us. It was based on personal family ties. They did not give us money to feed ourselves, they gave us sewing machines. They said: here is a machine and some jeans fabric, I will give you some machines, go and sell the product somewhere. And so, after about five months, we paid off the material that we got, and bought some more. . . . Our people were forced to do this. . . . And this is how we established hundreds of these small family owned businesses here. These businesses were usually located in family homes and were made up of two workers per one machine – usually the father and the mother, both of whom had learned how to do this job in the *Kombinat* – they had these skills and the know-how for this work. They just had no money to buy the machines, and this is how we created these small factories in Novi Pazar. Then, the children grew up slowly, and they also worked on these machines, and the production went on in this way. When Serbia was under sanctions, Novi Pazar experienced a boom. It saved us, this rescue from our relatives in Turkey, this initial help, which then turned into a business. This was not a gift. Thanks to that, we, as Muslims (*mi, kao muslimani*), withstood the economic situation here. Other cities did not have this opportunity, and the state could not help any other regions except Belgrade, so they all collapsed. They called Kragujevac the valley of death . . . in Prstenik, Niš . . . all the industries were no longer able to export anything from Serbia. The sanctions prohibited it, because of the war. . . . So, everyone went to participate in the wars, but we did not want to go. They first put pressure on us to go, but we did not want to. We did not . . . we did not want to go. And then, they let us be. They could not make us go.[15]

Other interviewees confirmed Asem's narrative of the crushing economic situation in Serbia during the 1990s. For instance, Leijla's daughter, a crestfallen middle-aged (Bosniak) lady, explained that locals were forced to help themselves:

> And then, you know, the textile and shoe factory closed. That's when people became self-employed, and started to work in their houses, bought machines, and sewed jeans. We all tried our best, as best as we could, to do something, some . . . anything . . . workshops, shoes . . . and you just work, get some more textile from Turkey, bring it here, buy some more machines, open a business. . . . do you understand? Sell (*Prodaješ*) your wares here, in Novi Pazar. There are so many who did just that . . . so many.[16]

Like Asem, she identifies the intersection between existing knowledge, namely, the work at the *Kombinat* and the possibility of procuring goods in Turkey. Locals turned to Turkey due to the deteriorating socioeconomic condition in Serbia and made use of their existing skills they had acquired locally. Trading, however, would have been unavailing if not impossible without material aid coming from Turkey.

Asem evidently portrayed the Bosniak community in Novi Pazar from a first-person perspective in his repeated emphasis of our people (*naši ljudi*), we (*mi*), us (*nas*), and so forth. Reflecting on Smith's deliberation on Bakhtin's *heteroglossia*,[17] one might thus suggest that Asem narrated his experience of the 1990s based on his audience that consisted of me, an outsider who was not versed in the social codes of his community. Asem, in other words, tailored his narrative to fit the initial contact and interview scene. Following this logic, Asem – deliberately or not – created a highly symbolic context for our first in-depth, semi-structured interview. Not only did he make sure to explain the origin and use of the roses in his yard, but he also arranged to demonstrate how they are dried before offering me the syrup for consumption. Humans, as previously argued by Max Weber, produce social actions that reflect their values.[18] Following the inner logic of this narrative and symbolic sense-making process accordingly, one may suggest that Asem not only displayed a degree of fealty toward the distant past by which he anticipated the future, but he had already absorbed it.

According to Asem's choice of words, the future of the Bosniak community did not belong to Serbia. In his words, "Our people could not expect anything from the state, and the state was disappearing." Yugoslavia, which, to be sure, did not accept the Bosniak national identity as titular,[19] seized to exist, and so did the Bosniak place in the emerging Yugoslav rump state. He said:

> I was very talented, and I had the possibility to play basketball. Back then, basketball used to be very popular in Yugoslavia. And we, as a sort of profile of those young people back during the 1980s, you know, as a sort of immodest example, I had, I can say, an ideal profile in the sense that I was a very good student, I did not participate in any conflicts, – beatings, theft – something our youth today is often implicated in. I had no problems and

didn't drink or smoke. This was somehow foreign to us, completely. We respected our parents, our professors, and were never in a situation. . . . we were afraid of meeting our professors on the street out of some sort of respect, because we did not want him to think we loiter around town, as opposed to studying. That was the sort of mentality back then. Back then, I played sports, and grew up according to some sort of model by which young people should be raised. It was truly a carefree time. When I was 16, I traveled to the Adriatic on my own, for the first time, without my parents. This means it was a carefree time. We were able to go wherever we wished. Yugoslavia was a truly wonderful country. One could not feel any of what is considered normal now. Now, the first thing people think about is who you are, where you come from, do you have money, or not, how . . . the criteria have changed totally. But I was raised in that other environment. We were not burdened with these things. Today, people are scared to become poor, of deprivation. Back then you simply had enough money. But money was not the priority. As a young man, I just wanted to travel, and if you were a good student, the parents give you just a little bit of money, and, I was an athlete, and this is how I got the chance to travel, as an athlete, all the time. We played competitions all over Yugoslavia, and we traveled a lot. I really liked that. I never experienced any problems just because I am a Muslim. I never felt excluded . . . never felt it was a problem. None of the girls minded, or anybody else. It was a non-issue. It was o.k.[20]

Asem emphasizes that he had never experienced any problems despite being a Muslim, and he even perceived himself as having had an ideal profile before the Yugoslav Succession Wars. His elaboration on the past suggests he identified with the Yugoslav state. Asem, one might argue then, perceived the system as inclusive, a system he was able to participate and thrive in. His experience stands in sharp contrast to the 1990s, given the regime-driven discourse and Belgrade supported proxy wars that induced animosity between Serbian and Bosniak Yugoslavs.

The loss of the republic is perceived as such by both Bosniaks and Serbs (and allegedly others). Bojana, a strong-willed, well-educated, and somber (Serbian) lady in her middle years, for instance, agreed with Asem about the reliable standard of living in Yugoslavia when compared to life in the Yugoslav rump state and Serbia at present:

Back then, the state was organized. Back then, people used to respect the law. One valued work and order (*znao se red i rad*). Now, nothing. . . . there is nothing. Everyone interprets the law in their own way. All of that was social once, the manufacturing plants, all those companies and all that.[21]

Questionnaire results (Figure 2.3) put these two statements further into perspective. For a total of 34.6 percent of survey participants, the former Yugoslav state remains very important, while 25.5 percent deem Yugoslavia as somewhat important. This means that a combined 60.2 percent of survey participants – roughly

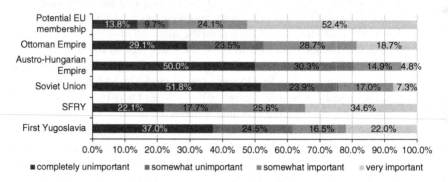

Figure 2.3 Perception toward past empires and supranational collectives

every other person and more – regard the former Yugoslav state as at least important. The perceived loss of Yugoslavia is thus a collective one and parallels a rupture that cuts across national affiliation. And yet, the Succession Wars brought about a retrograde affection with the nation-state, which amounted to a luxury for Bosniaks. Bosniaks, in other words, were faced with the violent territorial dispute Croatia and Serbia had fought in Bosnia and Herzegovina between 1992 and 1995. Bosniaks not only lost their social status as equal citizens in the rump state but also their existential well-being.

The Yugoslav rump state – consisting of Serbia and Montenegro – was, as emphasized by Asem, unable to lift its citizens out of the economic downward spiral. But locals in Novi Pazar helped themselves by invigorating transnational ties with the émigré community in Turkey:

> When Serbia was under sanctions, Novi Pazar experienced a boom. It (the market) saved us, this rescue from our relatives in Turkey, this initial help, which then turned into a business. This was not a gift. Thanks to that, we, as Muslims, withstood the economic situation here.

Novo Pazarci, Asem seems to suggest here, did not rely on or expect to receive aid from Belgrade. Instead, Asem indicates that locals organized economic structures that were based on personal networks. Other people in Serbia, according to Asem, did not have this possibility: "Other cities did not have this opportunity, and the state could not help any other region, save Belgrade, so they all collapsed." At the time, inferred from Asem's narrative, it appears that Novi Pazar, and the Sandžak region generally, existed from without the economic purview of Belgrade. Seen from this perspective, it comes as no surprise that Sulejman Ugljanin, then and still political leader of the *Stranka Demokratske Akcije* (SDA),[22] advocated autonomy for the region in October 1991.[23]

It is important to emphasize here that Asem, though speaking from a position of perceived weakness, narrates his experience as an "active agent."[24] 'Liberated' from the socioeconomic structures that governed Serbia at the time, the commencing economic boom made autonomy thinkable. Though latent, one may nevertheless point toward a possible correlation between the desire for autonomy in late 1991, and, according to Asem, the "booming market" that too started in 1991. Autonomy, in other words, became economically viable.

As seen in Figure 2.4, 50.9 percent of those who participated in the questionnaire agreed strongly with the statement that most of the goods sold on the Novi Pazar *buvljak* (flea market) came from Turkey, while 33.5 percent agreed with the statement. Meanwhile, 57 percent of all participants strongly agreed with the statement that this trade supplied Novi Pazar with goods during the 1990s, while 28.6 percent agreed with this same statement. This means that 84.4 percent – a great majority of participants – at least agreed with the statement that most goods that sustained the market in Novi Pazar came from Turkey, while 85.6 percent of all participants believe the market supplied Novi Pazar – and to a lesser degree Serbia (81 percent) and Montenegro (73.4 percent) – with goods during the 1990s.

Sustaining transnational relations with the émigré community thus seemed of vital importance. With the benefit of hindsight, one may posit that Belgrade's inability to safeguard Serbian citizens from the economic chaos induced anticipatory properties among the Bosniak community in Novi Pazar. The expectation in those

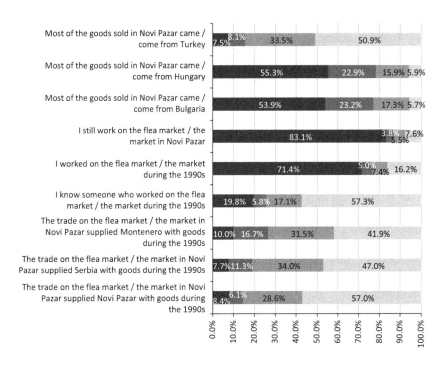

Figure 2.4 Origin of goods available on the market in Novi Pazar during the 1990s

Note: N = 500. Color range: strongly disagree, disagree, agree, strongly agree.

early months of 1992 was perhaps, in other words, a greater degree of autonomy – a prospect that was based on closer cooperation with Turkish businesses, and perhaps Ankara. What appears to emerge from the data then is an inverse power structure between the capital and Novi Pazar that set off a process of sociopolitical disengagement between locals in the Sandžak region, particularly in Novi Pazar, and Belgrade. Sociopolitical disengagement from Belgrade, meanwhile, seemed viable due to economic independence from Belgrade.

Asem provides us with an explicit sociopolitical example about local disengagement with the Serbian state. In the preceding quote, Asem explicitly emphasized the point that Bosniaks did not wish to join the Jugoslav Army. Another interviewee, Dubravko, agreed with Asem:

> So . . . the war was a period in which Serbs enlisted as army reserves. They were engaged in the army, while the Bosniaks did business. . . . they worked in business. But at that time, there was no turmoil here. Still, one knew the matter, and how (*znalo se i kako*), and we kept up neighborly relations, even friendships. The majority of people knew that something should have happened here. It was supposed to happen here, but someone prevented it.[25]

Dubravko, a middle-aged, educated, and heavy-set (Serbian) man whom I interviewed once in 2012, affirmed Asem's notion that Bosniaks – in part due to their business acumen – did not participate in the Yugoslav Succession Wars as recruits. Apart from agreeing with Asem about the apparently burgeoning disassociation of Bosniaks from Serbia proper, the tone of the respective narratives is instructive. On comparing the linguistic expression of the preceding passages, one is able to discern Asem's active if not assertive tone, compared to Dubravko's rather passive voice. Applying Smith's dichotomy of official versus contrasting voices to these passages,[26] one might conclude that Asem narrates a contrasting story line of the 1990s. Asem emphasizes a symbolic construction of past events, one in which Bosniaks were active agents and not passive recipients of repression and/or violence. Transnational trade relations were thus not only a tool by which to endure the economic downturn in Serbia, they also served as a centripetal force for the ongoing memory construction and reconstruction among Bosniaks. Dubravko, meanwhile, reproduces an official account of the past, one in which Serbian involvement in the war prevails trade with the Bosniak émigré community. Transnational trade relations in the form of material encounters thus produced contrasting memory patterns among Serbs and Bosniaks locally.

The following passage Dubravko recounts is especially telling:

> The war was a period in which Serbs enlisted as army reserves. . . . But at that time, there was no turmoil here. Still, one knew the matter, and how (*znalo se i kako*). . . . The majority of people knew that something should have happened here . . . but someone prevented it.

Dubravko is noticeably absent from his own narrative and communicates his experience from the perspective of an onlooker. He plays no part in the Serbian military-conscript or the Bosniak-business narrative and thus seems to assume the position of a passive outsider; he had no choice in the matter and to some extent accepted the socioeconomic situation that reigned at the time.

Asem, conversely, appears as an active agent within his own narrative:

> The sanctions prohibited it, war . . . so everyone went to participate in the wars, but we did not want to go. They first put pressure on us to go, but we did not want to. We did not . . . we did not want to go. And then, they let us be. They could not make us go.

Asem presents the collective refusal to fight in the Yugoslav wars as an active choice. It is interesting to note here that Asem refrains from naming either the state or Serbs who chose to partake in the wars – willingly or by coercion. Instead, Asem, in referring to Belgrade and Serbs as *they* in contrast to *we* and *us* Muslims and/or Bosniaks, creates a binary narrative that deflects continuity in belonging to Serbia. This becomes especially clear when compared to his description about the former Yugoslavia: "We were able to go wherever we wished. Yugoslavia was a truly wonderful country." Asem, in narrating his experience of the 1990s, displays restraint regarding Belgrade, and contiguity with transnational solidarity networks: *we*, as Muslims – he states – withstood the economic downturn because *our* relatives in Turkey rescued *us*.

The two narrative styles suggest a 'division of labor' within which Bosniaks partook in business dealings, while Serbs were expected to join the army.[27] By continuing with Ken Morrison's reflection on Emile Durkheim regarding the coordination of economic and domestic activities "for the purpose of survival," one recognizes how social processes conditioned anticipatory properties among the Bosniak community in Novi Pazar. Material encounters shaped this community to such an extent that locals could disengage from the state – even autonomy seemed viable at the time.

Asem, apart from establishing an understanding for how individuals narrate their experience of the 1990s in Novi Pazar provides us with fruitful insight into both failed and realized expectations of communal life in Serbia. Matti Hyvärinen, building his expectation analysis of narratives based on Bakhtin, stated: "life stories essentially recount the story of changing, failing or realized expectations."[28] Adopting Deborah Tannen and her list of evidence to frame expectations,[29] Hyvärinen catalogs the following terms by which to frame failed, changing, and/ or realized expectations:

> Repetition; false starts; backtracks, breakdown of temporal order of telling; hedges that flavor the relation between what was expected and what finally happened; indeed, just, anyway, and however; negatives; contrastives; modals; evaluative language; evaluative verbs; intensifiers, including laughter.[30]

Bosniaks in Novi Pazar repeatedly framed their bereaved national inclusion, and confusion thereof, within narratives of changing and failing expectations. Burhan, a very tall, sullen-looking, middle-aged (Bosniak) man, for instance, articulated his failed and changed expectations about communal life in Serbia as follows:

> Anyway, I think, I was . . . I was in the army when I was younger. I was, ahm . . . how do you say that, I remember the history of this country. . . . I don't know why. . . . why does this country belong to someone else, why is it not mine also? I fulfilled all my obligations to this country. I pay taxes, I obey the law, I served the army (as a young conscript). I don't know what more I could have given, or how someone else gave more to this country than me.[31]

Similar to Asem's recounted experience, Burhan displays an array of the afore-mentioned analytic categories that frame failing expectations of the Yugoslav community, including repetition ("I think, I was . . . I was"); false starts ("I don't know why . . . why does this country belong to someone else?"); and negatives ("I don't know what more I could have given"). Most illustrative is the break-down of temporal orders as Burhan seeks to make sense of his current position in society. Burhan explicitly recounts the Yugoslav history with himself as an active participant as a young man in it and contrasts this experience with his perceived exclusion from the Serbian state. His narrative mirrors Asem's experience and was not lost on younger generations, either. Erol, a young, educated, and contem-plative (Bosniak) man, for instance, observed:

> People usually did not keep tabs on others during socialism. . . . But my grandma told me that before that, people kept tabs on who is who because of the two Balkan wars here . . . those wars before the Yugoslav wars. They . . . they kept tabs on who is who . . . I mean, I don't know if they felt divided, but they kept tabs on each other, she said, about who practiced which religion, about . . . national customs, before the existence of Yugoslavia. Then, Tito came. That is when my mom grew up. . . . She remembers a totally different time . . . during which people sort of lost this national affiliation . . . and now, I don't know.[32]

Erol juxtaposes past societal configurations with the present situation by way of contrasting the narrated experiences of his grandmother and his mother to that of his own. It is remarkable that we have three generations in this narrative, all three of whom experience divergent expectations regarding their place in society. Erol's grandmother was an Ottoman subject that turned into a Yugoslav, while his mom was a Yugoslav that turned into a Bosniak – willingly or not. Erol, mean-while, often displayed bewilderment as to his own future as a young Bosniak man in Serbia during this in-depth interview and our numerous casual conversations between 2012 and 2019.

Asem who, like Erol's mother, grew up as a Yugoslav, expressly located the loss of community within the time frame of the 1990s:

> I told you, we knew immediately in the 90s when Slobodan Milošević went to war with Croatia, and then with Bosnia, that they would not help us. We had to turn toward ourselves, and we had no one else expect our family in Turkey. I told you, my father had lived in Novi Pazar, while two of his sisters left Novi Pazar to live in Turkey. This means our family was broken-up. This means we were able to relieve the pressure. We knew Serbia thought nothing good of us, and so we saved ourselves, we secured our economic foundation to have a life, to have jobs, to live, to survive. In other parts of Serbia, Kragujevac, Kruševac, Niš, people felt as though the government owed them something, that Belgrade must help them. They waited for the state to help them. They had no friends in Turkey. . . . we did not go to Turkey because the business was good. . . . we went because we had someone there. . . . we had no food. . . . they gave us a fishing rod, and not the fish. They gave us as much as they were able to give . . . one sewing machine, two, and you pay the debt whenever you can, to survive. When people noticed that survival could turn into a business, they started to expand. Then, they bought five machines, ten. Then, they had to leave their houses, because they worked in living and bedrooms where their daughters and sons slept. Pretty soon, these rooms turned into workshops, and the family members all had to sleep together in one room. And then, when they started to earn money, they established their own enterprises. . . . They had to construct new buildings, because they were not allowed to buy those abandoned companies.[33]

Asem articulates his shattered anticipatory horizon, regarding his place within the Serbian community, with clarity. Bosniaks, according to Asem, expected nothing from Belgrade. He stated unambiguously, "We had to turn toward ourselves to survive."

It is further instructive to analyze the breakdown of temporal sequences as presented by Asem:

> I told you, my father had lived in Novi Pazar, while two of his sisters left Novi Pazar to live in Turkey. This means our family was broken-up. This means we were able to relieve the pressure. We knew Serbia thought nothing good of us, and so we saved ourselves, we secured our economic foundation to have a life, to have jobs, to live, to survive.

Asem tied the 1950s, during which members of his extended family moved to Turkey, directly to the Bosniak community's economic survival during the Yugoslav Succession Wars. One might thus confirm a cognitive disruption with the Serbian state on the one hand and temporal continuity with the émigré community in Turkey on the other.

While Asem connected the trade to the historic migration of Bosniaks to Turkey and his extended family in Turkey specifically, others also identified the geographic location as fundamental to the successful trade during the 1990s. Saleh, a shrewd and well-educated young (Bosniak) man, explained: "It is this position of the city, our city in this border triangle between three countries, including Montenegro, Serbia, and Kosovo, that . . . that makes (šverc) smuggling possible, even to this day."[34] Leijla's daughter, too, ascribed geographic features to the flourishing trade of the 1990s. In her words:

> Here, we are between Montenegro, Kosovo, and Macedonia, right by our neighbors from the old State, and you could do some smuggling (*mogao si da prošvercuješ*) here, generally. You could make pretty good money doing that back then.[35]

These two statements are illuminating in that these two interlocutors do not simply assert a geographic location or proximity with neighboring states, they demonstrate intimacy with former co-nationals – their *neighbors from the old State.* Seen from this perspective, *šverc* was just another means for trading goods across newly created borders that had not existed before. These ties, in other words, did not subside because politicians decided to redraw the map.

Daud, a young (Bosniak) merchant without family members in Turkey, took this notion one step further:

> If you want to learn about trade here, you have to understand the history of this place, the history. I will tell you about it. Ras is about eight kilometers from here.[36] Ras, as the old town is called. This is the first Serbian city. This means, there was neither Belgrade, nor anything else here. There was Sveti Sava.[37] It was a Serbian city, and it was the first commercial place in all of Europe. When London had barely 8,000 inhabitants, Novi Pazar had 12,000. Novi Pazar was full of caravans from Byzantium and Rome, and they all came here to trade. Novi Pazar has an ancient commercial tradition, older than that of London, or that of Switzerland. Novi Pazar has a very old tradition of trading. Had it not been for the wars, Novi Pazar could have been Europe's Istanbul for trade. But the wars ruined everything.[38]

Daud, like Saleh and Asem, looks to the past to rationalize the economic boom of the 1990s. Daud, however, has no family members or friends in Turkey, which may be the reason for his emphasis on the geographic location over filial ties. And yet, his frame is decidedly historic. This pertains to all the above interlocutors who assign present-day properties to historic events of both filial and/or territorial nature. What sets Daud's narrative apart from Asem's, however, is the length of the historic view. Daud includes all of Novi Pazar's history, including the medieval past, though emphasizes that "Novi Pazar could have been Europe's Istanbul for trade" had it not been for the *wars* that ruined everything. By referring to the Byzantine Empire, Istanbul, the two Balkan wars, and the Yugoslav wars, Daud collapses the time-space continuum entirely to make sense of the present. Apart from assigning the present to the past,[39] Daud taps into a common narrative about Novi Pazar as a disempowered region and the necessity for local resilience in the face thereof. Serbia, as illustrated earlier, quashed local desires for autonomy in the 1990s, while both Montenegro and Serbia divided the Sandžak region during the Balkan Wars. And yet, it is this exact narrative that instills locals with a sense of pride:

> If all this had happened somewhere in Europe, in Germany, England, or France, people there would probably given up. But here, people can always make something from nothing! In Europe, they run to their government immediately, and the government helps them when they have problems, and then, the government helps them. Here, we cannot expect anything from our government.[40]

Self-sufficiency is thus a source of local pride and a narrative I encountered repeatedly. This account of aptitude simultaneously overlaps with narratives of perceived disregard, namely, indifference and neglect toward Novi Pazar by Belgrade, based on the predominantly Muslim background of locals. Interviewees, in other words, often invoked a narrative of necessity in the face of sociopolitical and economic negligence by Belgrade and took pride in their ability to accomplish self-sufficiency in the face of systemic collapse. In addition to providing locals with an impression of social continuity, trade relations replaced state support by Belgrade accordingly.

Given the fact that a potential 6 to 7 out of every 10 persons have family members who moved to Turkey at any point in time serves as an abstract, though no less important, backbone for the inner logic of transnational relations. It is important to recognize that locals understood themselves to be in a comparatively favorable position *because* Bosniaks had cross-border connections. Bosniaks, by following this train of thought, were not only able to opt out of what they perceived to be a vicious regime – and rightly so. Historical grievances also seemed corrected, as those Muslims who fled Southeastern Europe since the Austro-Hungarian annexation of Bosnia, and subsequent separation of the Sandžak region between Serbia and Montenegro, aided locals from a position of socioeconomic strength. As such, the practice of trading across porous borders – or *šverc* as locals called it – turned into a "shared event of practice" that fostered transborder connections. Traders did not simply distribute goods from Turkey in Novi Pazar; they also "re-transfer[red] cultural customs" across the border.[41] Trade, in other words, not only fulfilled material but also emotive needs, as becomes clear in the preceding narratives.

Synthesis

The Yugoslav Succession Wars provided ample reason to disassociate sociopolitically from Serbia proper within and of itself. Bosniaks in Sandžak, and Novi Pazar in particular, also had the possibility to connect with the greater Bosniak émigré community in Western Europe, for instance.[42] And yet, I did not come across narratives of symbolic and real transnational networks between émigré Bosniaks in Switzerland, Germany, or Sweden and locals. Instead, locals emphasized their failed expectations regarding Yugoslavia on the one hand, and the economic rescue in the form of material aid from Turkey on the other. The Yugoslav Succession Wars thus served as a rupture, a discontinuity of belonging to the subsequent rump state, as emphasized by a range of interlocutors.

The economic situation in the Yugoslav rump state – consisting of Serbia and Montenegro – spiraled out of control, and locals in Novi Pazar communicated the state would disregard them based on their religious affiliation. As a consequence, locals invigorated transnational ties with the émigré community in Turkey. Interlocutors repeatedly affirmed the positive effects of this market, including an economic boom during which other regions experienced severe existential insecurity. Trade relations, however, were more than simple business exchanges. These connections served as catalysts that induced anticipatory properties among the Bosniak community in Novi Pazar. As such, one might be inclined to argue that transnational trade relations induced local divisions between Serbs and Bosniaks. While interlocutors confirmed that Bosniaks mostly dealt in business while Serbs joined the army, however, all parties involved benefited from the trade.

For now, those migrants – or *muhadžiri*, as they are called locally – who emigrated through Novi Pazar, and on to Turkey, are especially important regarding the first narrative. Interlocutors frequently emphasized that family members in Turkey significantly contributed to the socioeconomic safety locally, so much so that political autonomy became thinkable. Seen from this perspective, Bosniaks were active agents who created fortunes out of thin air, as one of the informants stressed. Transnational trade relations were thus not only a tool by which to endure the economic downturn in Serbia, but they also served as a centripetal force for the ongoing memory construction and reconstruction among Bosniaks.

Notes

1 Voltaire (François Marie Arouet) and Theodore Besterman, *Miracles and Idolatry* (London: Penguin Books, 2005), 54.
2 Thomas Faist, "Transnationalization and Development," in *Migration, Development, and Transnationalization: A Critical Stance*, ed. Nina Glick-Schiller and Thomas Faist (New York: Berghahn Books, 2013), 74.
3 Nina Glick-Schiller, "A Global Perspective on Transnational Migration: Theorizing Migration without Methodological Nationalism," in *Diaspora and Transnationalism – Concepts, Theories and Methods*, ed. R. Bauböck and T. Faist (Amsterdam: Amsterdam University Press, 2010), 111.
4 Paul Ricoeur, *Time and Narrative – Volume 3*, trans. Kathleen Blamey and David Pellauer (Chicago: University of Chicago Press, 1990), 259–261.
5 Glick-Schiller, "A Global Perspective on Transnational Migration: Theorizing Migration without Methodological Nationalism," 111.

6 Горана Крстић и Божо Стојановић, *анализа формалног и неформалног трзиста рада у србији, у прилози за јавну расправу о Институционалним реформама у Србији* (Београд: Центар за либерално-Демократске Студије), 31–33.

7 Ana Džokić, Marc Neelen and Emil Jurcan, *Sta je u Pazaru zajedničko/What Pazar Has in Common(s)?*, (Serbia: Novi Sad, Daniel Print, 2012): 14–15.

8 All the identities and names of the interviewed partners are anonymized.

9 Asem, interviewed in the Sandžak region by Sandra King-Savic in 2012.

10 Robert Bideleux and Ian Jeffries, *The Balkans: A Post-communist History* (New York: Routledge, 2007), 196.

11 Ibid., 249.

12 Vesna Pešić, *Divlje društvo-kako smo stigli dovde* (Peščanik, Belgrade, Serbia, 2012).

13 Ibid., 373.

14 Susan L. Woodward, *Balkan Tragedy: Chaos and Dissolution after the Cold War* (Washington, DC: Brookings Institution Press, 1995), 125.

15 Asem, interviewed in the Sandžak region by Sandra King-Savic in 2012.

16 Leijla and her two daughters and grandson, interviewed in the Sandžak region by Sandra King-Savic in 2014

17 Andrea L. Smith, "Heteroglossia, 'Common Sense', and Social Memory," *American Ethnologist* 31, no. 2 (2004): 254.

18 Thomas Burger, *Max Weber's Theory of Concept Formation: History, Laws, and Ideal Types* (Durham, NC: Duke University Press, 1987), 36–37.

19 For a detailed analysis of the Bosniak identity see, for instance, Mustafa Imamović, *Historija Bošnjaka* (Preporod: Bošnjačka Zajednica Kulture Sarajevo, 1998).

20 Asem, interviewed in the Sandžak region by Sandra King-Savic in 2012.

21 Bojana, interviewed in the Sandžak region by Sandra King-Savic in 2012.

22 "Bošnjačko nacionalno vijeće," accessed October 31, 2017, https://www.bnv.org.rs/onama.php.

23 Serbia nullified the vote and local aspirations for autonomy based on the allegation of voter fraud. According to Belgrade, Muslims of Croatia and Bosnia and Herzegovina also took part in the voting process. For more information, see Milan Andrejevich, "The Sandžak: A Perspective of Serb-Muslim Relations," in *Muslim Identity and the Balkan State*, ed. Hugh Poulton (London: Hurst, in association with the Islamic Council, 1997), 174–177.

24 Smith, "Heteroglossia, 'Common Sense', and Social Memory," 254.

25 Dubravko, interviewed in the Sandžak region by Sandra King-Savic in 2012.

26 Smith, "Heteroglossia, 'Common Sense', and Social Memory," 254.

27 Émile Durkheim, *The Division of Labor in Society*, translated by George Simpson (New York: Free Press, 1965), 201–227, cited in Ken Morrison, *Marx, Durkheim, Weber: Formations of Modern Social Thought* (London: Sage, 2006), 159.

28 Matti Hyvärinen, "Analyzing Narratives and Story-Telling," in *The Sage Handbook of Social Research Methods*, ed. Pertti Alasuutari, Leonard Bickman, and Julia Brannen (Los Angeles: Sage, 2008), 456–457.

29 Ibid.

30 Ibid., 456.

31 Burhan, interviewed in the Sandžak region by Sandra King-Savic in 2012.

32 Erol, interviewed in the Sandžak region by Sandra King-Savic in 2012.

33 Asem, interviewed in the Sandžak region by Sandra King-Savic in 2012.

34 Saleh, interviewed in the Sandžak region by Sandra King-Savic in 2015.

35 Leijla, interviewed in the Sandžak region by Sandra King-Savic in 2015.

36 A medieval Serbian city in the Sandžak region. See, for instance, Kenneth Morrison and Elizabeth Roberts, *The Sandzak: A History* (London: Hurst, 2013), 7–16.

37 Sveti Sava was the Serbian archbishop between 1219 and 1233 and assumes an apostle-like saint position within the Serbian Orthodox Church.

38 Daud, interviewed in the Sandžak region by Sandra King-Savic in 2014.
39 Ricoeur, *Time and Narrative – Volume 3*, 260.
40 Daud, follow-up interview in the Sandžak region by Sandra King-Savic in 2014.
41 Thomas Faist, "Diaspora and Transnationalism: What Kind of Dance Partners?" in *Diaspora and Transnationalism – Concepts, Theories and Methods*, ed. Rainer Bauböck and Thomas Faist (Amsterdam: Amsterdam University Press, 2010), 11.
42 On the Yugoslav and Bosniak diaspora see, for instance, Alaga Dervišević, *Bošnjaci u Dijaspori – Historijat, Problemi, Analize i Perspektive*, Bosanksa Riječ (Sarajevo: Wuppertal, 2006); Paul Hockenos, *Homeland Calling: Exile Patriotism and the Balkan Wars* (Ithaca, NY: Cornell University Press, 2003); *Germans or Foreigners? Attitudes Toward Ethnic Minorities in Post-Reunification Germany*. Edited by R. Alba, P. Schmidt, and M. Wasmer. New York: Palgrave-Macmillan, 2003.

3 Novi Pazar as a mnemonic nucleus for the transmission of memory

The modern democratic constitution also requires citizens to agree on matters one cannot cast a vote on – trust, responsibility, and the common good.

H. Welzer[1]

In the previous chapter, I illustrated how residents of Novi Pazar narrate their experience of the economic downturn in Serbia. Locals repeatedly emphasized their surmounting the financial collapse by way of transnational trade relations between local and émigré Bosniaks in Turkey. In due process, informants, to frame it in Suzan Ilcan's words, "created ways in which alternative relations of belonging change(d) their home without moving anywhere."[2] Interlocutors not only highlighted the socioeconomic prominence of transnational connections, but by accentuating émigré kin-relations and belonging to the post-Ottoman realm they invoked mnemonic continuity. Trade relations, in other words, served as a centripetal force for the ongoing memory construction and reconstruction among Bosniaks in Novi Pazar. Informal market activities between Novi Pazar and Turkey were thus not simply a means to overcome economically induced predicaments but connected historical narratives to autobiographical experiences.

Maurice Halbwachs stated: "memory may be lost altogether unless it is brought to awareness again through contact with otherwise almost forgotten associations."[3] I argue that trading – alternative, material contacts – not only resurrected and to some extent re-created links between the local and Bosniak émigré community but also "brought to awareness those almost forgotten associations" in due process.

To answer the overarching question of how transnational practices between 1991 and 1995 shaped this communities' social relations *locally*, the question of how informants identify with the past must be examined. This question is at the core of the following section. I will identify the medium through which locals remember the past and analyze how autobiographical narratives differ from historic ones. Crucially, how do historicized narratives inform the present? I will examine these questions by answering the following two sub-questions. First, what are the vehicles by which interlocutors transmit memory in Novi Pazar? The town of Novi Pazar itself serves as a mnemonic nucleus, while families act as

DOI: 10.4324/9781003022381-6

carriers of memory. Second, what are the characteristics by which locals collapse the time-space continuum when narrating the past, and do these characteristics inform the present?

Following Halbwachs and his distinction between historic and autobiographical narratives,[4] I will analyze how lived experiences and invigorated commemorations – official and not – merge in local narratives, and how locals identify with this narrated past. I must, however, preface this section by emphasizing that it is not my aim to examine the Bosniak identity. Instead, I seek to filter out how agents identify their social condition through narratives.[5] Identification, as proposed by Rogers Brubaker and Frederick Cooper, is a fruitful tool to investigate why social agents emphasize certain narratives over others without falling into the trap of analyzing identity as a static entity. In Brubaker and Cooper's words:

[It] (Identification) invites us to specify the agents that do the identifying. And it does not presuppose that such identifying (even by powerful agents, such as the state) will necessarily result in the internal sameness, the distinctiveness, the bounded groupness that political entrepreneurs may seek to achieve.[6]

Like Rouse and Glick-Schiller then, Brubaker and Cooper encourage us to think beyond ethnicity as a bounded entity within which all group members share one and the same experience. Seen from this perspective, examining how locals identify and narrate the past is significant on account of hypothesizing the salience of transnational ties across time and space.

Social sites of belonging

Novi Pazar was an important trading town before turning into a space of transit with the onset of the collapsing Ottoman Empire. Migrants – or *muhadžiri*, as locals call those Muslim Slavs who emigrated from Southeastern Europe – migrated through the present-day Sandžak region to reach contemporary Macedonia, Albania, and finally Turkey. As such, the town itself serves as a mnemonic nucleus, while families serve as "vehicular units by which locals remember"[7] and engage with the past. I will unpack the two latter aspects in succession, starting with the statement that Novi Pazar itself serves as a mnemonic nucleus.

Looking in from afar, Novi Pazar appears like any other town in the Western Balkans where Muslims – practicing or not – constitute the majority of residents. The streets are lined with proper homes, unfinished *Gastarbeiter* houses and old, renovated, and/or new mosques dot the skyline (Figure 3.1). In Novi Pazar, imperial, communist, and national proclivities and/or ideologies continue to characterize the town in the form of architectural objects.

Standing at the center of town, one can see the wall of the old Ottoman fort on top of which stands a library and a relatively modern outdoor café (Figure 3.2).[8] The Amir-Aga Han looks as though no one ever bothered to renovate the structure since Ottoman officials retreated to present-day Turkey. Locals enjoy sipping hot

Figure 3.1 The town of Novi Pazar

Source: Picture taken by Joshua E. King.

Figure 3.2 Ottoman fort in Novi Pazar

Source: Picture taken by Joshua E. King.

brews within the shady though crumbling enclosure of what is left of the Isa-Beg hammam (Figure 3.3), and on the other side stands the massive socialist bloc that locals call *lučna zgrada* (Figure 3.4). After a ten-minute stroll from downtown Novi Pazar toward the direction of Raška, one reaches the St. Peter and Paul Church (Figure 3.5), and further out of town, perched on top of the hill overlooking Novi Pazar, stands the Djurdjevi Stupovi monastery (Figure 3.6). The remnants of old Ras, as well as the Sopoćani monastery, are within a 30- to 40-minute drive from town.

The Nemanja dynasty, the Ottomans, and the Socialist Federal Republic not only left their imprints in the form of cultural and religious practices that are still common to many post-Ottoman spaces, but also a material trail of structures that yet dominate the architectural landscape around a 20-kilometer radius of Novi Pazar.

Residents are proud of their legacy that is visible in cultural traditions and the surrounding heritage sites. After some time in town, locals began to flag me down, randomly, to initiate conversations about the city they inhabit, as was the case with an elegant, mustachioed, elderly gentleman who was sipping Turkish coffee in one of the cafés along the ever-packed pedestrian boulevard in downtown Novi Pazar. "This is our heritage," the man said proudly as he pointed up at the old Ottoman fort. "It's part of us. My family calls Novi Pazar home for seven generations! You can look it up in the archives if you want."[9] This sentence, *ovo je naša dedovina* (this is our heritage), was a decree whose presence was felt all around

Figure 3.3 Isa-Beg hamman in Novi Pazar
Source: Picture taken by Joshua E. King.

Figure 3.4 *Lučna zgrada* in Novi Pazar
Source: Picture taken by Joshua E. King.

Figure 3.5 St. Peter and Paul Church in Novi Pazar
Source: Picture taken by Joshua E. King.

Figure 3.6 Djurdjevi Stupovi
Source: Picture taken by Joshua E. King.

town in words and deeds, and was exhibited on signs, as is the case with this banner that hung from the Amir-Aga Han (Figures 3.7 and 3.8).

A middle-aged, tall, and lanky man with sunken eyes invited me to climb the
otherwise locked (so I was told) minaret of the Altun-Alem Mosque that was
built in the 16th century. The Altun-Alem Mosque is among the oldest and perhaps most famous mosques in Novi Pazar, in part due to its unique architecture
(Figure 3.9). The mosque has a single dome and a porch that is covered with
two smaller cupolas – similar structures can be found in Turkey. Altun-Alem is
placed in the midst of a courtyard that includes the original water well, a *maktab*,[10]
and gravestones engraved with Ottoman-Arabic calligraphy. As we climbed the
long, narrow, and dimly lit staircase of the minaret, the caretaker explained he
had renovated the mosque and its surroundings out of his own initiative, seeing
that Belgrade was not willing to refurbish historic buildings in town. "I was able
to renovate this mosque," he explained, "because we got donations from private
investors who sought to see this mosque restored."[11]

Looking down at the town of Novi Pazar (Figure 3.10), I was reminded of Peter
Sugar's description of Southeast European cities under Ottoman rule:

A bird's eye view of any city disclosed to the observer the plan of the city.
Its center was clearly distinguishable by the major mosques, large buildings

Figure 3.7 Pansion Amir-Aga Han in the center of Novi Pazar

Source: Picture taken by Joshua E. King.

Figure 3.8 *Ovo je naša dedovina*, banner hanging from the Amir-Aga Han in Novi Pazar

Source: Picture taken by Joshua E. King.

Figure 3.9 Altun-Alem Mosque in Novi Pazar
Source: Picture taken by Joshua E. King.

housing the chief markets, a fortress if any, and even a large open square. The size and height of structures in a given mahalles indicated clearly to which millet its inhabitants belonged. Not only were public buildings more substantially constructed then were the private homes, but their shapes were also indicative of their functions.[12]

It appears the public buildings were indeed constructed more substantially, as put forth by Sugar, seeing that bakeries, the hammam, han, water fountains, and mosques still stood intact after all these years – though dilapidated.

Figure 3.10 View of Novi Pazar from the Altun-Alem Mosque
Source: Picture taken by Joshua E. King.

Since the 1990s, such heritage sites, their maintenance and/or negligence thereof,[13] turned into contested sites of memory that are attached to cultural practices. Because, as Bourdieu maintained, material conditions endow social actors with "schemes of perception," one may extrapolate that locals imbue these buildings with meaning that mirror their social position within Serbia.[14] Indeed, the difference between the care for Orthodox heritage sites compared to that of the often ramshackle state of Islamic and cultural facilities from the Ottoman period is striking. As illustrated in the preceding images, Ottoman sites are often in tatters if not renovated with private capital, while Belgrade donated funds to renovate Orthodox heritage sites. A case in point is the renovation of the Djurdjevi Stupovi Church (1170) that was initiated by Zoran Djindjic.[15] The Djurdjevi Stupovi Church is, of course, integral to Serbian historiography, seeing that Stefan Nemanja himself ordered the construction of the church as a dedication to a saint who, according to Nemanja, rendered his victory over the Byzantines possible.[16] The church illustrates, in other words, a re-creation of Serbian nation-building processes that are based on Orthodoxy. This is significant because it symbolizes that Orthodox Slavs merit to be included in the social fabric of present-day Serbia while, drawing on interviews and casual conversations with locals, Muslim Slavs are not.

It comes as no surprise that Bosniaks turn toward historiographical sources that acknowledge their social presence in the very space they inhabit to overcome their marginal status. Heritage sites, because they symbolize belonging, are optimal sources that illustrate – quite literally – historic continuity. Perhaps Ilcan said it best when she stated: "belonging to a place is not an individual matter but an experience of being connected in and between social sites of social relations." As a consequence, heritage sites symbolize simultaneous and disputed claims to the space of Novi Pazar, which political entrepreneurs variously claim so as to highlight or dispute collective impressions of belonging among Serbs or Bosniaks, respectively.

Social sites and family narratives: chronicles of belonging in Novi Pazar

Both Serbs and Bosniaks in Novi Pazar tie narratives of belonging to social sites that highlight their respective historiography. In the following, I convey a dialogue between Erol and me that started with a chat about the 2012 election during which Tomislav Nikolić (SNS) won the Serbian presidency by a narrow margin of 49.54 percent. Upon my question about his consideration revolving around the recent election in Serbia, Erol replied:

EROL: A predetermined group of people won the elections, which means, Serbs won the election. I cannot understand this patriotism. If Nikolić won the election. . . . I don't know. . . . it also means that some Serbs voted for him. I hope they forged the elections. If this person won . . . this person who was a perpetrator of violence (*zločin*) in the 1990s. . . . It's not enough for them that their boss (Šešelj) is being judged in the Hague. He was their boss, the president of their party. Now he answers for his crimes in the Hague. I mean, what can I say about those Serbs that actually voted for him.[17]

ME: You say "a predetermined group won the elections," what do you mean by that? And, what do you think about the low voter turnout?

EROL: Well, now you're asking me about something that. . . . You came here to observe how people live in this town. Some people stereotype us, and the papers make this place look bad all the time. . . . Now . . . this guy won the elections. It is completely unimportant how many people turned out to vote for him, if they even voted, or not . . . he won. And this is an image that . . . you know, is difficult to change in a man. When I see that Nikolić won the elections, it is irrelevant how many people voted for him, because I already feel bitter. I already feel troubled about his victory. What can I say? Perhaps he will be decent. But, you know, these people did something. . . . Look, Vuk Drašković. . . . there is this footage that was recorded up by the St. Peters' church. . . . Drašković said: *the person who embraces the Turkish or any flag except the Serbian one, will lose their hand and their flag*. And this person is supposed to be a liberal politician . . . if they are Turks. . . . At the beginning, they were not as evil, but by the end, they were really evil, but not at the beginning. But that's war . . . every war is violent. There is no non-violence in wars. You kill someone to establish peace . . . but in a violent way. You know, the Turks were here for 500 years, and the Serbian churches were not ruined. You know, that kind of speaks for itself, that's again some evidence that makes you think about this situation. Even some Serbs cried when the Turks (*Turci*) left Novi Pazar.[18]

What Erol refers to in the preceding dialogue is the development of the Progressive Party that re-entered mainstream politics with Tomislav Nikolić at its helm in 2012. Vuk Drašković, together with Vojislav Šešelj and Mirko Jović, formed the Serbian National Renewal party (SNO), though Šešešelj later formed the Serbian Radical Party (SRS), half of which was renamed the Serbian Progressive Party (SNS) in 2008. For Erol, these men represent a group of people with nationalist ambitions and ideologies according to which non-Orthodox Slavs constitute a fifth column. Indeed, in the footage that was recorded at the St. Peter and Paul Church, Vuk Drašković is seen shouting:

> Every person that embraces, on this Rascian land, a Turkish flag, a Croatian flag, an Albanian flag, or any other flag except the Serbian flag, will be left without a hand, and without a flag![19]

According to Drašković, Albanians and Croats also constitute a potentially subversive element that undermines the Serbian nation-building process and thus the social fabric of Serbia. However, due to the question concerning transnational practices between local and Bosniak émigrés, I must focus on the Bosniak and/or Muslim community in the Sandžak region. It is interesting to note here that Drašković emphasizes Raška in his speech because the Petrova Crkva stands within a ten-minute walking distance from Novi Pazar, while Raška lies within 19 kilometers of the church. Novi Pazar, one might thus argue, is not an ideal site to propagate national unity from the perspective of nationalistically inclined politicians because it poses a misfit for the projection of an alleged Serbian homogeneity. Drašković's statement is, moreover, an explicit summons to assimilate lest one seeks to lose the claim to the land one lives on.

Both parties – Drašković on tape, and Erol during our in-depth interview and casual conversations – emphasize historic narratives that warrant belonging. Political entrepreneurs as well as locals, in other words, use – and rely on – the Ottoman Empire to either find meaning in, substantialize, or dismiss subsequent claims to this region in Serbia following the Yugoslav Succession Wars.

It is especially fruitful to recall Erol's earlier quote about his grandmother, who was an Ottoman subject, and his mom, who was a Yugoslav citizen. Both strands, the imperial and socialist narratives, conditioned his upbringing. Yet, when asked about the sociopolitical situation in Serbia, Erol identifies with the Ottoman past. "Even some Serbs cried when the Turks left," he explained. His understanding of present-day circumstances, and thus frame of mind, mirrors the narrative of his grandmother during which "people kept tabs on who is who because of the two Balkan wars here."[20] Though he did not experience the two Balkan Wars personally, Erol equates his social condition with that of his grandmother, who narrated the exodus of Muslim Slavs following the two Balkan and World Wars to her grandson. His social condition reflects that of his grandmother who experienced the World Wars and not the peace encountered by his mother. Erol, by paralleling the incident at the Petrova church with the exodus of the Ottomans, may thus exemplify the construction of social memory as hypothesized by Halbwachs who theorized that memory is "a social construction mainly, if not wholly, shaped by the concerns of the present."[21]

A second and related aspect in Erol's quote is strikingly clear; Erol distrusts political institutions in Serbia. He learned from his grandmother that Belgrade could not be trusted in the past and makes the same experience at present. Erol states: "a predetermined group won the elections and hopes they (Belgrade) forged the elections." His statement illustrates two critical points. First, Erol differentiates between governmental institutions and ordinary Serbs as he voices his hope that average citizens abstained from voting for Nikolić. Second, in floating the possibility of rigged presidential elections in Serbia, Erol alludes to a broken and potentially unreliable political system. The general welfare of the political establishment in Serbia, one may thus extrapolate, is not protected.

To put this statement further into perspective, Figure 3.11 illustrates the extent to which questionnaire participants distrust governmental institutions. Regarding the statement that Belgrade does enough for the equal development of all regions in Serbia, 51.6 percent of respondents strongly disagree and 26.9 percent disagree. This means a total of 78.5 percent of all questionnaire participants feel that Belgrade neglects to develop their region.

Equally telling is the high number of participants who feel their only chance to advance in their career depends on whom they know; 81.8 percent of all participants at least partially agree with the statement that a potentially successful career depends on personal relations. Based on these numbers, one may pose that misgivings toward Belgrade run deep in the region, a topic that recurred frequently during casual conversations and in-depth interviews. These numbers further suggest a strong patronage system in Serbia overall, a finding that correlates with research carried out by transparency international.[22] According to Andy McDevitt, the author of the study, 80 percent of Serbian citizens believe political parties are corrupt or extremely corrupt, and that self-censorship increased, while governmental institutions increasingly influence the media.[23]

Distrust, however, is not only directed at the political establishment in Belgrade but also toward local politicians and religious representatives in Novi Pazar. Asked if people feel they are valued for their intelligence and abilities *in their own region*, a total of 68.9 percent at least partially disagreed, while 76.6 percent agreed at least partially with the statement regarding career advancement if they come from a wealthy family.

When asked about misgivings or satisfaction with local politicians, interviewees frequently stated disillusion with electoral processes due to manipulation, as illustrated by Daud:

It's easy to be a politician like that. Politicians here just take advantage of what hurts people the most. They always remind you about the past, about how they burned the mosques one hundred years ago. They never talk about what we should do to get ahead, what they should do to make things happen. Why do they remind people of what happened a hundred years ago. . . ? Why are they politicizing this way?[24]

Daud refers to the Bosniak side of political and religious leaders who variously seek to utilize the symbolism of heritage sites to "persuade people to understand themselves, their interests, and their predicaments," to frame it in the words of Brubaker and Cooper.[25]

In Novi Pazar, there are two Islamic communities: the Islamic Community of Serbia (IZS) and the Islamic Community in Serbia (IZuS).[26] Both communities purport to represent all Muslims of Serbia and thus claim Islamic heritage sites.[27]

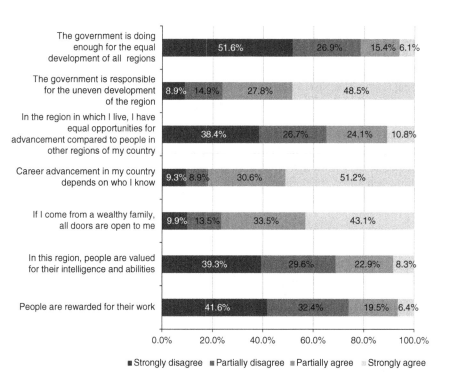

Figure 3.11 Opinions toward career options and government services

The political leadership in Belgrade supports the IZS due to Serbian territorial integrity; in contrast, the IZuS is oriented towards Sarajevo.[28] Yet, the existence of two Islamic communities in Serbia must be understood from the perspective of fluctuating border regimes and the way in which distrust in governmental institutions shape local communities. At the local level, disputes that surround the representation of the Islamic community in Serbia serve as a prism through which we understand that locals do not simply endorse decrees because they are couched in religious terms. To the contrary, locals seek to escape the straitjacket of national boundaries and partisan policy makers, as illustrated by questionnaire results and the preceding statement by Daud.[29] Individuals possess agency to choose whether they seek to concede to persuasion efforts of political entrepreneurs and, significantly, they are also shaped by their families.

Both Daud and Erol grew up in Novi Pazar, are nominal Muslims of similar age, though they do not share one and the same view. Erol, as exemplified earlier, regularly referred to historiography and narratives as told by his grandmother when seeking to make sense of his own social position in Serbia. Daud, inversely, ordinarily referred to his nuclear family – his children, wife, and brother – and beheld the present to question the political stagnation in Belgrade but also locally. Daud, moreover, consistently emphasized his Serbian citizenship and general indifference toward Turkey despite taking regular trips to Istanbul to procure wares for sale in Novi Pazar. One of the explanations for the disparity between Erol and Daud might be their upbringing and perception of the past: Erol was co-raised by his grandmother and mother, Daud primarily by his parents. This is an important difference one must consider when assessing the strength of transnational relations in Novi Pazar; this will be examined in the next section. For now, we must reflect the consistent tenor that runs through all the narratives: distrust toward political institutions en masse.

Daud raises an important question about "why they (politicians) politicize the way they do." I would like to reformulate his question to inquire when place-making turns into forced homogenization practices. The answer comes from Asem who, when asked about his assessment of the current sociopolitical situation and his place in it, replied:

> Now, there are several elements that explain the current political climate, including nationalism, radicalism, and all that. This was not simply the result of our wish, or because we wished for this situation to develop in this way, or because we wanted to air our grievances, no. This current situation is a result of our defense against the Serbian nationalism we experienced during the 1990s. Meaning, some guy called Šešelj appeared on the political scene, some guy called Vuk killed people just because they were Muslims. We lived here in Serbia, and waited for our turn. . . . And, as a sort of resistance, we, our . . . our people created some sort of platform, to protect ourselves from that, because people were physically annihilated. Bosnia was right here, our neighbor, and we saw what was happening there, and so many family members from there came here . . . every day . . . they stayed with us for a while . . .

but we were scared from the government, because people would have been beaten. . . . This was all done in secret. This is why I say, conditionally, Bosniak nationalism, Muslim nationalism. It was not just created because we planned this, because we complained about some invented reason, no. It was created as an antipode, a protection against the strong nationalism that was propagated by Slobodan Milošević, because of the nationalism propagated by Šešelj, and Vuk Drašković.[30]

The platform locals created to protect themselves against Serbian nationalism, as suggested by Asem, thus not only caused local ruminations and a reorientation toward the past to understand the present, but also led to a nationalist countermovement. As a result, interlocutors frequently demonstrated resignation and apathy toward, but also emancipation from, political institutions – local and national. Locals, it seems, entered a depoliticized stage in which political information and historiography disseminated by way of official channels lost significance.

For instance, Siniša, a stylish, very well-educated and outspoken young (Serbian) man, argued:

For the first time we have local Bosniaks, Muslims, not atheists, who say: Look, I appreciate and respect your opinion, and I also wish for my rights to be respected, but I don't want to be told how to live. I want to live freely and in tune with 21st century values. This actually leads to democratization the way it has in BiH were Bosniaks say they don't need anybody telling them that they are Muslims. They know that by themselves, too. They don't need a mufti to tell them they are not good Muslims.[31]

Because religious and political leaders seek to influence locals, informants often emphasized aversion toward officially sanctified historiography, as was the case with Mirijam, who emphasized oral history as opposed to official sources provided by the government:

I always consider both sides, the side of those people that are manipulated, and those that are armed to carry out inhuman acts, things from which they will never recover. . . . That's what interests me. I am telling you, history is like that. Anyway, I believe in the history that is told by the simple people here. You know . . . ahm . . . all that government wants to do is exploit history.[32]

Interlocutors regularly refer to external forces that seek to manipulate and/or persuade individuals to adopt particular perspectives. This was the case with Drašković, who instructed Muslim Slavs to embrace the Serbian flag, and a nationalizing group of Bosniak political and religious leaders as described by Asem.

History – mythologized versions thereof that are tied to specific cultural artifacts – is a powerful agent that carries local narratives, especially when infused into still existing heritage sites. Yet, humans are not monoliths who absorb messages of political entrepreneurs without reflection. Individuals are influenced by their social circumstances but also conditioned by their family history, as illustrated by Daud and Erol.

Erol, who had a very close relationship with his grandmother, emphasized the 500-year history of the Ottomans when asked about national elections, highlighting that Ottomans never destroyed Orthodox Churches. Daud, who does not have relatives in Turkey but goes to Istanbul regularly, rarely stressed family narratives, even when directly asked about them. Instead, he ordinarily chose to focus on the duties the government fails to fulfill. It is important to understand this differentiation because it sheds light on how interviewees view the past and the salience locals confer upon informal historic narratives and non-state, 'alternative social networks' in turn.[33]

Collapsing the time-space continuum

Overall, 69.5 percent of 500 questionnaire participants confirmed to have family members who migrated from Novi Pazar to Turkey. It is through these filial relations and the connected narratives of migration – forced and voluntary – that locals "take up contact with the past."[34] Overall, 69.5 percent of all questionnaire participants have family members who migrated to Turkey, while 46.4 percent of them connect with émigré family members on a regular basis (Figure 3.12). This

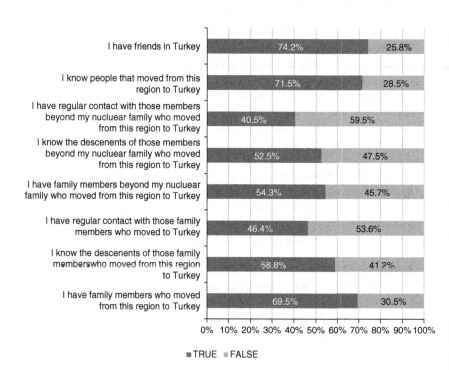

Figure 3.12 Transnational connections with Turkey

means a little less than every other person has connections to members of their family who moved to Turkey since the first wave migrated in 1876/78. Transnational contacts, however strong they may be, are couched within the physical and tangible heritage sites left over from the Ottoman era and revitalized by way of the Yugoslav Succession Wars. As such, tacit knowledge about the migration to interior Ottoman lands resurfaced where it acquired a public value. Tacit knowledge about earlier migratory waves allowed for operationalizing transnational practices for symbolic but also practical means. As such, the first narrative as hypothesized in the previous chapter is substantialized because these relations present a seemingly chronological extension between the past and the present.

Interlocutors, as illustrated earlier, associate the presence of the Ottoman Empire in Southeastern Europe with the still existing, though often decaying social heritage sites in Novi Pazar. In turn, social heritage sites connect present-day concerns tangibly with memories narrated by elder generations who not only seem to re-experience the past but also confirm the social condition younger individuals experience at present. Halbwachs theorized that older men and women

are in a most favorable position to evoke events of the past as they really appeared. But if these events recur is this not because they were always there?[35]

Senior citizens, by preserving the past, link younger generations to a history they did not experience by themselves. Under the un-'favorable' conditions that were the Yugoslav Succession Wars, links to the émigré community turned into salient connections because they confirm existing assumptions among locals that Bosniak citizens had no place in society. Younger generations, in other words, experience a present that mirrors the past as narrated by elders; a feedback loop between social sites and unofficial, or rather orally transmitted history, is created. Such links are powerful because, as stated by Halbwachs:

Memory gives us the illusion of living in the midst of groups which do not imprison us, which impose themselves on us only so far and so long as we accept them.[36] . . . In short, the most painful aspects of yesterday's society are forgotten because constraints are felt only so long as they operate and because, by definition, a past constraint has ceased to be operative.[37]

In the case of Novi Pazar, past constraints turned operative once more when nationalistically inclined political entrepreneurs seized heritage sites to denounce all affiliation with the *Turks* (i.e., the Ottoman Empire). Though not sequential, events following the collapse of the Ottoman Empire, including the exodus of loved ones and abolition of favorable social conditions that subjects of the Porte enjoyed, are strung together into a seamless chronological narrative in which the Kingdom of Serbs, Croats, and Slovenes and the subsequent Jugoslav State imprisoned the Sandžak region by imposing themselves upon Bosniak Muslims. Ergo, life – or a reconstructed recollection thereof – was better under the Porte, and might be favorable under Turkish rule. Painful memories of loss and eradication of commonly held values were thus a focal point around which interlocutors spun their narratives to understand present circumstances. This is especially the case for elder generations. Mustafa Imamović, too, argued along these lines and stated that elder generations "suffered the most, because they still remembered the Turkish administrative system" and feared persecution.[38] Senior citizens raised by parents who remembered the collapse of Ottoman governing structures thus present an especially significant link to this past. These individuals connect the past to the present in the form of narrative transmission.

Leijla is one of those individuals who was raised by parents who experienced the Ottoman Empire. Though she does not know the exact date of her birth, she states she is "somewhere in her upper nineties." She wears her long white hair in a bun and speaks so softly that all activity seems to grind to a halt when she does. Her two daughters sat beside her and listened intently as she spoke of migration, expulsion, and the two Balkan and World Wars. Both of her daughters nodded empathetically as Leijla rummaged in her memories upon my asking if there were people she knew who had migrated to Turkey:

> Indeed, child (*bogumi jeste, sine*). Yes, there have been a lot of families who left. My two sisters left also. I was the third daughter. I stayed here. Mom and dad both died . . . and I got married when my sisters left for Turkey. Now, everyone has grown old. I grew old, my sisters grew old, our kids are old. . . . I don't even know when they left here anymore . . . can't remember the year anymore . . . which year.[39]

During our conversation, I learned that Leijla's sisters left for Turkey sometime during the early 1930s. Speaking from a first-person, past-tense perspective, Leijla conveys a personal autobiographic experience in the preceding quote. Later on, during our taped conversation, Leijla mixed her lived experience with historicized events the way I encountered in younger generations when they spoke of the Ottoman Empire:

> Back in 1912, there were beatings, fighting . . . that was somewhere around 1912. . . maybe. I don't know. It doesn't even matter which year it was. . . . When the Austrians came, that's when everybody left immediately. . . . some fled to Turkey, after that, people started to leave.[40]

Though Leijla was not sure when she was born, it is not likely that she remembers the outbreak of the first Balkan War. To her, however, these events seem to present a logic continuity of past incidents that were conveyed to her when she herself was a child. Her repeated oblivion for time is, to be sure, a sign of old age. Yet, it is also indicative of how the past blends together to form the present when people are asked to narrate their experience from memory.

During the Balkan Wars in 1912/13, Serbia and Montenegro unified, upon which the Sandžak of Novi Pazar ceased to exist officially. Since then, the region is no longer a legal entity but a mental map that symbolizes a common history among Bosniaks.[41] Reflecting on the Balkan Wars, Sabrina Ramet stated that conflicts between Bosniaks and Serbs were of class nature but also ensued as a form of revenge against subjects who were formerly loyal to the Porte:

> Some violence had a class nature with Serbian peasants seizing land from Muslim estate-owners. But Muslim peasants were also targeted, because they were Muslims. Most of Serbia's troops had had no experience of living among Muslims, and had been brought up to think of Muslims as such almost as mythical symbols of the enemies of Serbia. In addition, such sentiments were reportedly fanned by the Serbian boulevard press.[42]

As a general note, one might note the striking similarity of this quote when considering the 1990s. In reflecting on the quote in isolation, in other words, one might mistake this assessment for a description of the Yugoslav Succession Wars. Be that as it may, interlocutors deliberated both of these aspects, including the general fear and class disparities upon my question how and why people left Southern Serbia, and Novi Pazar in particular:

> They went to Turkey because they were scared. Do you know what was happening here back then? It was the agrarian reform. They took from the officers (*Aghe*) and the chieftains/governors (*begs*) who had a lot – and the others where workers (*čifčije*). They worked for them for money, for a little bit of money. But they had a lot of money. Eh, then the state (*država*) took everything, and divided it up equally. But they were used to living . . . but they also left because they were scared.[43]

Though Leijla does not remember these events of her own accord, she was intent on conveying how she *felt* about the Balkan Wars, the subsequent dispossession and cycle of retribution that followed: "the things I experienced here . . . I remember this fear," she repeated over and over.[44] Notions of pain and fear, such as the one described by Leijla, are not communicable through history books or debated in public. Instead, these are transferred within the family unit or swapped among close acquaintances.

Interviewees emphasized affectual reactions they either experienced, as was the case with Leijla, or heard by way of narratives transmitted by parents and grandparents, as was the case with Erol. Past grievances, in other words, were not aired in public, as emphasized by Asem:

> And that's this fear, do you understand. . . . Some *četnik* slaughtered my grandfather here. . . . he was only 13 when the *četniks* killed his father. This is all public knowledge, but nobody talks about it in public.[45]

After the unification of the Serbian, Croatian, and Slovene Kingdom (KSHS) in 1918, the agrarian reform continued to herald retributions against Muslims.

Local Serbian peasants avenged former landholders "very often with the nod-ding encouragement of Serb authorities."[46] Rich and poor Muslims were equally targeted by Serbian paramilitary and voluntary militia groups who were set to profit from the emigration of local Muslims, and peasants used the general law-lessness at the time to seize land, as described by Husnija Kamberović.[47] Signifi-cantly, local Muslims organized a revolt against dispossession which, however, was swiftly quashed by the newly minted monarchy.[48] As a consequence, Muslim Slavs continued the migratory process to interior Ottoman lands that had started in 1876/78.

Interviewees emphasized how they felt about these events, because they were not present to witness them in person. Both Leijla and Asem highlighted fear as a salient component that led to the large migration of local Muslims to Albania, Macedonia, and interior Ottoman lands in general. Yet, these events are so far in the past that hardly anyone alive between 2012 and 2018 could remember these events personally. Narrative transmission practices within families were thus likely strong. Leijla's interview is illustrative of this possibility, given her blend-ing of autobiographical and historicized narratives.

Because the 1990s seemed like a recurrence to elder generations, narratives of the past not only came to mirror present circumstances but parallel each other across generations. Here, a statement given by Leijla's daughter is especially edifying:

> They . . . were under the Turks for a long time. A long time. 500 years. Now, they are convinced that those of us who stayed here, are some sort of sub-Turks (*pod-Turci*), or whatever else they think we are. That is how they think . . . that we should pay for something they had experienced.[49]

Leijla's daughter grew up in the former SFRY and never experienced the govern-ing structures of the Porte. And yet, her statement reads as though she grew up during the collapse of the Ottoman Empire and encountered subsequent retribu-tions against Muslim Slavs herself. It is instructive to recall Hyvärinen's expecta-tion analysis of changing, failing or realized expectations here.[50] Leijla's daughter states, "now they are convinced" that Bosniaks are sub-Turks. She speaks, in other words, in the present tense, and states that Orthodox Serbs avenge Muslims for their collaboration with the Porte at present. Between the narrative memory reconstruction of her senescent mother and her own experiences of the 1990s, one might argue the social conditions within which Leijla grew up after the turn of the century mirrors her own.

Narratives oscillate between the past and the present, a process that is invigor-ated by local skepticism toward governing structures. Oral history thus acquires additional weight, as iterated by Mirjam:

> I don't consider the official history, only what Bosniaks tell each other unoffi-cially, the memory of Bosniaks. And there is so much that happened here dur-ing the 20th century. . . . I mean, this is not a long historical period. When you

look at it from the perspective of historical times, then, I guess, it is somehow short. But so much happened here, and nearly every family has relatives who moved from the Sandžak (region) to Turkey. I am talking about the Sandžak region now, but this happened to all Bosniaks in Southeastern Europe. All this also happened in Bosnia, in Macedonia . . . since 1912 when the Balkan Wars started, since the Ottoman Empire left this region. When the Turks stopped to govern this region, many of the Islamized peoples here (*islamizirani narod*) found themselves within new borders. A lot of them . . . they had a really hard time to adjust. They were like fish on land. . . . One people (*jedan narod*) were suddenly supposed to divide into four, five new states.[51]

Besides confirming wariness with officially sanctioned historiographies, Mirijam taps into a significant narrative in this quote, namely the common supposition that all Bosniaks lived as one under the Ottoman Empire. Following the logic of this recurring conjecture among informants, Bosniaks constitute a diaspora – one community that was forced to espouse monarchic and subsequent supranational and national values to fit into newly created states. It is difficult to overstate this last argument. Local Bosniaks learned about the seemingly recurring past from individuals who narrated the breakup of an empire by way of violent expulsion, state-led misappropriation of property, and fear on the basis of their belonging to an ostracized religious group. This recurring experience of the past, however, connects locals not only with their history but also with the entire Bosniak diaspora that was subject to the same developments. Locals in Novi Pazar are, according to this logic, not subject to Serbia but belong to this very diaspora that was left scattered around Southeastern Europe and Turkey following the collapse of the Ottoman Empire.

Because the newly minted monarchy of Southeastern Europe was to avoid existing cohesion with the antiquated Porte, borders replaced millets while Muslims were stripped of their privileges. Economic privation, and new state structures were consequently a recurring topic that informants addressed. According to Mirijam:

The borders constantly changed! Up, down, up down . . . and the people were constantly on the move, now to the left, then to the right. You know, the Ottoman Empire existed here for about 500 years. During that time, they strengthened their power here. But those institutions were not held by Turks. Those institutions were mostly in the hands of those who had converted to Islam. I am not going to talk about who is a Bosniak, are they this or that . . . no. Anyway, they were landowners before all else (*pre svega*). In the Balkans, those included Albanians, Klefts, Illyrians, and all those who embraced it (Islam). . . . eh, and those people, as Islamized (*kao islamizirani narod*) peoples had, how to say, privileges. Of course, the main rights. And they were in those Ottoman institutions, which is why, when the Ottoman army moved out, they were left without their state, and stripped of those privileges.[52]

Mirijam repeated time and again that she did not consult history books to learn about the past. Instead, she was intent on listening to oral testimonies given by locals. Her interview corroborates the above assumption by which locals swap stories to learn about a past with which interviewees identify at present. Mirijam also raises the important aspect of privileges and the loss of property.

The loss of property following the collapse of the Ottoman Empire was a regular topic I encountered in casual conversations and interviews. Omar, an older, very tall and hefty gentleman, for instance, explained:

> They came here, and they started to kill people. They took the properties from families. Then they gave the land to the other people, the Austrian Slavs . . . all the Imams became jobless because of this development.[53]

The loss of property is evidently tied to reprisals by which Orthodox peasants seized land from the former beys – a development that is further tied to the abolishment of religious institutions. Seen from this perspective, the abolishment of religious institutions was not simply an act of seizing land and mosques. Instated, the act of seizing heritage sites implies a loss of common values. To put it in Mirijam's words, Bosniaks "were like fish on land" after the creation of nation-states in place of the old Ottoman Empire. Omar and Mirijam thus both substantiate Bourdieu's theory that material conditions endow social actors with "schemes of perception."[54] Omar elucidates that heritage sites were not simply structures made of concrete, but tied to a specific way of life Ottoman subjects were accustomed to:

> Usually, people who were considered to have enough means of their own and for their families paid into a foundation in the form of zakāt,[55] to support the community, schools, and other things. Families used to have their own school, madrasas, here. But . . . those institutions were taken away from Bosniak families, and those properties fell apart.[56]

Like Leijla's daughter, Omar portrays the sociopolitical transformation as though he was himself present at the time. Whether relations exchanged anecdotes within the family unit or not, narrative events about the consequences following the collapse of the Ottoman Empire impressed themselves on the public conscience to such an extent that interviewees perceive them as their own.

In addition to emphasizing the loss of property and depletion of income for religious institutions, Omar's statement implies a forced acquiescence on the side of the Bosniak community, an aspect that also recurred in Leijla's interview:

> Everything was settled . . . those who had possessions, those who had to leave, where to, and how they had to divide [into the different parts of] Yugoslavia.[57]

Leijla, Omar, and Mirijam seem to suggest here that Bosniaks were no longer able to exercise their own autonomy. Bosniaks – as was the case with individual

Muslims who identify with other nationalities at present – were told to leave their home, their friends, and a way of life they knew. This is an important aspect, because it bears an aspect of ambiguity. Muslims who moved to interior Ottoman lands were forced to leave their home. And yet, early émigrés managed to preserve a way of life by doing so. An interview excerpt from Amer, a young descendent from a Bosniak and Albanian family that had settled in Turkey during the 1920s, is insightful here:

> My grandmother had lived in this one village ever since she came here (to Turkey). So we went to visit there for Bayram. They were Republicans, they were part of the Turkish Republic. They felt and called themselves Turks.[58]

At that time, Novi Pazar was no longer a viable trading town and lost its economic significance.[59] When Amer's grandparents left Southeastern Europe, Novi Pazar turned from a place of trade into one of transmigration for Muslims who sought to leave Southeastern Europe.[60] This was especially the case during the second migratory wave. The Turkish state was instrumental as regards the migration of Muslim Slavs, seeing that Ankara passed the Law on Settlement that allowed members of Muslim communities to migrate and settle in Turkey. The Law on Settlement stipulated:

> Those who are accepted as '*muhacir*' are given Turkish citizenship by the Council of Ministers. Muhacir are people of Turkish descent or those who either come as an individual to settle in Turkey or who make their application as a group.[61]

Kemal Kirişci, however, draws attention to the fact about the inexistence of clear criteria that defined Turkish 'ethnicity and culture'. Instead, according to Kirişci, it was "the Council of Ministers that (is) [was] empowered to decide which groups abroad qualified as belonging to Turkish ethnicity and culture."[62] Muslims fell into two groups upon migrating to Turkey: *iskânli göçmen* and *serbest göçmen*.

Iskânli göçmen depended on state support for their resettlement.[63] Migrants of this group were, according to Kirişci, settled into predetermined areas because the state allocated land to these émigrés. This type of state support, however, subsided in the 1930s as land became stretched thin.[64] *Serbest göçmen*, by contrast, included migrants who left their residence of origin on their own behest. They were stipulated to apply for resettlement before leaving and were free to settle anywhere in Turkey upon receiving a visa.[65] Amer's grandparents belonged to this early group of migrants who moved to Turkey for good. People of these early waves migrated to the Republic as Ottoman subjects and subsequent Turks, not as Bosniaks.

There are several explanations as to why the Sandžak region turned into a space of transmigration, including safety and bureaucratic reasons. Asem stated, for instance, that Novi Pazar was "still considered safe at the time."[66] Jovanović indicates administrative reasons, seeing that Sandžak was a place where locals give up their citizenship – a stipulation lest one sought to apply for a visa in Turkey. By the 1950s, he states, "a river of émigrés traveled through Sandžak, and on to Macedonia."[67]

The last wave of Muslims left Southeastern Europe in the wake of WWII.[68] Turkey and Yugoslavia had by now signed the Turkish-Yugoslav convention in 1938 and arranged further population exchanges in the form of the 'Gentlemen's Agreement' in 1953. These two documents facilitated the emigration of Muslim Slavs to Turkey, provided they spoke the Turkish language or else ascribed to republican values. Bosniaks were particularly welcome in Turkey as these groups were thought to assimilate to Turkish values and norms with ease. Here, the previously mentioned reconciliation between Turkey and the Yugoslav Republic spurred the second large emigration wave from Southeastern Europe to Turkey, a period that lasted well into the 1960s when this wave slowly abated.

With the outbreak of the Yugoslav Succession Wars, Bosniaks again migrated and fled Southeastern Europe. Relying on a report from 1994, Kirişci states that 20,000 Bosniak refugees settled in Turkey, some of whom moved in with relatives in Istanbul.[69] The greatest number, however, settled into the prefabricated housing for the Bulgarian refugee wave of 1989, which was provided by the United Nations Human Rights Council (UNHRC). A mix of government and non-governmental authorities, including hospitals and schools, the Anatolian Development Foundation, and private citizens provided these refugees with aid in the form of schooling, care for injured Bosniak soldiers, and vocational training.[70]

Asem did not elect to leave Novi Pazar during the 1990s, and he gave the following answer when asked about his decision to stay in Southern Serbia:

> On my mom's side, they came to Novi Pazar sometime in the 1890s. . . . My mom's side is Albanian, and they came to live here before 1900. My grandpa on my mom's side was a tailor. He ran his own cooperative. He had three brothers, and they all lived together under one roof. After the great war, sometime in 1922, or 1923 – that is when people from here started to move to Turkey – two brothers of his also left. My grandfather stayed here. Those two that left were sent to Izmir where the Turks had driven out the Greek population, by the island there. When the generation of the 1950s started to emigrate, they went to Pendik by Istanbul. And, ahm, somehow, as is the case in any war, I know for example how it was in this war, during the bombing, I also stayed here. My older brother and my younger sister both left for Turkey, they couldn't live like this. You can't persuade people, or explain, why they should stay or leave. Nobody knows how they react in such a situation, to this fear, somehow. . . . Look, I told you about my son; Before he was born, I didn't think that I would experience his birth as something that would make me this happy. When he was here, I was happy. But I didn't know what it would feel like before he came. This is the same principle. Just the opposite. Bombing. At that time, I had three children, my oldest son was eight, my daughter was four, and then there was the baby. Now, when I consider the whole situation with some logic, I would tell myself to leave. But then, you couldn't get me

out of here. No chance. My older sister also stayed, but my older brother, and my younger sister, they both went to Turkey. We have a house there in Turkey, by the sea. So, they left. They were there during the bombardment. They left in April and returned by September. I went after the bombardment ended. I went there to recuperate for a month, and after that we all came back together. Those are strange times, when you experience such things. So, there is no clear answer to your question about why I stayed. It just happens. There are no big conclusions here. You just don't plan for these things, never. And, I can imagine these people back then. . . . When someone is forced to leave . . . there was misery, poverty, there was not one particular reason. Just fear for one's life. You could basically disappear overnight. The next day, there would be rumors about how they shot you, as in, this guy disappeared, that guy disappeared. . . . And people weren't even supposed to ask what had happened to whom. And the rumors about what exactly happened just keep spreading because people couldn't talk about it openly out of fear about their disappearing, too. . . . Think about it, Sandra, what if I told someone that I am selling my house, or anything else, and I leave, and you can be sure that there are thieves around, and people purposefully scare you away because your house is right downtown, because they want your house. . . . And because of this, you have nowhere else to go when some official doesn't hand you out the documents that allow you to leave the country. So, he stays where he is. We can't understand their motives from this distance. Look, it's still the same, we, as a country in general, we don't have a defined direction. What we want to do, who we are, what is it that we actually want!? If we at least knew what we do not want, what we no longer are. . . . This would actually open a path toward the future. If we were able to say, this is right, and this is wrong, to admit it was a crime that some person was liquidated 70 years ago. I didn't read these things in a book; I learned these things by listening to my family members. This means there was someone who's name was četnik (*znači, tu je bio neko ko se zvao četnik*), and don't ask me if a soldier is responsible for his own actions or not. This someone killed my grandfather. And now, I am supposed to have a sort of approach to this as if it never happened. But it is all connected.[71]

This quote is, to be sure, exceedingly long. Yet, it was imperative to keep this answer together for two specific reasons. First, Asem corroborates all narrative strands that recurred in casual conversations and in-depth interviews, as illustrated here. These include the significance of heritage sites, and loss of property, autonomy, and safety – or rather the lack thereof – among Muslim Slavs in Southern Serbia. Second, and connected, is the fact that Asem illustrates the extent to which interviewees collapse the time-space continuum to understand their current sociopolitical situation. Nearly all interviewees oscillated between past and present narratives during casual conversations and in-depth interviews – Asem articulated this aspect most clearly. Instead of handing me a simple answer as to why he chose to stay in Novi Pazar during the war years, he lunged into a full-fledged historic explanation that he couched into previous decisions his fam-ily members made in the past. His narrative is a clear and chronological continuity to a non-sequential past. This is especially clear when reconsidering his favorable description of the former SFRY. Yet, upon my inquiry about his decision to stay, he clearly displayed affinity toward the social condition as experienced by family members who left the Sandžak region out of fear.

The extent to which interviewees string narrated atrocities together with auto-biographical experiences of the 1990s is striking. Cognitive connections with the émigré community – based on memory transmission within the family unit – form a bedrock for the continuity of social relations among Bosniaks for two reasons. First, connecting with the émigré community served the purpose of "symbolic or normative anchoring" by which interlocutors superseded their loss to the Yugo-slav community.[72] Second, family relations with the émigré Bosniak community in Turkey assumed the character of a collective diaspora experience and herit-age with which locals identify, even in the absence of strong personal relations to émigrés. The fact that much of the local Ottoman heritage stands in tatters serves as powerful and very public reminder for the marginalization of Muslims in Southern Serbia. Though many local Bosniaks had not emigrated themselves, they nevertheless identify with and to some extent exhibit a diasporic experience as a result. Narratives by which locals learn about the past are, crucially, tied to the loss of cultural heritage sites and private property, as illustrated earlier.

And yet, not all interlocutors share the same experiences. It is thus important to recall Marsden, who cautioned that individuals construct associations of and with the past based on present circumstances, while heeding Brubaker and Cooper's invitation to go beyond ethnicity as a bounded entity that connects individuals. As such, it is instructive to illustrate, shortly, that maintaining rapport with the émigré community was difficult if indeed impossible at times.

The maintenance of kin relations across space and time

Considering the maintenance of kin relations from our perspective seems an easy feat. Bearing in mind the first large-scale migration from Southeastern Europe to interior Ottoman lands and Turkey took place around the turn of the century, how-ever, renders the uptake of relations across newly forming state borders difficult. Interlocutors variously confirmed this notion. Upon my asking if Leijla managed to stay in contact with her sisters after they left Novi Pazar, she answered:

> I went to Turkey twice. I was there for a month . . . perhaps I have even been there three times. But I went later, now there is public transportation. Back then, you had to travel for months at the time to get there, and you didn't know how. She (my sister) also came here, later. You know, people were afraid of coming back here, of being stuck here when you returned . . . it's hard from me. . . . I cannot talk about that . . . that one sister that left . . . both of my sisters left.[73]

Structural difficulties thus hampered efforts to sustain contact among family members. Once family members emigrated, moreover, individuals feared to return, which further strained filial connections over time.

Finding relatives in Turkey after they migrated, moreover, bore its own difficulties because émigrés received new identity cards, at times along with new surnames upon arrival. This was the case for Amer's family:

> My grandmother has a different surname than her brother. They came at different times to Turkey. I am not sure who came first, but they came at different times, and were situated in different locations in Anatolia at first. So, they had to find each other. I don't know how, but they did.[74]

While this seems inconsequential for Amer himself, reconnecting with relatives in Novi Pazar was exceedingly difficult because he did not know the last name of his relatives.

Language serves as an additional and decisive factor that permits relations to uphold connections across time and space, or not. Amer, for instance, explained:

> My mom's dad was born in Novi Pazar, so, of course, this is the birthplace of a beloved person for the whole family. But, I think this is not enough to feel that connected. . . . I mean, she does not know the language. She would have to know Albanian and Bosnian. And me, I don't speak Albanian, or Bosnian either. So . . . even if she came here, she won't understand anything.[75]

Following this logic, Amer feels fealty toward the birthplace of his ancestors, so much so that he traveled to Novi Pazar to discover his roots. Yet, he questions whether this serves as a glue that is strong enough for the continuation of a common bond across space and time. One might therefore argue that socialization processes in Turkey and Yugoslavia, respectively, superseded ethnic ties.

Synthesis

Informants clearly identify with the past as demonstrated earlier. The seemingly salient tradition of narrative transmission of historiographical experiences within the family unit is especially notable. Halbwachs stated that memories might be lost lest they are resurrected by way of nearly forgotten associations.[76] The Yugoslav Succession Wars served as one such association that brought these recollections to the fore with full force. Because narrated experiences recounted by elders to some extent mirrored the experiences of younger individuals at present, the Yugoslav Succession Wars served as an indicator that history indeed recurred. Muslims and/or Bosniaks lost the right to own much of the estates they owned prior to the collapse of the Ottoman Empire following the Balkan and World Wars, as was the case across the border in Bosnia during the Yugoslav Succession Wars. As a consequence, heritage sites (and private property) are an important piece to the puzzle, seeing that they serve as visible and public reminders about the marginalized status Bosniaks and/or Muslims inhabit(ed).

Both Serbian as well as Bosniak and/or Muslim political entrepreneurs capitalize(d) on cultural and religious heritage sites to emphasize historiographic presence and thus social belonging. Yet, locals are no longer content with and distrust officially sanctified historiographic accounts. As a result, locals turn to narrated sources of historiography to understand their social circumstances at present. Transnational connections build a focal point within these narratives, seeing that Bosniaks ascertain their place within the larger, scattered diaspora experience. As such, local Bosniaks – while belonging within the jurisdiction of Serbia – find a symbolic anchor within the transnational connections that link them with the émigré community in Turkey by tangible means.

And yet, it is vital to acknowledge and stress that this is a symbolic anchor – an anchor that is not based in or determined by a purportedly common ethnic denominator. Socialization processes and the tradition of narrative transmission within the family unit, for instance, influenced the degree to which individuals identified with the past, as illustrated with Erol and Daud. Structural barriers further illustrate the difficulty by which locals were able to uphold kin relations. Time and structural factors variously served as stimuli or detracting factors that allowed for kin relations to stay intact, or not. Amer and Leijla illustrate this point vividly. Overall, one can ascertain that Asem is the closest to his family. This can be explained by the fact that his family members migrated to Turkey in the 1960s and again in the 1990s. As such, one might confirm the earlier statement that Bosniaks of the third wave migrated to Turkey as Bosniaks and no longer as co-Turks. Individuals of this last large migratory wave migrated to an established state and come closest to our current understanding of migratory patterns to established states. One might thus further argue that this last group – Bosniak migrants belonging to the third wave – builds the core of individuals with which local Bosniaks connected during the Yugoslav Succession Wars.

Notes

1 Harald Welzer, *Wir sind die Mehrheit: für eine offene Gesellschaft* (Berlin: Fischer Taschenbuch, 2017), 10.
2 Suzan Ilcan and Inc Ebrary, *Longing in Belonging: The Cultural Politics of Settlement* (Westport, CT: Praeger, 2002), 9.
3 Maurice Halbwachs and Lewis A. Coser, *On Collective Memory*, The Heritage of Sociology (Chicago: University of Chicago Press, 1992), 23–24.
4 Ibid.
5 Rogers Brubaker and Frederick Cooper, "Beyond 'Identity'," *Theory and Society* 29, no. 1 (2000): 12.
6 Ibid., 14.
7 Lewis A. Coser, *Maurice Halbwachs: On Collective Memory* (Chicago: University of Chicago Press, 1992), 62.
8 During my last visit to Novi Pazar in 2019, the outdoor café made way for archeological excavations.
9 Field notes, greater Sandžak region, 2012.

10 Elementary school where children learn reading and writing, grammar, Quran recitation, etc.
11 Field notes, greater Sandžak region, 2012.
12 Peter Sugar, *Southeastern Europe under Ottoman Rule, 1354–1804* (Seattle: University of Washington Press, 2006), 76.
13 *Serbia's Sandžak Still Forgotten.* The International Crisis Group (2005), https://www. refworld.org/pdfid/425e8bf14.pdf.
14 Pierre Bourdieu and Richard Nice, *Outline of a Theory of Practice* (Cambridge: Cambridge University Press, 1977), 116.
15 *Serbia's Sandžak Still Forgotten.*
16 Kenneth Morrison and Elizabeth Roberts, *The Sandzak: A History* (London: Hurst, 2013), 18.
17 Erol, interviewed in the Sandžak region by Sandra King-Savic in 2012.
18 Ibid.
19 RUDAR 7, "Vuk Drašković, speech at the St. Peter's Church" (December 13, 2014).
20 Erol, interviewed in the Sandžak region by Sandra King-Savic in 2012.
21 Coser, *Maurice Halbwachs: On Collective Memory*, 62.
22 Andy McDevitt, *Fighting Corruption in the Western Balkans and Turkey: Priorities for Reform*, Transparency International – The Global Coalition against Corruption (2016), 10, https://images.transparencycdn.org/images/NISWBT_EN.pdf.
23 Ibid., 19, 20, 24.
24 Daud, interviewed in the Sandžak region by Sandra King-Savic.
25 Brubaker and Cooper, "Beyond 'Identity'," 5.
26 Parts of this section were published in 2017. See Sandra King-Savic, "Serbia's Sandžak: Caught Between Two Islamic Communities," *Islam in Central Asia and Southeastern Europe* (2017).
27 For a detailed analysis of the religious and political movements in the Sandžak area, see Aleksander Zdravkovski, "Politics, Religion and the Autonomy Movement in Sandžak *(1990–2014)"* (PhD Dissertation, Institute for Sociology and Statistics, Norwegian University of Science and Technology, 2017).
28 The *Sandžak – Nacionalna Revija za Politiku I Kulturu* that is published monthly gives interesting insights into current and past discussions on local politics and questions of representation. The magazine is available in print, and online at http://revijasandzak. com/?page_id=34.
29 Parts of this section were published in 2017. See King-Savic, "Serbia's Sandžak: Caught Between Two Islamic Communities."
30 Asem, interviewed in the Sandžak region by Sandra King-Savic in 2012.
31 Siniša, interviewed in the capital city by Sandra King-Savic in 2012.
32 Mirijam, interviewed in the Sandžak region by Sandra King-Savic in 2015.
33 Susan L. Woodward, *Balkan Tragedy: Chaos and Dissolution after the Cold War* (Washington, DC: Brookings Institution Press, 1995), 125.
34 Coser, *Maurice Halbwachs: On Collective Memory*, 61.
35 Halbwachs and Coser, *On Collective Memory*, 47.
36 Ibid., 50.
37 Ibid., 51.
38 Mustafa Imamović, *Historija Bošnjaka* (Preporod: Bošnjačka Zajednica Kulture Sarajevo, 1998), 426.
39 Leijla, interviewed in the Sandžak region by Sandra King-Savic in 2015.
40 Ibid.
41 King-Savic, "Serbia's Sandžak: Caught Between Two Islamic Communities."
42 Sabrina P. Ramet, *The Three Yugoslavias: State-building and Legitimation, 1918–2005* (Bloomington: Indiana University Press, 2006), 49; *The Other Balkan Wars: A 1913 Carnegie Endowment Inquiry in Retrospect* (Washington, DC: Carnegie Endowment

for International Peace: Brookings Institution [distributor], 1993); and the updated version with a new introduction, George F. Kennan and International Commission to Inquire into the Causes and Conduct of the Balkan Wars, *The Other Balkan Wars: A 1913 Carnegie Endowment Inquiry in Retrospect* (Washington, DC: Brookings Institution Press, 1993).

43 Leijla, interviewed in the Sandžak region by Sandra King-Savic in 2015.

44 Ibid.

45 Asem, interviewed the Sandžak region by Sandra King-Savic in 2015.

46 Ivo Banac, *The National Question in Yugoslavia – Origins, History, Politics* (Ithaca, NY: Cornell University Press, 1994), 367.

47 Husnija Kamberović, *Bošnjaci, Hrvati i Srbi u Bosni I Hercegovini i u Jugoslaviji – U Stalnom Procepu*, (Beograd: Helsinški odbor za ljudska prava u Srbiji, 2017), 64–65.

48 Morrison and Roberts, *The Sandzak: A History*, 96–97.

49 Leijla, interviewed the Sandžak region by Sandra King-Savic in 2015.

50 Matti Hyvärinen, "Analyzing Narratives and Story-Telling," in *The Sage Handbook of Social Research Methods*, ed. Pertti Alasuutari, Leonard Bickman, and Julia Brannen (Los Angeles: Sage, 2008), 456–457.

51 Mirijam, interviewed the Sandžak region by Sandra King-Savic in 2015.

52 Ibid.

53 Omar, interviewed in Bosnia and Herzegovina by Sandra King-Savic in 2014.

54 Bourdieu and Nice, *Outline of a Theory of Practice*, 116.

55 Zakāt is a form of taxation and/or almsgiving, and one of five pillars practicing Muslims observe. Zakāt is levied on six types of property, including (1) cash, gold, and silver; (2) merchandise; (3) natural resources; (4) ancient treasures; (5) livestock (not including swine); and (6) crops. Zakāt is usually levied at a rate of 2.5 percent, except on ancient treasure, which is taxed at a 20 percent rate. For more information see, for instance, Frederick Mathewson Denny, *An Introduction to Islam* (Upper Saddle River, NJ: Pearson, 2006), 115–116.

56 Omar, interviewed in Bosnia and Herzegovina by Sandra King-Savic in 2014.

57 Leijla, interviewed the Sandžak region by Sandra King-Savic in 2015.

58 Amer, interviewed in Bosnia and Herzegovina by Sandra King-Savic in 2016.

59 Morrison and Roberts, *The Sandzak: A History*, 96.

60 Sabina Pačaric, *The Migration of Bosniaks – The Case of Sandžak* (Sarajevo: Center for Advanced Studies, 2016), 55.

61 "Law no. 2510/1934 Settlement Act," ed. European University Institute – Robert Schuman Centre for Advanced Studies Global Nationality Laws Database, http://eudo-citizenship.eu/databases/national-citizenship-laws/; see also Rainer Bauböck, Bernhard Perchinig, and Wiebke Sievers, "Citizenship Policies in the New Europe: (Expanded and Updated Edition)" (2009): 434, http://www.oapen.org/download?type=document&docid=340017.

62 Kemal Kirişci, "Post Second World War Immigration from Balkan Countries to Turkey," *New Perspectives on Turkey* 12 (1995): 61.

63 Ibid., 62.

64 An exception was made for the massive migratory wave coming from Bulgaria in 1989.

65 Kirişci, "Post Second World War Immigration from Balkan Countries to Turkey," 62.

66 Asem, interviewed the Sandžak region by Sandra King-Savic in 2015.

67 Vladan Jovanović, "Iz FNRJ u Tursku," *Peščanik*, June 24, 2013, https://pescanik.net/iz-fnrj-u-tursku/.

68 Edvin Pezo, "Komparativna analiza jugoslovensko-turske Konvencije iz 1938. i 'džentelmenskog sporazuma' iz 1953. Pregovori oko iseljavanja muslimana iz Jugoslavije," *Tokovi Istorije 2* (2012): 114.

69 Kirişci, "Post Second World War Immigration from Balkan Countries to Turkey," 71, and footnote no. 20.
70 Ibid., 72.
71 Asem, interviewed the Sandžak region by Sandra King-Savic in 2015.
72 Elizabeth Shove, Mika Pantzar, and Matthew Watson, *The Dynamics of Social Practice: Everyday Life and How it Changes* (Los Angeles: Sage, 2012), 75.
73 Leijla, interviewed the Sandžak region by Sandra King-Savic in 2015.
74 Amer, interviewed in Bosnia and Herzegovina by Sandra King-Savic in 2016.
75 Ibid.
76 Coser, *Maurice Halbwachs: On Collective Memory*, 23–24.

Part III

4 Recontextualizing narratives of *šverc* within the discourse of economic collapse

In Part II, I retraced how Bosniaks identify and narrate events related to the practice of *šverc* to examine the salience of transnational ties between locals and the émigré Bosniak community across time and space. Due to the experience of the Yugoslav Succession Wars, locals reconstructed a narrative in which life had been safe under the Porte and perhaps favorable within a Turkish sphere of governance. Senior citizens in Novi Pazar are instrumental in this process. They were raised by parents who remembered the collapse of Ottoman governing structures and present a living link to a past that yet exists physically in the form of social heritage sites in Novi Pazar. Transnational relations, in other words, are couched into a "shared event of practice" that connects present narratives to the past, thus serving the purpose of sense-making by which locals understand their socio-political situation at present.[1] To answer the overarching question of how transnational practices shaped this communities' social relations *locally*, I will reconstruct a sociopolitical and economic version of events as reported by the *Večernje Novosti*[2] newspaper between 1993 and 1995 in this chapter. Reconstructing sociopolitical and economic events between 1993 and 1995 serves the purpose of embedding experiences as narrated by interlocutors in Novi Pazar within a larger, national frame.

Novosti is a fruitful source by which to reconstruct and analyze a version of sociopolitical and economic events in Serbia. Serving discursive functions that shaped nationalizing processes before the outbreak of the Yugoslav Succession Wars started, the paper, for instance, leaked the infamous SANU memorandum.[3] During the war, the paper enjoyed the highest circulation rates across national boundaries and within Serbia. By 1990, *Novosti* sold up to 222,282 copies and thus led circulation by numbers ahead of other prominent papers, including the *Večerni list* (ZG), *Politika ekspres* (BG), and *Politika* (BG).[4]

Regarding the time frame, I chose to view newspaper articles published between 1993 and 1995 despite the United Nations enacting of sanctions on Yugoslavia in 1991[5] and rising inflationary rates during the 1980s.[6] Belgrade ordained a media crackdown between 1991 and 1995, which manipulated the nature of news Serbian citizens consumed.[7] In their effort to quash anticipated dissent among journalists, the Serbian regime purged the media staff following the electoral victory of the Socialist Party in 1993.[8] By 1994, *Borba* (resistance) was the only reliably

DOI: 10.4324/9781003022381-8

independent newspaper, which nevertheless ousted regime disloyal individuals in December 1994.[9] Concurrently, previous research recorded a reduction in the formal economic sector, and a minimum per capita consumption by 1993.[10] Between 1993 and 1994, individuals in the Yugoslav rump state experienced galloping inflation rates of up to 313 million percent per month,[11] while the Dayton Peace Accords in 1995 heralded an end of sanctions and a steady, albeit sluggish stabilization of the market thereafter. As such, examining the time frame between 1993 and 1995 allows for insight into the socioeconomic state of Serbia when inflation, sanctions, and informal-market activities intersect with a governmental crackdown on the media.

Coding for *šverc*, for instance, suggests the prominence of smuggling increased between 1993 and 1994, for the term appears 2.5 times more often between those years. By 1995, the term *šverc* appears 5.5 times more often when compared to 1995. In 1995, the paper discussed *šverc* 215 times in one year.

One might further assume that even though the socioeconomic situation improved in 1995, *šverc* had already turned into an ordinary practice that did not subside with the Dayton Peace Accords. Because Belgrade used informal channels to penetrate the sanctions, political actors cultivated transnational trade relations so long as the state benefited from the sanctions-busting businesses. Belgrade not only approved of but fostered small-scale *šverc* to penetrate the internationally imposed trade sanctions on Serbia during the first half of the 1990s. Perhaps Momčilo Grubač said it best when he explained the Serbian regime accepted criminal activities as a source of state stability.[12] Belgrade was thus initially unwilling to dismantle informal trade practices for the sake of state stability and proved unable to quash informal trade practices thereafter.

Utilizing the narrative frame of interlocutors, I further coded for the terms 'Ottoman' and 'Turkey' to analyze how the news portrayed Ankara and the Ottoman past. Further terms, including weapons, drugs, cigarettes, Islam and Muslim, borders, gray and black market, and (consumer) prices are utilized here for three reasons. First, interlocutors regularly referred to terms such as Turkey, Islam and Muslim, borders, and *šverc* when narrating experiences of the 1990s. I therefore apply these terms to recontextualize local narratives about the 1990s. Second, smuggling practices include the terminology of *buvljak* (a type of flea market) and *šverc* because the availability of goods occupied locals in their everyday lives, while smugglers brought coffee, cigarettes, and other consumer goods across the shifting borders of the Yugoslav rump state. Discursive schemes about informal goods, including weapons, are coded for because interviewees narrated experiences of governmental intimidation practices against Albanian and Bosniak citizens of Serbia based on their alleged clandestine harboring of firearms during the Succession Wars. Third, utilizing the coded words demonstrates how regimeloyal representatives portrayed the practice of *šverc* in the paper.

To narrow the analytic frame, I also coded for Belgrade to compare the discourse about *šverc* to that of smuggling in Novi Pazar by utilizing the Atlas.ti coefficiency table (Table 4.1).

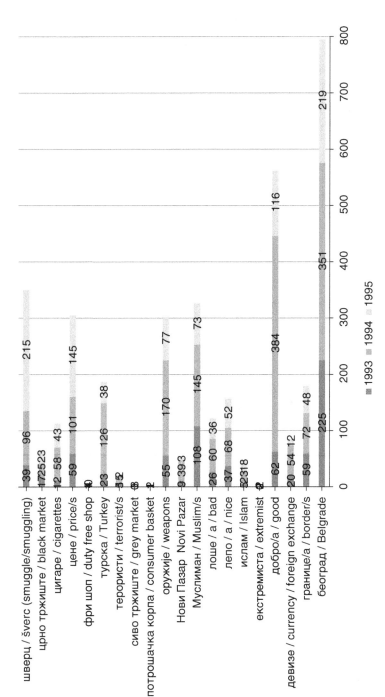

Figure 4.1 Coded terms, *Večerne Novosti*

Table 4.1 Atlas.ti coefficiency table

	Београд *Belgrade*	*Муслиман* *Muslim*	*Нови Пазар* *Novi Pazar*	*Осман* *Ottoman*	*Турска* *Turkey*
Београд / Belgrade	0	4	11	1	7
границе / borders	8	3	3	1	6
Девизе / foreign currency	7	0	0	0	0
Добро / good	18	8	2	0	9
Дрога / drugs	42	2	5	0	20
Екстремиста / extremist	0	0	2	0	1
Ислам / Islam	0	15	2	2	5
Лепо / nice	19	1	4	0	1
Лоше / bad	12	5	0	0	0
Муслиман / Muslim	4	0	22	0	28
Нови Пазар / Novi Pazar	11	22	0	1	19
Оружје / weaponry	10	39	11	1	28
Осман / Ottoman	1	0	1	0	4
потрошачка корпа / consumer price	0	0	0	0	0
сиво тржиште / gray market	0	0	0	0	0
Терористи / terrorist	0	1	0	0	3
Турска / Turkey	7	28	19	4	0
фри шоп / fri šop	0	0	0	0	0
Цене / prices	25	0	0	0	5
Цигаре / cigarettes	12	1	0	0	4
црно тржиште / black market	6	0	1	0	2
Шверц / šverc	13	3	2	1	13

To gauge discursive qualifications about Islam and Muslims, as well as Turkey, I coded for additional, evaluative attributes including good, bad, and nice.

Following Ruth Wodak and Martin Reisigl, I analyzed the newspaper articles through the lens of a discourse-historical approach (DHA) to gain distance from but also to triangulate the data collected in the field.[13] Utilizing a DHA approach allows for a 'socio-diagnostic critique' of social actors that shaped local practices by way of locate the 'manipulative character' the government and regime loyal actors employed during the 1990s.[14] To answer the overarching question of how transnational practices shaped social relations in Novi Pazar, the aim of the following section is thus twofold: I first reconstruct the socioeconomic and political ambience that prevailed in Serbia as presented by the paper to 'recontextualize' the narratives of locals in Novi Pazar. I do this by way of examining the coded terms in Figure 4.1.[15] In a second step, I analyze 'discursive qualifications' about *šverc* in Novi Pazar by utilizing Table 4.1.[16] Doing so allows for greater insight into the sociopolitical and economic situation that defined Novi Pazar's in-state and transnational character.

A discursive analysis of *šverc* in Serbia

Between 1993 and 1995 (Figure 4.2), *Novosti* discussed the topic of prices 305 times.[17] Fluctuating and rising prices, especially, were a recurring theme in the paper during the years under investigation. In 1993, and thus the initial period of the sanctions regime, the paper seemed to portray the emptying stores and rising prices with little concern. In fact, one might argue the paper illustrated the burgeoning informal market activity with a sense of benevolence, if not adventurism. On April 26, 1993, for instance, the paper seemed to guide potential customers to the various *buvljaci* where goods were available and reasonably priced.

> On Belgrade's most famous flea markets (*buvljacima*), the Zeleni Venac,[18] the Boulevard of the Revolution, and the New Belgrade Block 44, smugglers (*šverceri*) and customers alike appeared in droves. The supply of merchandise was as good as usual – reaching from light bulbs, batteries, hygienic products, women's and men's vests, over coffee, cigarettes, and flour. For only 30,000 dinars (the price for these goods was twice as high in the stores) customers can buy a 100-watt light bulb, while the cheapest batteries for watches are about 40,000 dinars (there are none at the stores). The best offers concern prices for hygienic products – four rolls of toilet paper cost 100,000 dinars, domestic soap of 150 grams cost between 25,000 and 30,000 dinars. Foreign soap costs between 40,000 to 80,000 dinars [original parentheses].[19]

Figure 4.2 Večerne Novosti, December 7, 1994: 7

Buvljaci were, judging from this article, well stocked on a regular basis. Using a positive evaluative adjective, the paper defined the supply *as good as usual*, suggesting that *šverceri* commonly offered domestic as well as foreign products. Regular stores, meanwhile, ran low on goods. This is interesting considering UN resolution 757 that banned trading with companies *and individuals* from the rump state from 1992 onward.[20] *Šverceri* thus turned into valued members among the community because these individuals procured the most basic of goods, including toilet paper and soap, despite international sanctions. Smugglers were not, in other words, viewed *and* portrayed as deviating from social norms. Instead, the practice of *šverc*, and thus smugglers themselves, developed into necessary agents whose practices enabled a semblance of normalcy during the sanctions years.

It is especially useful to consider the terminology used in the clipping in Figure 4.3. Smugglers and citizens came in droves to procure goods at the (as usual) well-stocked *buvljak*. One might argue that by 1993, one year after the international community enacted the sanctions regime, smuggling was no longer simply necessary. Buying smuggled goods, and relying on the availability thereof, became an ordinary feat in a citizen's everyday life. Moreover, because smugglers imported foreign products across international borders, including the soap as described in the news clipping, governmental agencies were surly aware of the sanctions-busting enterprises. The government, then, as suggested by Grubač, relied on smugglers to warrant state stability.

In addition to guiding citizens to available goods, the paper also discussed price hikes. Tables discussing and comparing prices for commodities, such as Figure 4.3, appeared at regular intervals to inform consumers about and illustrate rising prices. Expenses for the most basic staple food items, including bread, milk, feta cheese, yogurt, and so forth, increased exponentially. Sugar prices, for instance, increased by an incredible 205 percent between March and April of

Намирнице	количина	март 93.	април 93. поскупљење у %	
хлеб тип 500	800 г	6.656	19.734	196
млеко	лит.	9.560	15.220	59
сир бели	200 г	10.884	19.494	79
јогурт	1/2 лит	11.517	17.389	51
путер	125 г	12.021	31.116	59
уље	300 г	4.952	12.039	44
шећер	100 г	982	2.998	20?
јаја кок.	4 ком	8.764	18.760	114
шункарица	300 г	23.464	64.725	17?
месо свињ.600 г	64.523	79.420	23	
кромпир	кг	13.600	18.700	38?
црни лук	200 г	2.490	3.067	23?
јабуке	кг	13.050	22.000	68?
супа кок.	кес	21.757	39.536	82?
парадајз	1/2 кг	3.750	100.000	2.567
Укупно:		207.970	461.198	123

Figure 4.3 Večerne Novosti, December 7, 1994: 7

Figure 4.4 Večerne Novosti, May 5, 1993: 9

1993. The price for bread increased by 196 percent. All the while, unemployment rose to 39 percent in 1993 from an initial 14 percent in 1991.[21]

The *potrošačka korpa* (consumer price index), illustrated here by way of Figure 4.4, increased steadily, while income and employment contracted. On September 23, 1993, a kilogram of white bread cost 300 million Serbian dinars,[22] and on October 20, 1993, Belgrade was out of bread altogether.[23] Meanwhile, the dinar further devalued in 1993, and the paper regularly published announcements about current black-market exchange rates in regions around the rump state:

> Black mark exchange rates continue to grow! Yesterday, the price for a Deutsch-Mark was the highest in Podgorica, Kruševac, and Sombor where

the Deutsch Mark was offered at a rate of 4.200 Dinars, and sold at a rate of 3.700 and 3.800 Dinars. Exchange rates for the Deutsch Mark were the lowest in Kragujevac, where dealers sold the Deutsch Mark for 3.700 dinars, and bought the Deutsch Mark at a rate of 3.300 and 3.400 Dinars. In Leskovac, the Deutsch Mark cost 3.800 dinars, and sold for 3.300 dinars. . . . The official purchasing price for the Deutsch Mark is 405,07, and for the dollar 658,19 Dinars.[24]

By September 23, 1993, the hyperinflation had reached such high levels that *Novosti* announced the bank would render the 1 million dinar bill as 1 dinar from here on out. The mint, in other words, simply shaved off six zeroes from the banknote – a move the paper caricaturized by way of assigning an etc. (i.t.d., *i tako dalje*) next to the number on the bill to indicate indignation with the bellowing insignificance of paper money (Figure 4.5).

At the time, very low and/or altogether missing wages and disappearing pensions induced the creation of the second or informal-market economy. The second economy got under way in earnest during the early 1990s and soon flourished to account for 30 to 40 percent of Serbia's entire economy.[25] It is the intersection of this hyperinflation, price hikes, and the regular announcement of the black-market currency exchange rates in different regions around Serbia that normalized black marketeering and informal practices. Exchanging Serbian dinars in privately owned offices and on the street proved simply more profitable compared to exchanging the worthless dinar in state-sanctioned institutions, as illustrated in a news clipping from October 31, 1993.[26] Official exchange rates in the state-owned banks, according to the article, were twice as low compared to the value received in private exchange offices. One hundred German marks, for instance,

Figure 4.5 Dinar Briše Lire, Novosti, September 23, 1994: 4

yielded between 14,000 and 14,800 dinars in unofficial exchange booths, and half as much at state-sponsored institutions. "It is difficult to buy decent clothes for half of this sum," the journalist of this piece stated. "Prices for an ordinary sweater, for example, start at about 8.000 Dinars. Quality products cost twice as much. The only product that is cheaper, are jeans."[27]

Among the goods that cost exponentially more compared to prewar and sanctions years was coffee. Coffee, according to a newspaper clipping of July 15, 1994, was either inexistent or hopelessly overpriced.[28] The cost for coffee hovered around 7–8 dinars before Dragoslav Avramović developed the program to curb inflation on January 24, 1994. On July 15 of that same year, the price for coffee stood at about 20 dinars for 1 kilogram. In other words, the price for coffee increased by 185.7 percent within six months. It is worth quoting the reporter of this particular piece in his own words:

In those countries in which we tend to buy our coffee, the prices have not even doubled. In our country, the price for coffee increased by 300 percent since the beginning of the inflation. This renders the import of coffee the most profitable job – after petrol.[29]

It appears the reporter at once doubts the legitimacy of the price hikes while suggesting to readers they might turn a profit by joining the coffee trade. Trading coffee, to be sure, was not illegal in itself. Yet, under international law, trading goods beyond the borders of the Yugoslav rump state was indeed illegal due to the international sanctions regime. UN Security Council resolution 757 stated in no uncertain terms that states ought to prevent individuals from importing all products and commodities to Yugoslavia, except for medical purposes and comestibles as stipulated by the UN.[30]

By 1994, the paper regularly discussed *šverc* in connection with the practice of smuggling drugs, including marijuana, cocaine, and heroin. According to a news clipping from March 27, 1994, "drugs continued to travel from Turkey to Europe, across our country, despite the embargo. There were attempts to smuggle narcotics across Romania," but, as stated in the article, "it was too risky." It is worth quoting the article here due to the (again) mixed message in the paper:

There is great pressure on the shipment of narcotics to Italy. Traders and smugglers are lamenting the slowdown, of course, because transit through Yugoslavia has reduced. Customs officers at the border have time to inspect every passing vehicle closely, especially those that seem suspicious.[31]

As was the case with the coffee, the paper seemed to offer guidance to readers by implying that smugglers ought to avoid certain border crossings in view of the likelihood of increased inspection. This is an apparent practice as seen during the initial period of the sanctions regime whereby papers informed potential shoppers about anticipated delays on borders crossings.[32]

In all, the paper discussed drugs 42 times in connection with Belgrade and five times in relation to Novi Pazar. On February 6, 1994, the paper announced "Belgrade had turned into the largest market for drugs in the Balkans."[33] As was the case with much of the reporting during the period under investigation, the paper sent contradictory messages about drugs. On July 28, 1994, an article in the paper explained:

> Hashish and marijuana are the cheapest drugs that can be bought on the street. At present, the price for weed starts at two dinars (German Marks) on the streets of Belgrade. One gram usually yields two joint-cigarettes. The use of cannabis is almost impossible to determine. Young people smoke weed at parties. But middle-aged, or older people also smoke weed. It is difficult to calculate the number of those who tried weed, or smoke weed on a regular basis. Marihuana and hashish are mainly domestic products, which is why it is inexpensive. This weed is known as *domaćica*.[34]

Domaćica alludes, most likely, to the double meaning of *domaće*, which means homegrown and/or domestic, relating to the production of goods. *Domaćica*, as an abbreviation from the stem, means homemaker and/or housewife. In connection with the title of this article, one might extrapolate the paper meant to sound a warning about the increasing dependency of drugs among the citizens of Serbia: "there is no such thing as a harmless drug" (*nema naivne droge*). And yet, the word *domaćica* sounds benevolent in itself, while the paper instructs readers that 1 gram of marijuana yields two joints. One might argue that this way of reporting sends mixed messages to readers.

Over the course of the 1990s, the drugs trade became more volatile as diverse groups sought to control the market in Serbia. Wads of money as well as drugs were found and sold in various flats and bunkers in and around Belgrade,[35] while turf wars led to multiple deaths in the capital city.[36] Even a cursory analysis of the news implies that Belgrade failed to fulfill the social contract. The state was unwilling or unable to root out the increasingly harmful and deadly trade in drugs. Instead of employing state-sanctioned forces to root out criminal gangs, Belgrade used its monopoly of power to wage a war in Croatia and Bosnia.

Belgrade was certainly aware of the legal and illegal aspects of *šverc* as well as the prospering businesses enjoyed by a segment of the population while others scraped by to make ends meet. It seems likely for legislators to have pushed for humane living conditions for all citizens in the Yugoslav rump state had it been for the unity of the socialist state as relentlessly propagated by Belgrade. Unity, however, was not the primary concern of leading representatives. Instead, politicians instrumentalized nationalism to enrich themselves, as substantiated with the murky trade of cigarettes.

Misha Glenny stated the "gigantic marketplace for smuggled cigarettes" could only function the way it did due to the "approval of the government in Belgrade, which meant Slobodan Milošević himself signed off on it."[37] In addition to governmental involvement in the cigarette smuggling business, the trade was so lucrative that even tobacco companies, including Philip Morris and R.J. Reynolds, joined the scheme.[38] It is interesting to remember that Milošević, in his effort to present his government as a responsible agent to the international community, adjusted his rhetoric on the war toward the end of 1993. Milan Milošević stated:

In this new media projection, it was the radicals and extremists who were the war-crime culprits. They were now referred to as 'war-profiteers' and 'criminals'.[39]

The effects of this policy were quickly propagated through the paper. On February 27, 1994, *Novosti* declared the "one-month long campaign 'Borders 94'" heralded the dismantling of a smuggling ring. "Serbian smugglers, according to the paper, had used supply lines in Teslić (Bosnia) to smuggle goods to Muslims":

Serbs sold weapons, munitions, flour, coffee, cooking oil, sugar, cigarettes, petroleum and gasoline to Muslims – their enemies. Their actions impoverished and broke Republika Srpska from within.[40]

Smuggling was not *only* a simple activity that rendered life bearable for ordinary citizens as demonstrated by this news clipping. Smuggling was a highly politicized practice the regime sanctioned at the very least, or governed at most. Illustrative of this possibility is the paper's free and positive reporting on the sale of goods despite international sanctions in 1993, while smugglers turned into a fifth column that aided the alleged enemy of the Serbian people in 1994. To be sure, the Serbs mentioned in the clipping smuggled goods behind enemy lines. Yet, the outrage in the article rings hollow considering that smuggling was an ordinary practice in 1993, while smugglers turned into vilified criminals that broke Republika Srpska from within in 1994. Moreover, criminals and paramilitary groups, including Arkan Ražnatović, the likely most infamous war profiteer with close ties to Belgrade, were known to smuggle counterfeit currency and looted goods while trafficking oil and drugs across enemy lines.[41]

It is with the benefit of hindsight that we know about war profiteering and cooperation between Bosnia, Serbia, and Croatia. Glenny, for instance, documented weapons deliveries from Bulgaria and Romania to Bosnia and Croatia across Serbian territory, while Bosnians, Albanians, and Croats sold oil to Serbia against extortionate prices.[42] Andreas stated, "organized crime, business, and the security apparatus became closely integrated to evade international sanctions, generate war profits, and carry out ethnic cleansing."[43] As such, the alleged outrage in the preceding news clipping is not only misplaced but also absurd given that the apprehended smugglers traded in cooking oil, sugar, and flour as well as, to be sure, weapons – while state-sanctioned paramilitary groups, including the *Crvene Beretke* and *Tigrovi*, pillaged villages and smuggled goods between Bosnia and Serbia under the protective cloak of Belgrade.

Citizens of Serbia not only paid the price for the faltering economy in form of exorbitant price hikes for comestible and elastic goods. Citizens also lost money by way of state-sanctioned pyramid schemes.[44] At the center of this heist were Jezdimir Vasiljević, known as *Gazda Jezda* (Jezda the boss), and Dafina Milanović. Both Vasiljević and Milanović as well as their respective institutions, the Jugoskandik and Dafiment Bank, superseded black-market exchange dealers on the street by luring citizens with high interest rates. R. T. Naylor explained that Belgrade needed hard cash to acquire strategic though high-priced and hard to come by goods under international sanctions. Encouraging the creation of state-sanctioned banks that offered interest rates of up to "15 percent per month on German Marks and Dollars" thus opened the possibility to soak up the sought after hard currency.[45] After a falling out between Milanović and the regime, Milanović escaped Serbia while citizens flocked to the Dafiment Bank to demand their savings. Those savings, however, were inexistent. On February 5, 1994, *Novosti* reported:

> Although it is objectively not easy to determine the strange path the money took out of the pockets from the citizens and into the banks of Dafiment, Inos, Stefani, and the vaults of other smaller banks, it is now evident that the financial chaos was also due in large part to the factual or non-factual competence of state institutions. True, the committee stated it tried to prevent the work of Gazda Jezda and Dafina, but they also gave up on it. Now the committee seeks to replace these institutions or powerful individuals who made these decisions.[46]

Assessing the sociopolitical and economic situation through this short overview of the *Novosti* paper illustrates that Serbia turned into an epitome for Donald Cressey's *Theft of the Nation*. Belgrade was no longer discernible from paramilitary groups, 'businessmen', and related individuals that characterized the sanctions-busting years between 1993 and 1995. As such, I characterize the Yugoslav rump state as a "strong-weak" hybrid state, to frame it in Radniz's words. Serbia was a powerful militarily state in possession of a large weapons arsenal and an extensive web of military and paramilitary personnel. And yet, the rump state proved economically weak, seeing that Belgrade was unable or unwilling to curb the massive unemployment and hyperinflation rates.

It is further interesting to recall the news clipping in which Serbs provided Bosnians in Teslić with elastic goods and weaponry because these connections confirm that national and ethnic identifications wither when criminal organization grow. Instead, as illustrated by von Lampe's research on transnational crime networks, trust and the primary interest in turning a profit prevails.

In view of the deteriorating socioeconomic and political situation in Serbia, it comes as no surprise that citizens all over Serbia built and relied on solidarity networks.[47] Diminishing enforcement capacities by the state, as suggested by William Haller and Alejandro Portes, left Serbian citizens to their own devices. As a consequence, the 'frontier economy' rendered economic exchanges dependent on private networks, which were freely reported in the paper.[48] Discursive reporting by the paper in due process normalized *šverc* in a state that broke the social contract between governing forces and the population.

An analysis of 'discursive qualifications' about *šverc* in Novi Pazar

Overall, the paper discussed the terms 'borders' and 'border crossings' 179 times between 1993 and 1995. Most debates revolved around the topic of border closures and delays upon attempting to pass. On May 9, 1993, the paper informed readers that

the United Nations imposed new measures, stipulating that passenger cars may pass the border, while larger vehicles and trucks are subject to inspection. Only UNPROFOR trucks may traverse the border unhindered.[49]

At the time of this announcement, Novi Pazar was, according to the paper, already among the best-outfitted towns across Serbia:

The best-supplied city in Serbia is not, as you would expect, Belgrade – no – it is Novi Pazar. In the shops, mostly private, you can buy all the goods you desire, both domestic and foreign. The merchandise comes from all over and enters Novi Pazar via Turkey and Macedonia. For example, imported laundry detergent is 30 percent cheaper compared to domestic laundry detergent. Rice, cooking oil, and all other foods can also be purchased, and are affordable. Clothing and footwear are similarly inexpensive: the best jeans cost between 15 and 20 German Marks, shirts cost around 20 German Deutsch Marks, and sneakers cost anywhere between 10 and 20 German Marks.[50]

The article continues to cite a "*Novo Pazarski biznismen*" who explained that people from all over Serbia came to Novi Pazar to obtain goods – sometimes up to 10,000 people. "The exchange rates were the best in all of Serbia, although increased financial inspections in the region slowed down commerce," the *biznismen* explained.[51] Despite financial inspections, however, Novi Pazar continued to attract shoppers and smugglers alike. Novi Pazar was thus indeed, as previously stated by interlocutors in Chapter 1, a successful and thriving town that seemed to prosper due to, or because of, international sanctions. Lyon similarly stated: "overnight, a new class of wealthy entrepreneurs – both Serb and Bosniak – sprang up, although many Serbs remained in low-paying state sector jobs."[52] Nevertheless, Serbs and Bosniaks cooperated in their business dealings, as illustrated by *Novosti*. On November 19, 1994, the paper again reported Belgrade managed to cut off a *švercerski lanac* (smuggling ring) that connected Istanbul to Novi Pazar and Belgrade.[53]

By the end of 1993, the paper no longer engendered enthusiasm about the market in Novi Pazar, but notified readers that

Novo Pazarci were known to have traded weaponry even before the war.[54] People of the Pešter highlands were especially prone to trading guns with and for the Albanian mafia. Weapons arrived from all over the world, including Austria, Turkey, and other 'eastern' countries.

Assuming a rather sinister tone in the main article, too, the journalist reported:

> Some peddlers turn into millionaires overnight. All of the goods are sold untaxed, which deprives the state of revenue. Serbs do not take part in this trade, because they do not have relations with people in Istanbul, where most of the goods on the market come from.

An interviewed trader, however, defended the merchants:

> Customs officers and tax collectors should not bother us right now, because, owing to relations of the Muslim population, all of Yugoslavia is supplied with goods. But, we all pay our dues. It is not true that we easily enrich ourselves, on the contrary. We spend our days and nights on wheels, and along the road, we have to bribe everyone – from the customs officer to the policemen. At one border crossing, a drunken customs officer stopped 30 truckers from Novi Pazar. He then demanded we buy his boss a Mercedes. We all had to pitch in a thousand German marks. We cannot disclose the name of the customs officer or the particular border crossing, because we have to pass through there again. It is better to give a thousand marks, than to lose a full truck that is sometimes worth one hundred thousand dollars.[55]

"Most of the people who come to shop here don't care that Turkey is among those states, which most often attack Serbia. Muslims," the article continues, "commit an act of genocide in the Sandžak region: With the enormous revenues from šverc, they increase their property by way of buying out local Serbs."[56]

One is left wondering about the overall accuracy of the coverage. On September 5, 1994, for instance, the paper claimed that Ugljanin (SDA), the political engineer behind the sought-after autonomy in 1993, paid locals for their continued loyalty. Ugljanin had fled Novi Pazar for Turkey in 1993 in fear of Serbian secret forces and allegedly bribed locals with up to 7,000 German marks to spread propaganda in favor of Bosnia, the SDA, and himself.[57] Yet, why would one need to bribe individuals with 7,000 German marks when people became millionaires overnight, as propounded by the paper? Either the *biznismen* exaggerated the general income among smugglers in Novi Pazar, the paper falsified the numbers, or the ousted politician offered no bribes. Perhaps the truth lies somewhere in between.

Novi Pazar, as this side-by-side comparison of the two articles clearly demonstrates, morphed from a prized market town at the beginning of 1993 into a pariah bazaar with a potential to dismantle the social fabric of Serbia. The paper, in other words, indicted the *entire* Muslim population for war profiteering: with the revenues from *šverc*, Bosniaks and/or Muslims sought to expel the Serbian population from the Sandžak region. It is ironic, of course, that the townspeople of Novi Pazar – predominantly Bosniak – enjoyed financial success as a result of the Yugoslav Succession Wars. The extraordinarily successful practice of *šverc* among this population, in other words, turned into an unintended consequence, for it connected the Muslim and/or Bosniak population to Istanbul, as confirmed in the preceding clipping: "owing to relations of the Muslim population (with relatives in Istanbul), all of Yugoslavia [was] supplied with goods." This connection, one might argue, reinforced the extreme nationalism of Belgrade that sought to enlarge its political territory.

It is significant to recall here the second segment of the previous section. Bosniaks narrated their loss of property after the collapse of the Ottoman Empire: the new government "took the properties from families. Then, they gave the land to the other people," as narrated by Omar, for instance.[58] Following the Succession Wars, Bosniaks felt as though Belgrade deprived the Muslim population of belonging to Serbia by renovating Orthodox heritage sites. In the preceding article, the paper claims Bosniaks "committed genocide" by purchasing Serbian property, thereby forcing the Orthodox population out of Novi Pazar. *Šverc* thus directly intersects with the making of historiography as Yugoslav successor states sought to redraw their respective political borders based on purported historical claims.

Serbian claims to ensure continued authority over territories, including the Sandžak region, appeared most often in connection with historicized events dating to the Ottoman past. "Serbian forces could stop the war in Bosnia immediately, but the Muslims do not wish for the war to end," the paper reported in a clipping on February 5, 1994.[59] Arguing the borders ought to remain as they currently appear on the battlefield, the paper documented a claim by Vojislav Šešelj that SDA[60] members sought to "bring the war to ancient Raška. All Muslims who live in this country must be loyal citizens. There is no Sandžak as they claim, because we have thousands of soldiers who are ready to defend their homeland." One might argue the government used the paper to send explicit warnings to locals in Novi Pazar. "This is old Raška," the clipping reads, "and as such it will remain."

The paper frequently discussed the SDA, the sought-after autonomy for Sandžak, and discursive portrayals of Muslims as 'extremists' in connection with Turkey proper. In an article dating to February 3, 1994, for instance, the headline stated "REBELLION FINANCED BY THE TURKS . . . formation of paramilitary forces financed by Turkey":[61]

The Montenegrin ministry of internal affairs discovers the hellish plans (*pakleni plan*) of an organized uprising on a daily, or rather on an hour-by-hour basis. The SDA planned an armed uprising in northern Montenegro and in those parts of Serbia, which Muslim extremists call Sandžak.[62]

This article illustrates the discursive qualities about Muslims of Sandžak most clearly. Characterizing Muslim citizens of Serbia as extremists was likely to sow distrust among the majority population of Serbia that was inundated by false propaganda from the outset of the Succession Wars.

One must put this fear in perspective. There are an estimated 9 million people in Serbia, 100,000 of which are Muslims – both practicing and not. There is not only a great numerical imbalance one ought to consider in this alleged threat the paper termed 'hellish plans'. Serbia indisputably possessed a larger weapons arsenal and the manpower with which to quash the alleged threat, had there really been one. One might also argue that Belgrade, by waging a war against its neighbors in pursuit of expanding Serbian borders, ignited a self-fulfilling prophecy. Bosniaks would not have connected with the Bosniak émigré community in Turkey had it not been for the relentless propaganda spread through the news as well as governing institutions.

On March 4, 1994, the paper published an article under the title "Dreams of Greater Turkey."[63] Ankara, according to the article, used its superior geopolitical location to foster relations with Washington as American forces employed their forces to attack Iraq during the Desert Storm mission. Both Walker and Kirişci echoed this notion. Turkey indeed enjoyed a favorable geopolitical position following the end of the Cold War. "Ankara was not satisfied with this feat, but harbored dreams of greater Turkey," the paper reported:

> Imperialists of all right-wing parties seek to re-impose control over all areas previously under held by the Ottoman Empire, reaching from the Black Sea to the Caucasus, Central Asia, Macedonia, Kosovo, over the Sandžak, Bosnia and Albania. True, those are unrealistic dreams, but these topics nevertheless occupied Turkish policy makers.[64]

Of course, the irony lies in the fact that Belgrade supported the realization of greater Serbia by violent and political means when this article appeared.

Historiography served the purpose of substantializing territorial claims. On August 2, 1994, the paper reported 'new' findings about the history of ancient Ras.[65] Stanko Ravić, a historian and publicist from the region, according to the paper, found that "ancient Ras – the capital city of medieval Serbia – was falsely believed to be located out of town." Instead, Ravić asserted,

> the capital of ancient Ras lay beneath Novi Pazar. Jovan Cvijić and Constantine Jireček falsely, and without substantial proof, located ancient Ras outside the city limits of Novi Pazar. When the Muslims occupied Southern Serbia then, they built Novi Pazar on top of ancient Ras.

Serbia was unable to attack citizens within its own borders. An attack on citizens within Serbian state borders would serve as a valid pretext for an invasion of Serbia under international law.[66] Belgrade, in other words, was not able to 'cleanse' the Sandžak region of unwanted elements because doing so would have nullified Serbian state sovereignty. Instead, Belgrade embarked on a campaign to ensure Serbian state sovereignty over its territory by way of propped-up historical claims.

Synthesis

Serbia was a strong-weak hybrid state during the time under investigation. Unable to provide citizens with the most basic of goods, including toilet paper, soap, and cooking oil, the state allowed for a flourishing of informal market practices. At the same time, Belgrade supported paramilitary and military offensives to enlarge Serbian territory beyond state borders. Two specific unintended consequences resulted from this hybrid governing structure.

First, Belgrade was unable to control the sprouting informal market activities while (at least) partaking in the illegal trade of cigarette smuggling. Novi Pazar, paradoxically, profited from this trade. Though the paper, and perhaps the *biznismen* themselves, might have exaggerated the profits of the smugglers, the revenues resulting from the business of *šverc* were likely substantial. It is significant that locals initiated trade by way of contacts with relatives in Istanbul. Especially striking is the fact that the paper reported this feat by emphasizing that Serbs do not partake in this trade due to inexistent connections with Turkey. Regarding the increasingly negative reporting of the market in Novi Pazar in view of Belgrade's efforts to portray Novi Pazar as the original Ras demonstrates Serbian determinations to break with the inclusive past of SFRY. It comes therefore as no surprise that Bosniaks envisioned a sociopolitical and economic future in connection with the Turkish state. The paper played a critical role in this process. Serving as a mouthpiece for Belgrade, the paper illustrated to Bosniaks that they no longer belonged to the Serbian state. Bosniaks, moreover, deprived the state of critical revenue by withholding taxes, according to the paper. This is, of course, absurd given the extent of *šverc* that reigned all through the 1990s in all of Serbia.

Second, because *šverc* was evident in all of Serbia, and reported as such by the paper, the practice of smuggling across borders became normal. Smuggling was not a deviant form by which individuals made a living but necessary due to the exceedingly unpredictable economic situation in Serbia, especially during the first half of the 1990s. Belgrade proved unable to control the practice of *šverc* after 1995.

Bosniaks in Novi Pazar, as this chapter illustrates, participated in an in- and out-of-state experience at the same time. Bosniaks were, like citizens in all of Serbia, involved in informal market practices. The paper, meanwhile, increasingly depicted Bosniaks as a pariah that collaborated with Turkey, which *regularly attacked the Serbian state.*

Notes

1 John Law, *After Method – Mess in Social Science Research* (New York: Routledge, 2010), 56.
2 Hereinafter *Novosti*.
3 Sabrina Petra Ramet, *Balkan Babel: The Disintegration of Yugoslavia from the Death of Tito to the Fall of Milosevic* (London: Hachette, 2002), 19–20.
4 Ibid., 41–42.
5 "Resolution 721 of 27 November 1991" (1991), https://documents-dds-ny.un.org/doc/.
6 Susan L. Woodward, *Balkan Tragedy: Chaos and Dissolution after the Cold War* (Washington, DC: Brookings Institution Press, 1995), 106–107.
7 Vladimir Petrović, "Uloga medija u učvršćenju vlasti Slobodana Miloševića," *Istorija 20. veka*, no. 2 (2013): 183–204.
8 Marcus Tanner, "Belgrade Sacks Anti-Milosevic Journalists," *Independent* (1993).

9 "Scooping the Dictator; Serbia's Last Independent Newspaper Fights for Its Life," *Washington Post* (1995).

10 Jens Stilhoff Sörensen, "The Shadow Economy, War and State Building: Social Transformation and Re-stratification in an Illiberal Economy (Serbia and Kosovo)," *Journal of Contemporary European Studies* 14, no. 3 (2006): 322.

11 Mladen Dinkić, *Ekonomija Destrukcije: Velika Pljačka Naroda* (Beograd: Stubovi Kulture, 1996), 42–43.

12 Momčilo Grubač, "Organizovani kriminal u Srbiji," *Zbornik radova Pravnog fakulteta u Splitu* 46, no. 4 (2009): 702.

13 Martin Reisigl and Ruth Wodak, "The Discourse Historical Approach," in *Methods of Critical Discourse Analysis*, ed. Ruth Wodak and Michael Meyer (Los Angeles: Sage, 2009), 87–121.

14 Ibid., 88.

15 Ibid., 90.

16 Ibid., 94.

17 Please note, these numbers are not absolute. It is possible that I missed several mentions of prices (the same is true for other topics I coded for) in the paper, seeing as the first viewing in the National Library in Belgrade was done manually.

18 Urban neighborhood in Belgrade.

19 Е.В.Н. 4:4, "нема шта нема," *Вечјерне Новости*, April 26, 1993, 7.

20 "United Nations Security Council Resolution 757," ed. United Nations Security Council (1992), https://www.un.org/.

21 Predrag Jovanovic and Danilo Sukovic, "A Decade under Sanctions," *Transparency Serbia Documents* (2002), http://www.transparentnost.org.rs.

22 D. Nedeljković, "Novosti," September 23, 1993, 5.

23 James Lyon, "Serbia's Sandžak under Milošević: Identity, Nationalism and Survival," *Human Rights Review*, no. 9 (2008): 298.

24 8: 167, "Novosti," *Novosti*, October 7, 1993, 3.

25 David A. Dyker, "Economic Overview: Serbia," *Europaworld*, accessed March 8, 2012, www.europaworld.com.

26 S. Pasić, "8: 32, Novosti," October 31, 1993.

27 Ibid.

28 M. Milić, "5:256, из цезве кипи цена," *Novosti, July 15, 1994, 7.

29 Ibid.

30 "United Nations Security Council Resolution 757."

31 M. Stevanović, "5: 324: дроги – дупла рампа," *Novosti*, March 27, 1994, 11.

32 J. C., "8:161: Нови прелаз риђица," *Novosti*, October 24, 1993.

33 D. Nedeljković, "1:290, Београд постаје највеће тржиште дроге на балкану – Хероин из – Немачке," *Novosti*, February 6, 1994, 6.

34 Miljana Aksić, "5:228, Нема наивне дроге," *Novosti*, July 28, 1994, 20.

35 5:867, "подземље пере рук," *Novosti*, October 21, 1994, 10.

36 5:429, "дрога за шанком," *Novosti*, August 15, 1994, 19.

37 Misha Glenny, *McMafia: Seriously Organised Crime* (London: Vintage, 2009), 48.

38 Marko Hajdinjak, *Smuggling in Southeast Europe. The Yugoslav Wars and the Development of Regional Criminal Networks in the Balkans* (Bulgaria: Center for the Study of Democracy, 2002), 41.

39 Milan Milošević, "The Media Wars," in *Burn This House: The Making and Unmaking of Yugoslavia*, ed. Jasminka Udovicki and James Ridgeway (Durham, NC: Duke University Press, 2000), 124.

40 "1:56, одмотава се српско-муслиманско трговачко клупко на Теслићком ратишту – Ровови пуним- шверца," *Novosti*, February 27, 1994, 4.

41 R. T. Naylor, *Patriots and Profiteers: On Economic Warfare, Embargo Busting, and State-sponsored Crime* (Toronto: M&S, 1999), 360; see also N.P. Vreme & B92,

"Jedinica – Film o Crvenim beretkama ili kako je ubijen Djindjić 1–3" (March 9, 2018), https://www.youtube.com/watch?v=n-UO7lm_5S4.

42 Glenny, *McMafia: Seriously Organised Crime*, 40–41.

43 Peter Andreas, "Criminalized Legacies of War: The Clandestine Political Economy of the Western Balkans," *Problems of Post-Communism* 51, no. 3 (2004): 7; see also Andrew Feinstein, *The Shadow World: Inside the Global Arms Trade* (New York: Farrar, Straus and Giroux, 2011), 5, 69, 418; Katherine C. Sredl, Clifford J. Shultz, and Ružica Brečić, "The Arizona Market: A Marketing Systems Perspective on Pre- and Post-war Developments in Bosnia, with Implications for Sustainable Peace and Prosperity," *Journal of Macromarketing* 37, no. 3 (2017): 7.

44 Slobodan Sociološki pregled Vuković, "Ekonomska Struktura Društva I Kontinuitet Vlasti U Srbiji," *Sociološki pregled* 1–2 (2000): 9.

45 Naylor, *Patriots and Profiteers: On Economic Warfare, Embargo Busting, and State-Sponsored Crime*, 360.

46 Vladan Dinkić, "1:388, Trka za Markama," *Novosti*, August 15, 1994, 10.

47 Alejandro Portes and William Haller, "The Informal Economy," in *The Handbook of Economic Sociology*, ed. Neil J. Smesler and Richard Swedberg (Princeton, NJ: Princeton University Press, 2005), 403–425.

48 Ibid., 410.

49 M. M., "4:281: нема робног промета," *Novosti*, May 9, 1993, 11.

50 E.B.H., "4:26, нема шта нема," *Novosti*, April 26, 1993, 7.

51 Ibid.

52 Lyon, "Serbia's Sandžak under Milošević: Identity, Nationalism and Survival," 85.

53 Z.V.L., "5:82, шверц у излогу, порез у – џепу," *Novosti*, November 19, 1994, 11.

54 S. Pasić, "8:161, Кроз Руке – Милион Марака," *Novosti*, October 31, 1993, 10.

55 Ibid.

56 Ibid.

57 Miroljub Nićivorović, "5:135; статус или новац," *Novosti*, September 5, 1994, 21.

58 Omar, interviewed in Bosnia and Herzegovina by Sandra King-Savic in 2014.

59 P. M., "1:101: Нема ништа од Санџака," *Novosti*, February 5, 1994, 12.

60 SDA, *Stranka Demokratske Akcije* (Democratic Action Party), headed by the late president Alija Izetbegović, with an offshoot in Novi Pazar, headed by Sulejman Ugljanin.

61 Milutin Sekulović, "1:129, побуну плаћали турци," *Novosti*, February 3, 1994, 12.

62 Ibid.

63 N/A., "5:88, Снови о великој Турској," *Novosti*, March 4, 1994, 26.

64 Ibid.

65 Pavle Pavlović, "5: 132, Стари Рас Нови Пазар," *Novosti*, August 2, 1994, 14.

66 James Ron, "Boundaries and Violence: Repertoires of State Action along the Bosnia/Yugoslavia Divide," *Theory and Society* 29, no. 5 (2000).

5   Speaking about the practice of *šverc*

Gordana, an attractive, well-kept (Serbian) lady in middle age, receives me at the entrance to a beauty salon. Tucked away on an innominate back street, one would never know the place is there unless someone specifically received instructions about its existence. No sign announces the presence of this parlor to potentially interested passersby. The only give away is a bleached-out cardboard placard picturing two women with 1980s hair. Standing beside the aged poster, Gordana receives me with a smile as I climb the stairs to the parlor. Once inside, I am engulfed in the smell of facial tonics, hot wax, and creams. Ladies, young and old, sip strong coffee in the small but neat waiting room and chat about their daily business, Novi Pazar, and their appearance. This parlor is like any other I frequented anywhere in the world.

Gordana is all graceful smiles, though the depiction of her hometown packs a punch. Gordana is not registered as gainfully employed and thus works 'under the table'. She does not, in other words, receive any social security benefits, and frequently invokes her fear of old age. "I have no idea how to pay my bills when I grow old . . . when I am no longer able to work." She earns approximately 300 euros per month. Her husband and son, too, earn about 300 euros monthly and contribute to settle the bills. Her son never finished his education and works odd jobs here and there. "He was never all that interested in finishing his education because the job prospects around here are grim. Sure," Gordana continues, "he never liked going to school in the first place. Besides, people in Serbia can earn a lot more money by doing some job 'under the table'." She explained on another occasion: "Take this salon; it belongs to a girl that fled the war during the 1990s. She relocated to Novi Pazar. I am convinced," Gordana maintains, "this girl is connected in some way. Her store is not registered, and no financial inspector ever shows up to review this place."

Besides working in the salon, Gordana attends to clients in the privacy of her home. She usually receives one or two clients per day, though she is not registered as doing so with labor services. "Is this why all the stores around here taped the '*uzmite račun*' (request receipt) poster on their wall?" I asked Gordana. "Nobody will give you a receipt, she scoffed, nobody. Ok . . . if some inspector comes, or some tourists, or people like you," she added consolingly:

> But that's peanuts anyway. The truth is this; there is a lot of money in Serbia. Look at all the fancy cars everywhere, Serbia is full of Jeeps, BMWs,

DOI: 10.4324/9781003022381-9

Audis. . . . all the hotels and resorts are always full! These people are all doing *šverz*, and not the smalltime kind we are doing. No. Only the people with shady dealings (*oni koji muvaju i muljau*) have that much money. They started back in the 1990s. But they are still doing business. How else could they have that much money to afford houses and those kinds of cars? You cannot afford those kinds of things by simply doing a bit of *šverc* out of a clothing booth (*gde malo prošvercuješ*). These people fill their bags with other things, besides clothes and shoes, I mean. You simply cannot make that much money by selling shoes. If there were as much money in the shoe business, I would immediately quit this job to sell shoes! No, no. If you have a normal job, like me, nine to five, then you are nobody in this town, in this entire country. Take my neighbor, he is endlessly (*beskrajno*) in and out of jail, and every time he goes to prison, he comes out a wealthier man. When you go to jail, your net-worth grows. In this country, incarceration rewards you with a plaque of honor. Going to prison means you have earned your keep in certain circles.[1]

During the Yugoslav Succession Wars, *šverc* turned into an ordinary occupation. Since the breakup of Yugoslavia, informality is increasingly practiced on two levels; people like Gordana continue to perform legal tasks informally. Others engage in illegal business. What emerges in the case of Serbia then is an intersection between transnational practices and opportunistic crime. Portes and Haller's concepts on informal economies and von Lampe's paradigm of transnational crime illustrate that sanctions-busting was necessary before turning into a normal, everyday practice. *Šverc* further reveals the ongoing contestation over the maintenance of cultural values among the citizens of Serbia in Novi Pazar – Bosniak, Serbian, and Roma alike.

Understanding *šverc* as a practice that afforded agents with a degree of "symbolic or normative anchoring," *šverc* served as a sense-making tool by which Bosniaks reconnected with the Bosniak émigré community in Turkey.[2] This narrative was prevalent during earlier stages of the ethnographic study, though not exclusively. During later stages of this research project, informants increasingly voiced apprehension about the market. This twofold ambiguity about the market signifies a connection to, first, a fulfilling social obligation, namely the necessity to supply the town of Novi Pazar (and Serbia) with goods. In turn, the social obligation nourished locals from the perspective of belonging when considering the re-established connection between the local and émigré Bosniak communities. Understood as such, the symbolic function of *šverc* served the purpose of (re) producing a distinction between the Bosniak community in Serbia and Belgrade.

Second, *šverc* is associated with inimical normative behavior that is anathema to the symbolic function of (re)producing *communitas* between locals and Bosniak émigrés in Turkey. During later stages of my fieldwork, interviewees and informants suggested *švercerci* of all backgrounds embraced Milošević because traders got rich in the process. News media, too, took up this narrative. For instance, Sanja Kljajić, a reporter for *Deutsche Welle*, declared the "talk of brotherly relations" between the Turkish émigré and local Bosniak population a myth.[3]

Evidently, *šverc* contains two normative components with at once virtuous and morally deplorable properties. Rouse, considering Stephen Turner,[4] stated:

> Actors share a practice if their actions are appropriately regarded as answerable to norms of correct or incorrect practice. Not all practitioners perform the same actions or presuppose the same beliefs, but some are subject to sanctions for actions or beliefs that are inappropriate or otherwise incorrect.[5]

Šverc was (is) both appropriate and inappropriate for the outlined reasons. It is significant that locals sanctioned *šverc* during earlier phases of the fieldwork, while predominantly connecting informal practices with the Milošević regime during later fieldwork stages. I will demonstrate this inherent ambiguity to answer the overarching question of how material encounters influence social relations in detached spaces in the following section. Two sub-questions inform this segment: how does the narrative about *šverc* change when probing into the actual *practice* of smuggling goods, and are informal material encounters connected to an ensuing sense of anomia?

Filtering out how the two narratives differ will demonstrate that *šverc* cut(s) across ethnic, religious, and political boundaries. People do not divide into neat ethnic and/or national enclaves despite the rupture the Yugoslav Succession Wars brought about. Local and émigré Bosniaks, purportedly an ethnically homogenous group, do not simply associate based on their common descent, and neither do Serbs. Instead, I will demonstrate that the everyday experience of living in a corrupted system trumps ethnicity.

Šverc as a narrated practice

For the most part, I conducted situational interviews during later stages of the fieldwork to gauge and categorize statements given during autobiographic interviews. Who practiced *šverc*, what materials were smuggled, and do people involved in *šverc* divulge this information readily and freely?[6] Informants at times welcomed the chance to talk about their experiences, whereas other interlocutors tired of sharing after some time. Senad illustrates both alternatives in his disparaging of the Milošević regime and the 1990s in general, while habitually talking himself into a frenzied rage when he started:

> Now I have to talk about this again. . . . I'm just kidding . . . relax. ahm . . . the time of Slobo's (Slobodan Milošević) regime during the 1990s, well, to tell you the truth . . . people usually only remember the positive things in life. I think that is human nature. They want to forget about the nasty things that happened here. They prefer to remember the positive things. But people in Novi Pazar have somehow an actual reason when they say their lives were great . . . they made loads of money . . . they had everything they wished for when Slobo was in power. Because that was a time when the town of Novi Pazar really flourished, because they smuggled goods. Everyone traded on

the market. All of Serbia came here to buy goods on the market, all of Montenegro. People in Novi Pazar earned up to 500 Deutschmarks at the time, and you were able to open businesses with that money.[7]

This excerpt is significant for Senad clearly places himself from without the performance of *šverc, and* to some extent the experiences made by his compatriots during the 1990s. He uses descriptive terminology and emphasizes *they* want to forget, *they* prefer to remember, and *they* smuggled goods. Senad externalizes the market and signals his non-involvement during this situational interview in 2016. A direct comparison with a quote about the market from 2015 reveals insightful discrepancies with the previous statement:

I only sold a few things with my friends. We were kind of kidding around. We were kind of trying to fit in, it was more a kind of joking around instead of real work, even though, back then, those were serious earnings. I mean, you could literally, *easy* (original emphasis) earn 120 Deutschmarks just like that. That's almost as much as 500 current Euros, more perhaps. People started whole businesses with 500 Euros then. The inflation was *huge* (original emphasis), do you understand? And, the market was going every day. And like this, you go down to the market two, three times a week for a couple of hours, and make 500/600/700 Euros, eh, Deutschmarks. That's a huge amount of money for those times.[8] But me, I only did that with friends, kind of. I went to Bulgaria once with some aunt, to buy something on the market there. . . . I didn't know how to do that. I am not really a merchant. I am . . . I mean, people carried enormous bags across the border, and I took two puny bags with me . . . and then, I turned out to be the most suspicious person on the border! Those guards on the border saw something white, and assumed I am smuggling drugs across the border.[9]

Even more glaring is the discrepancy between the first autobiographic interview in 2012 in which Senad unambiguously stated: "I am educated, but even I sold coffee on the market between 91–93." As such, there is a clear regression in the narrated involvement between the first autobiographical, and subsequent two situational interviews in 2012, 2015, and 2016.

Senad, a candid interlocutor in and out of the field, adjusted his narrative about his own involvement in the market. One can draw two conclusions based on the apparent reversion; first, Senad iterated a common narrative that accurately described the 1990s from his perspective. During the Succession Wars, individuals traded on the market informally. Even the newspaper echoed this sentiment as illustrated in the previous chapter. *Šverc* was state sanctioned, served the purpose of "symbolic . . . anchoring," and was, above all else, normal.[10]

In the previous excerpt, Senad states: "We were kidding around. . . . we kind of tried to fit in, it was more a kind of joking around." The fact that Senad and his friends tried to fit in, as he calls it, reveals that locals acquiesced to the apparent status quo in which a majority of people made a living by informal means. This finding correlates with the survey data, according to which 57.3 percent strongly agreed and 17.1 percent agreed with the statement of knowing someone who had worked on the market during the 1990s. Every other person knew someone who worked on the market, at the least.

As is the case with interviews, however, the questionnaire data in Figure 5.1 exhibits crucial inconsistencies. Of the respondents, 74.4 percent at least agree with the statement of knowing someone who had worked on the market. Meanwhile, 71.4 percent strongly disagree with the statement "I worked on the market during the 1990s." Two scenarios might explain the potential numerical disparity here: first, questionnaire participants overestimated how many of their acquaintances worked on the market; second, contributors conceivably shied away from disclosing their *own* involvement in the market. In light of the retraction apparent in the interview passages with Senad, one might argue the latter. Interview data and casual conversations with informants corroborate this option as interlocutors predominantly emphasized the large-scale involvement on the market during early stages of the ethnography. "Everyone worked on this market," as Senad and other interviewees repeatedly emphasized. As such, the high number of those who divulged to know someone who had worked on the market during the 1990s testifies to the commonality of *šverc* at the time. Interviewees and questionnaire data thus confirm Rouse's hypothesis that "actors share a practice if their actions are

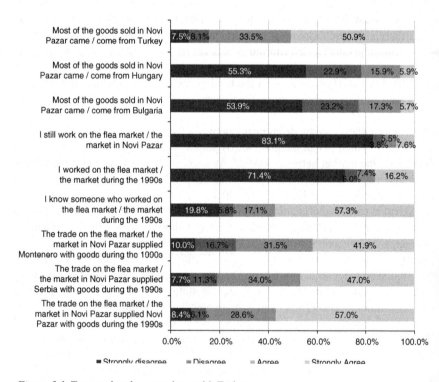

Figure 5.1 Transnational connections with Turkey

appropriately regarded as answerable to norms of correct or incorrect practice."[11] Because Rouse positions the learning and emulation of habits at the intersection of individual agency and maintenance of cultural values, one may postulate that locals "view(ed) the organization of informal enterprise as a normal part of life and involvement in the underground economy as a justifiable form of resistance," to put it in Portes and Haller's words, incipiently.[12]

Conclusion two is therefore more likely; interlocutors do not like to disclose their involvement in the market. Senad squarely acknowledged his involvement in the market at first, though points to his being aware of the informality and/or to some extent illegality thereof. This is especially noticeable when he states: "those [guys] saw something white, and assumed I am smuggling drugs across the border."

Locals, in taking the argument one step further, are not comfortable to divulge their personal involvement in the market because they knew their survival mechanism implicitly propped up the Milošević regime financially. A short conversation I had with Senad illustrates this perception:

ME: Would you say this market was good or bad for the town?

SENAD: I say it was good, yes, in a way. But, it was only good for Novi Pazar, not so much for the rest of the Sandžak region. The other towns in Sandžak did not have that possibility. For Milošević, it was good because the people of NP could somehow penetrate the sanctions, the blockades from the side of Turkey and Bulgaria, and sometimes from the side of Hungary. People from Serbia and Montenegro came here to Novi Pazar to buy stuff with their private cars and buses and took the goods back to their towns where they re-sold what they had bought here. This means that about 250 buses descended on Novi Pazar daily! *In addition* (original emphasis) to private cars! Only to buy merchandise! This was good for Milošević because they penetrated the sanctions, and the regime allowed for this to happen. There was no regular economy . . . the system did not function. From time to time, Milošević sent his people to Novi Pazar to collect money (*da reketiraju*) from those people who owned workshops. This means (*znači*) they went from workshop to workshop to collect a sort of tax. But this was no regular tax, it was extortion. It was all under the table, and the sum they took was completely random. Of course, it kind of matched the size of the workshop's income. Still, this happened randomly. These people would come whenever they needed money. Perhaps every two to three months, or perhaps once in every four to five months. For us, this was good because we did not pay regular taxes. People employed for instance (*lupam*) 50, 100, or even 500 workers, but, according to official numbers, there were only about two or so workers employed in the workshops. All of the salaries were paid under the table. No taxes.[13]

I asked Senad the same question three years later, to which he replied:

This (market) was good for the state, the regime, and Milošević. They literally robbed the state, plundered it. And they were under sanctions, do you understand? This means all of the official business conducted here was *šverc*.

The government was under sanctions, and Novi Pazar was some sort of a door through which to bring in goods . . . ehm . . . illegally . . . by doing *šverc*. What I mean to say is this, they all smuggled. Do you understand? Half of Novi Pazar was a flea market (*buvljak*) back then. This means the market started here, and reached all the way up to the municipal building, and back down toward the Raška river. I am telling you, about 70 percent of all the people from Novi Pazar worked on this market back then. Whoever was able to do anything ended up working on the market. Those who did not travel to Turkey told others who did what to buy for them, for instance coffee, or anything, you know. Then, you go there, buy a bag, take it to the market, measure the quantity in kilos, and sell it to customers on the market. The government tolerated this. And what did they do, they came here from time to time, when Slobo (Milošević) decided to send his goons, to collect their so-called taxes, they literally racketeered. This was no ordinary tax, they racketeered the market, the workshops. They also seized goods, took it from us. They would come here, and just kind of size up some-one's company based on the size and the workers there, and come up with some mystery number the owners would have to pay, say 200,000 Deutschmarks, 300,000 Deutschmarks . . . and that's how he sent them two or three times per year. That was lucrative for the state, not the state, of course, but for Slobo and his people who lined their pockets, do you understand? But it was also good for our people here. Do you understand? If we had to pay taxes here, had to pay insurance for the workers, to register them and so on, that would have been really very expensive. But this way, the earnings were bigger. There could be for instance 200 workers who worked in a workshop, but registered were only two. People saved money by not paying social contributions for employees. Life was great here, it was a great life here in Novi Pazar back then.[14]

Both statements are similar in form and tone. And yet, it is significant that Senad insinuates that *Slobo* – as he used to call Milošević during our interviews and casual conversations – was a criminal who racketeered the state for financial gain. Locals know this and emphasized trading with the émigré Bosniak community in Turkey as a symbolic anchor, as opposed to highlighting their forced cooperation with the regime.

Three specific quotes stand out as notable in these interview passages. First, Senad states the trade "was only good for Novi Pazar, not so much for the rest of the Sandžak region." Recalling that nearly all Bosniak and/or Muslim families have kin in Turkey, one is left wondering about this apparent asymmetry. One possible answer might be the geographical location that favored the flourishing of this market – Novi Pazar was (is) better accessible compared to the rest of the other five municipalities on the Serbian side of the Sandžak region.[15] The *Kombi-nat*, too, was in Novi Pazar, as was the existing market infrastructure. Therefore, Novi Pazar primarily served as a trading hub, while functioning as a centralizing force for the unity of Bosniaks in Serbia. Novi Pazar, in other words, consti-tuted an economic powerhouse much as the town preserved the narrated unanim-ity of the Sandžak region. External threats, including the war in Bosnia as well as nationalistic posturing and threats emanating from the paper, contributed to this rallying around the flag reaction. Bosniaks, in other words, gravitated toward Novi Pazar for economic, and later symbolic reasons. As such, isolating *šverc* from the sense-making account provided in Part II allows for the possibility to go beyond narratives of kin and ethnic unity to examine these inconsistencies.

Ethnic and/or national solidarity respectively, second, was not the raison d'être for the Milošević regime or the local and Bosniak and/or Muslim community. Instead, it served as a means to an end – personal enrichment for Belgrade and survival for the Bosniak community. Senad explained that *šverc* was "lucrative for Milošević and his people who lined their pockets. But it was also good for our people here." Both communities profited from this market for which cooperation was necessary – coerced and/or willingly. Location, moreover, was crucial, too. One might therefore postulate the emerging market resulted due to a geographically auspicious location and involuntary cooperation with the Milošević regime in addition to kin-relations.

Third, Senad estimated a nearly identical number of participants who were active on the market: "70 percent of all the people from Novi Pazar worked on this market." Senad thus echoes questionnaire results and corroborates the earlier assertion that interlocutors highlighted symbolic anchoring that produced a distinction between local Bosniaks and the Belgrade regime, as opposed to 'cooperation' with the government. Leijla's daughter, more to the point, stated:

> It was like this through all the wars here. Our countries (*naše zemlje*) fall apart . . . Srebrenica . . . everything. And ours (*naši*), cooperate with them (*glavu uz glavu sa njima*), and traaaaade, loooot . . . they created empires! Economic empires. But how can you explain that to people. . . ? The way it is now . . . unfortunately . . . it has always been . . . still. . . . This means you can always find someone, some group to manipulate, to poison.[16]

It is with this argument in mind by which one recognizes the extent of the two narratives illustrated in this book. *Šverc* indisputably heralded a reconnection between local and émigré Bosniaks in Turkey. Yet, this connection was not built on universal kin relations alone but was also constituted due to pragmatic choices the government, in part, enabled so long as Belgrade profited therein.

Practicing *šverc*

A conversation at the local NGO contextualizes the aforementioned findings further. The local NGO is a meeting place where like-minded people gather to talk about job opportunities, the government, and upcoming projects. An array of people frequented the locale during my time in the field, most of whom had opinions about the government, the market, and Turkey they cared to share. One attendee explained upon my inquiry as to how one goes about when seeking to smuggle goods:

> To put it in the simplest, and most logical way possible, we had a leg up on everybody else in Serbia because we could call our relatives in Istanbul or in

the other cities. Perhaps they themselves had nothing to offer, but they could ask around (*da se raspitaju*) for good prices for windowpanes, textiles . . . anything, anything we could sell. This is why the government let us do our thing here – they needed us (*mi smo njima bili potrebni*).[17]

It is interesting to note the specific commodity this interlocutor mentions: windowpanes. Considering that Serbian citizens bought windowpanes on the market in Novi Pazar, one can reaffirm a segment of the population benefited during the sanction years. Purchasing windowpanes is useless, in other words, unless one builds or renovates a house. While this observation seems tangential, one ought to recall the segment of the population in Serbia that lost their savings, jobs, and livelihood at the time. Building and renovating houses stands in stark contrast to the former. At any rate, this field note further relates that locals in Novi Pazar served as middlemen, able to provide potential merchants with initial contacts and access to merchandise before traveling to Turkey to obtain goods.

Building upon interviews from 2012 through 2015, I sought to learn about the actual doing of *šverc* in subsequent interviews between 2015 and 2016. By 2015, in other words, I had moved from coding how locals narrated *šverc* to analyzing "the basic social process"[18] that guided practitioners to bring the inherent contradictions that surround narratives of *šverc* to the surface.[19] Settings such as the one above were valuable because of the ready possibilities to question potential interviewees and casual interlocutors about the details concerning *šverc* in view of transnational family relations.

During one such episode, I met Saleh, a polite young man in his mid-thirties. After a few casual conversations, Saleh told me about the family business his father established during the 1990s. His family initially roasted coffee they had imported from Turkey. "Our house basically turned into a workshop where we roasted coffee for the market in Novi Pazar," Saleh explained, thereby confirming Asem, who stated that people often turned their homes into workshops during the war. Saleh was a boy back then, though distinctly remembers the collective family effort during the war years. "We all wore those huge coats so that we could stuff coffee into our pockets on our way to the market, and money on our way home. I remember . . . I remember, there was a lot of money everywhere . . . in all of our jackets . . . the pockets, the pants . . . everywhere. . . (*svuda*)."

ME: How did this market work?
SALEH: I usually went to the market with my parents. My younger sister also came with us, and the both of us were there, in these huge crowds . . . there were always huge crowds of people. A lot of people came from all over Serbia. Thousands. Especially every Tuesday and Sunday, those were the official market days.[20]
ME: How did your family get the goods here, and how did you grow the business?
SALEH: My father had a great idea, he bought his own minivan, to import things from Turkey with it. There was a lot of money in that business. He transported things from Turkey for certain people (*za odredjenje ljudi*) from Novi

Pazar. There was a lot of money in that business. . . . After some time, he bought another van, then he bought a trailer, and his business grew gradually. He transported more and more things, and went to Turkey more often, twice a week even. Later . . . he later sold the vans, bought a big lorry, and continued to do business with Turkey. I went with him a few times, and he brought this jeans material, and other things, but mostly textile, because people bought this material from Turkey either to produce goods, or to peddle them wholesale. There were big profits in that business . . . I mean huge. It was all normal, and it kind of went on like this for quite some time. My father bought another truck, and even expanded his business. Then he bought another truck, and on and on until we had kind of a small freight company. All of that fascinated me.[21]

Saleh and his family were set to leave for Germany when the Succession Wars started but decided to stay for a range of reasons, including his grandmother's old age. The Yugoslav Succession Wars were thus perceived as a clear rupture that locals sought to escape. Instead of escaping, however, Saleh and his family began to do business. During our numerous casual conversations, Saleh repeatedly explained, "I had a nice childhood, because of this business, we were never left wanting for a thing." Conversations and interviews about the specificities of market practices filtered this very experience of liminality to the surface: locals appreciated the market for its protective properties though were aware of potential liabilities, including the legal and ethical risks, as well as the potential bodily harm during the first half of the 1990s. In Asem's words:

This was basically that concept during those difficult war years in Serbia. . . . This economy saved us. Simple. We were independent from this terrible economic situation that reigned all over Serbia. But we knew they [Belgrade] would go to Kosovo, and we, as Muslims, we knew we were in a dangerous situation for the war might have spilled over into Sandžak . . . when we were surrounded by tanks.[22]

Juxtaposing these statements yields remarkable insight; Asem and Saleh describe memories that took place during the same time frame. If one were to separate the statement given by Saleh from the situation described by Asem, one might assume Saleh describes the simple success story of his family business. Especially intriguing is how Saleh portrayed his childhood. He was never left wanting at a time when want loomed large. Traveling to Turkey and standing beside his family members on market days was as normal for Saleh as it was to carry large wads of cash knowing that tanks surrounded the city, as illustrated by Asem. Saleh, one might argue, was born into a system in which informality served formal functions – a system that was governed by trial and error.

It is fruitful to use an analogy introduced by Diane Vaughan here.[23] Vaughan, reflecting on Bourdieu, illustrates the normalization of deviance by way of depicting an anomaly during flights by NASA (US National Aeronautics and Space Administration):

> The first decision to fly with an anomaly justified others; . . . The immediate social context was important to their construction of risk. . . . having an anomaly was not in itself a signal of potential danger, but in fact the norm. When the first unexpected booster anomaly occurred, a cause was identified, a corrective action taken, and the boosters defined officially as an "Acceptable Risk" for the next launch.[24]

Applying Vaughan's example of flight to the problem at hand, one might argue that locals decided to fly with the anomaly that was the broken Yugoslav system – that is, locals examined their social context to find solutions to remedy the economic and social malady. For this, Bosniaks called acquaintances and kin to locate goods for the market in Novi Pazar, which in turn required people who were willing to risk the drive across increasingly scrutinized borders. Because Belgrade and Yugoslav citizens variously penetrated the sanctions regime, for instance, the UN initiated a Sanctions Assistance Mission to monitor the shipment of goods coming to and leaving the Yugoslav rump state.[25] Saleh's father is a case in point here. He grew his one-man business into a trucking company for the import of goods from Turkey with great success. Not only does this example demonstrate that local businessmen thrived under international sanctions. Instead, the financial success resulting from this anomalous economic and social situation justified the construction of further risks. Evading international monitoring missions, bribing border guards, and additional acceptable risks encountered along the way became the norm, as the following excerpt demonstrates:

ME: How did smugglers get those goods across the border? I mean, did the border guards check the vehicles?

SENAD: The border guards, well, the border guards were bribed. The border guards in Yugoslavia, Bulgaria, and Turkey were all bribed. That is how it was. I mean, look, it was easy back then. Now, those merchants that were successful, those who traded, they cooperated directly with the state. They imported whole convoys full of things, lorries. And they traded, but not only with Turkey. The Turks did not care (*pa Turke baš briga*). They just sell stuff. I mean, what, you go there, give them cash, and take your wares. Nothing special. . . . What I mean to say is that these family relations were, above all else, and this is perhaps a bit simplistic, but these family relations helped. If I had no one there, no family members, I have to look for someone. I don't know where I am at, but the people who live in Istanbul know, and they can help you to prepare the terrain. They provide you with goods, facilitate the job. And this is why it was easier for us who had family relations there, compared to others who did not, like those people in Kragujevac, Čačak, and Kraljevo. It would have been hard for them to go to Turkey, because they have no one there. Isn't it. Ehm . . . and that is why we had an advantage, in the beginning . . . in the beginning, we had a big advantage, do you understand, that is how it was.[26]

Again, one is able to draw a correlation between the discourse presented in the previous chapter and the events as narrated by Senad. Locals indeed bribed the border guards on their way to Turkey as reported in the paper, which indicates a degree of cooperation across national, religious, and 'ethnic' affiliations. Trust surpassed ethnic affiliation as the necessity of protecting one's business magnified the necessity of collaboration.

Trust was a crucial precondition for the continued success, as emphasized by interlocutors. One had to trust the middlemen locals called in Turkey, truckers relied on the effective and continued use of bribing customs officers, and locals required trusting truckers who brought the ordered goods to the market. Frontier economies thus develop an internal logic that is shaped by, and in turn shapes social relations. In the case of Novi Pazar, the ability to call acquaintances and kin facilitated access to goods. External and internal events – transnational and national – defined the further course of social relations which, as illustrated in the previous excerpt, included the regime: "Those who traded . . . cooperated directly with the state." Consequently, the successful continuation of this frontier economy hinged on the unintentional and/or intentional cooperation with Belgrade. An excerpt of Saleh's portrayal of the 1990s illustrates this most clearly:

I don't know how to explain this, but I distinctly remember. . . . I remember at some point, our things were taken from us. We were suddenly no longer allowed to import goods from Turkey, this was the reason we were given. There was no concrete reason. But we kept on working, people kept importing goods from Turkey. But then, I remember, the government confiscated our products, along with our truck at the border. My dad's trucks were impounded. . . . I don't know how many trucks they took . . . but they put them somewhere . . . and I remember that Mihalj Kertes used to be the head of the border control agency back then. His name was often mention in connection with the Zemun Clan. I know he was implicated in everything that happened during the 1990s, and in the beginning of the 2000s . . . but I don't know much else about that. But I know that all of my dad's friends mentioned his name . . . Mihalj Kertes . . . Mihalj Kertes. . . . He did all that . . . decided . . . he was in charge of all that.[27]

Mihalj Kertes (Bracika), former customs administration director for the Federal Republic of Yugoslavia between 1993 and 1995,[28] is variously connected to criminal machinations in the academic as well as popular literature. A WikiLeaks cable, for instance, designated Kertes a close associate of Milošević and Stanko Subotić (Cane), the latter of whom is labeled "as a leader of the smuggling group."[29] In all, the cable designates eight leaders that headed smuggling groups, two of whom include Mira Marković and Marko Milošević.[30] "Most of these groups," according to the cable, "operated under the patronage of Milošević's secret services and their illegal profits were used for financing the regime and the accumulation of personal wealth."[31] Miloš Vasić, author of *Atentat na Zorana*,[32] and contributing writer to *Peščanik, Vreme*, and *B92*, echoed the WikiLeaks cable. Discussing *šverc* in a *Peščanik* article, Vasić states one cannot mention the name Kertez without also talking about Jovica Stanišić, Badža Stojičić, Arkan, Hadži Struja, Milorad Vučelić, Marko Milošević, and Vanja Bokan.[33] These individuals are known for their involvement in the underground economy as well as the atrocities they dealt as they looted villages during the Succession Wars in Bosnia. As such, it comes as no surprise that locals seek to emphasize connections with the Bosniak émigré community in Turkey over their unintentional cooperation with these criminal groups. Saleh, though indicating incomplete knowledge about Kertes, knew about the role Kertes played in the 1990s. This is especially evident in his citing the Zemun clan, one of the most infamous criminal gangs in Serbia during the 1990s.[34] And yet, people nevertheless had to make a living, as testified by Saleh:

> That was really hard, when they took away our trucks . . . and we, we were literally. . . . everything was on stand-by in our family. But then we learned about the whereabouts of the trucks, learned where they had taken the goods and all that, but nobody dared to do anything about it. That was during Milošević's time. He knew exactly what was going on. He knew who was doing what . . . all of that . . . ahm, and then . . . after a couple of months, I mean, they wanted to see what had happened to those trucks . . . and someone had discombobulated all the parts. The trucks stood on cinder blocks, without tires, without anything inside them.[35]

Following Portes and Haller, one can identify two of the three typologies that categorize informal activities in Novi Pazar. First, locals indeed "increased managerial flexibility to reduce labor costs."[36] Local workshop owners employed hundreds of employees but registered two, for instance. Directors thus increased their earnings as Belgrade compelled managers to pay a random tax in lieu of registering employees. Second, *šverc* was organized around "capital accumulation . . . through mobilization of [their] solidarity relationships, greater flexibility, and lower costs."[37] This is what Woodward called the modus vivendi: Bosniaks in Novi Pazar turned to "alternative social networks," their relatives in Turkey, to acquire goods.[38] To be sure, one might question the effectiveness of the bureaucratic apparatus in Serbia during the war years. And yet, judging by interview data and casual conversations in the field, managers appreciated the low labor costs: "People saved money by not paying social contributions for employees. Life was great here, it was a great life here in Novi Pazar back then."[39]

The economy in Novi Pazar was informal, and not a criminal endeavor par excellence. Relying on the data collected in the field, most people traded in elastic goods, such as textiles, coffee, and cigarettes. Yet, deliberating the underlying connection to and/or dependence on the criminal netherworld that was tied to the Milošević regime, one must point toward the intersection of criminal foraging as defined by von Lampe[40] and informal practices that sustain(ed) the political and social stability in Serbia as defined by Portes and Haller. Given the under-lying cooperation between locals and the Milošević regime, the third criterion, "activities . . . taking place outside the pale of state regulation," is not met. Though agents procured goods from without the purview of state regulation, merchants depended on the state for the successful continuation of *šverc*, as demonstrated with the example given by Saleh. Recalling Belgrade's desire of divesting the regime from the tainted business of *šverc*, Milošević sealed the borders in 1994. Saleh's father serves as a case in point here. Even if he did not cooperate with the state directly, his enterprise prospered only so long as the state profited from such businesses in social, financial, and political terms.

Another facet came into view upon repeatedly querying interlocutors about the practice of trading with kin in Turkey. Senad stated: "the Turks did not care (*pa Turke baš briga*) with whom they traded, they simply sold goods." Situational interviews and repeated meetings with interlocutors allowed for clarifications and a reevaluation of initial statements. Asem, too, reassessed the relations between Turkey and Novi Pazar upon my inquiry about the specificities of trading practices:

ME: Did the people in Novi Pazar mostly import jeans material because they had personal connections with family members in Turkey? I mean, did this trade start because of personal partnerships between Novi Pazar and Turkey?

ASEM: This is how it came about (*znaš kako*), I think, Turkey, what Turkey does as a state, you know, they perceive us as consumers. We don't even count for one thousandth of their capacity. This means, we are not really that useful as consumers for their market in some strategic sense. They have some big customers, huge companies that sell their goods all over the world. They are focused on those customers. What we do is look at what the big companies do, look at the trends. For instance, Zara. So, we look at the colors, the cut, and then we order perhaps one thousand, or even twenty thousand meters from a certain material. But then you have Zara, and they order three million meters of the same material. We are just peanuts for their market . . . but still, this is great for us, you know? We can hire people, give them a job, we are able to create a value, to sell goods, and to earn money this way.[41]

During our first interview, situational interviews, and casual conversations, Asem often emphasized family connections as a key element that saved the Bosniak community during the war years. Trading, as emphasized by Asem, served the purpose of connecting with kin and shielded locals from experiencing the economic hardship other citizens of Serbia experienced. In contrast to earlier narratives in which he stressed family and kin relations, Asem describes the connection between Turkey and Novi Pazar as a business connection in the previous excerpt. Turkey, in other words, no longer appeared primarily as a symbolic anchor during later conversations and interviews but as a place of transaction. Asem's choice of words is especially intriguing here. He uses the word 'Turkey', thus implying a distance that characterizes a transnational business transaction that is void of personal connections. To be sure, personal connections still enabled locals to do business, yet the sense-making properties evolved into a secondary narrative upon repeated inquiry about the actual practice of trading.

Three possible developments might explain this shift in emphasis. First, during the initial fieldwork phase, I recorded autobiographical interviews. Interviewees narrated life events as they chose. During latter fieldwork stages and after initial coding between 2012 and 2014, I identified *šverc*, Turkey, transnational family and trade relations, and rupture as key concepts by which to understand how social relations transformed in Novi Pazar. I therefore asked questions pertaining to emerging key concepts, which might have shaped subsequent conversations with interlocutors. Second, when we first met, Asem was employed, drove a sleek car, and appeared at our meetings in nice suits. Always courteous, welcoming, and an excellent source of reliable insider knowledge, he lost his job during latter stages of the fieldwork, which influenced not only his frame of mind but also his willingness to disclose information at times, as well as his overall disposition toward Turkey. During latter stages of the fieldwork, Turkey began to cooperate with the Serbian state and routed investment through official channels, as documented on the Turkish Cooperation and Coordination Agency (TIKA) website, for instance.[42] It is in this example that we can see most clearly that transnational relations occur between two states, as previously emphasized by Faist. They do not, in his words, transpire on a "magic carpet of a de-territorialized space of flows."[43] Adapting this statement to the argument at hand, one might argue the Turkish and Serbian states co-opted existing transnational kin relations to legitimize cooperation and access to their respective markets. However, this argument lies beyond the scope of this book. What remains is the fact that a range of interlocutors increasingly voiced their view of relations with Turkey as transactional. An excerpt from a situational interview with Daud is illustrative of this perception:

ME: How did these family connections help? Did émigré Bosniaks in Turkey donate goods for the market in Novi Pazar, or how did this work?

DAUD: A gift from a Turk (*Turčin da ti da džabe*)?! He will lease it to you, he might give you a loan, but you will have to pay him back. You know what my grandfather used to say? "Why were the Turks not the first to land on the moon? Because there was no money up there (laughs). . . . there was no money on the moon. . . (laughs)." Had there been money, the Turks would have been the first ones to go up. Eh . . . for free . . . no way! Ok, he will give you something if he trusts you, if he knows you, but you have to pay it back. But without paying the money back, no chance.[44]

Like Asem, Daud narrates the connections between Turkey and Novi Pazar from a transactional perspective when asked about the specificities of the trade.

A third option is Asem's overall disillusion with the Serbian state – a disillusion harking back to the rupture that came about the Yugoslav Succession Wars, and the subsequent dislocation of the Bosniak (Albanian, Roma, Hungarian, etc.) population from the Serbian state. It is instructive to recall that Asem felt connected to the Yugoslav state as he grew up. He no longer, however, recognizes the state he once called home. Transnational relations with the émigré community thus offered much needed respite and relief and the potential for financial autonomy from the Serbian state. Yet, it became increasingly clear that Novi Pazar would remain within the sovereign state borders of Serbia. Turkey now cooperated with Belgrade, and the local community, too, had already changed beyond recognition. According to an excerpt from 2012:

> Today, if you are a good student, you are seen as a nerd. Being good at school is no longer in. Now, you have to be bald, unemployed, you have to be a troublemaker, to argue with professors . . . that's what is in now. . . . There are a few who also want to advance, but there are not enough of us here. There are not enough intellectuals here, with real knowledge, educated people with diplomas.[45]

Asem, as this excerpt demonstrates, was critical of the state from the outset. Yet, during our initial interviews and casual conversations, Asem displayed a spirit of optimism. His job imbued him with a sense of security and autonomy, which he lost at a later stage of the fieldwork. Again, this might seem tangential. Yet, given the reliance on oral testimonies, ethnographers must take contemporary circumstances into account when analyzing the sayings and doings of interlocutors.

Anomia

Emela and I sit in a cafe bar and sip our lemonades as she tells me about a bar club (*kafana*) that is located behind her house:

> There are a bunch of girls there. I can always hear a noise (*galamu*) coming from inside that place, but nobody ever asks what is going on there. My hairdresser is located close-by, and the lady who fixes my hair also cuts the hair of the girls who live in this place.

Emela is a tall, very well-educated and progressive (Bosniak) lady, always dressed in the latest fashion and bent on leaving Novi Pazar for good. "The other day," Emela explains,

> my hairdresser told me about those girls . . . there is this one girl from Prijepolje, she must be really pretty (*izuzetno lepa djevojka*). The hairdresser told me this girl is held against her will, that she is being forced to work as a prostitute. They are giving these girls drugs to sedate them. All those girls start out looking nice, but then they start to look really bad . . . after some time.

Emela looks into the distance, and we sit in silence for the next couple of minutes. The afternoon sun beats down relentlessly. The air-conditioning inside the café bar is equally relentless. Both of us are wearing sweaters inside as the sun swelters outside. Emela breaks the silence and picks up where she left off a couple of minutes earlier:

> There are several establishments in Novi Pazar that purport to be hotels, but in reality, these places are bordellos. In Novi Pazar there are only a few places where you can go, the Hotel Atlas, Tadj, and perhaps the Oxa. But even they rent out rooms by the hour. It is difficult to go after those guys, because some policemen, judges, and politicians protect the owners of those establishments. I think they are connected to this trade, the trafficking of humans.[46]

A report by the Organization for Security and Co-operation in Europe (OSCE), published in 2008, found that victims of trafficking in Serbia often come from neighboring towns or even the same town in which they are trafficked.[47] According to the human rights report published by the Council of Europe, 296 trafficking victims were officially recognized between 2013 and 2016.[48]

"The worst thing," Emela tells me,

> is that black marketeering (*krijumdjiranje*) became normal for me. I know that this or that guy did this or that job in the 90s. . . . they made a ton of money (*gomilu para*). They live like kings now. It is normal for me to know that this or that guy has shady deals or deals with illegal substances. Everybody knows! Those are public secrets (*to su javne tajne*).

Emela throws her hands up in the air and exclaims, "I don't care about them anymore. And that," she says emphatically, "is what is wrong with this place. The new normal is the old abnormal."[49]

The trial and error system that started in earnest during the 1990s, I contend, laid the basis for the rising anomia, seeing that society lost its power "to regulate [the] social equilibrium by setting the acceptable level of social restraint."[50] An excerpt from an interview with Ekrem serves as an indicator here:

> If you look at all of Serbia, you will notice that everyone in this society (*celo ukupno društvo*) took a wrong turn. Those people who try to live normally . . . there are only a handful that remained normal. They all want something sensational; they all want to be, I don't know . . . they generally worship the wrong idols. Idols are those people who used to be criminals during the 1990s. . . . Why? Because people think they are cool. They had the best cars, the most beautiful girls, and everyone wanted to be with them, be like them. . . . Everything some normal boy or girl wanted back then, they had. This means, all the things these people did were presented as though they were normal, legal. This Arkan guy was a criminal, who knows what he did . . . he indirectly ruled Serbia. He had a nice house, right next to the Red Star stadium so he could watch the [soccer] games from his home. . . . He got married to Ceca. She was . . . I don't know, the most sought-after woman in Yugoslavia, I think. . . . I mean, there are those who like that. . . .

So, people around here looked at them, and thought, aha, Arkan has all these things. . . . O.k., I will be like Arkan, and the girls started to look and behave like Ceca. . . . I think only a small percentile remained normal.[51]

Robert Merton, deliberating "socio-cultural sources of deviate behavior," stated:

The dominant pressure of group standards of success is, therefore, on the gradual attenuation of legitimate, but by and large ineffective, strivings and the increasing use of illegitimate, but more or less effective, expedients of vice and crime. The cultural demands made on persons in this situation [poverty] are incompatible. On the one hand, they are asked to orient their conduct toward the prospect of accumulating wealth and on the other, they are largely denied effective opportunities to do so institutionally.[52]

Merton's deliberation on anomia is highly fruitful because one recognizes the social structure in Serbia was not deviant, but normal. In other words, deviancy was built into the very institution of the Serbian state. Racketeers collected 'taxes' from shop owners who smuggled goods – counterfeited and otherwise – border guards were bribed, and local idols included Arkan, a war-criminal,[53] and his (now widowed wife) Svetlana Ceca Ražnatović, a turbo-folk singer who is frequently connected to criminal machinations in Serbia.[54] What started as a trial-and-error system, in other words, transmuted into a normal organism of expectations that carried legitimate "prospect(s) of accumulating wealth" by illegitimate means, however legally. Senad, in describing the general atmosphere in Novi Pazar during the 1990s, explained:

I mean, you could get drunk here, enjoy and throw out money by the fistful if you wanted to . . . some people simply made so much money in such a short time that they had no way of developing a sense of boundary, their sense of normal got lost. They thought it would go on like this forever. because all this happened, the black market developed. These people simply did not think ahead. They threw money out with both hands, spoiled their children, education was no longer deemed necessary.[55]

Interlocutors, albeit narrating the past, often connected the period of the 1990s to the present. Illustrative of this is that interlocutors repeatedly argue the value of education declined in the 1990s, a characteristic that also pervades the present. Gordana serves as an example here, speaking about the past, she related her son, too, decided to discontinue his education to 'work under the table' at present seeing that a person that works in "a normal job . . . nine to five[, then you are] is (a) nobody in this town, in this entire country." Other interlocutors concurred with this sentiment, echoing Gordana's and the above assertion that "education was no longer deemed necessary: diplomas can be bought. If you know the right people, you can get employment. . . . I feel like having a diploma is just important for the bureaucracy."[56] This correlates with questionnaire data, according to which

51.2 percent strongly agree and 30.6 percent agree with the statement that career advancement in my country depends on who I know (Figure 5.2).

Education, it seems, is secondary in this system that evidently values connections over merit. Present circumstances thus factor into the answers and perceptions interlocutors relate to researchers. One might argue, therefore, interlocutors see no difference between the past and the present – that is, the sociopolitical system as described by Ekrem did not change substantially since the 1990s.

During my time in the field, Senad used to say:,

> We have a saying here in Novi Pazar; '*para nema ni babu ni majku*' (money has neither a grandmother nor mother). The criminals and the politicians have always worked hand in hand, without political support, the criminals could not have functioned the way they did.[57]

Interlocutors, as demonstrated with this statement, and illustrated in the questionnaire data, distrust(ed) Serbian governing institutions, and perceive politicians as self-serving rather than serving the electoral body in Serbia:

> Political parties. . . . All that matters is if they are Serbs, Bosniaks, Hungarians or Croats. Everything is decided by nationalists. Not because they are nationalist – of course, they are not all nationalists. Slobo was for instance

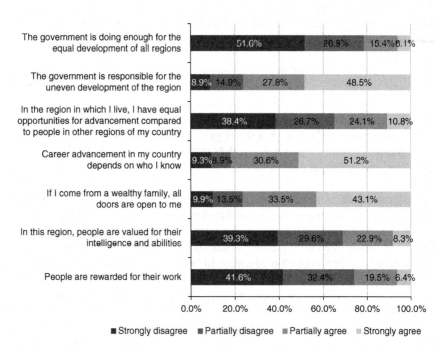

Figure 5.2 Potential for development and satisfaction with governmental services

in my view not a nationalist, even though some would like to call him that. He *was using* (original emphasis) the nationalist wave, but he was above all a criminal individual, a bandit, a crook! He stole from the population. This horrible inflation did not come from nowhere! The war did not simply come out of nowhere. The way I see it, there was no national, religious, or any other reason except that some criminals saw the opportunity to make a *lot* (original emphasis) of money. Of course, the war *was* (original emphasis) a war for those people that fought and lost relatives etc. But for those that made money off of it, the war was a welcome opportunity to make money. The war was generated so that they could steel as much money as possible.[58]

Judging from the data collected in the field, this distrust is rooted in the 1990s and the connection between the criminal netherworld and the Milošević regime. Senad even declares the Milošević regime as criminal instead of nationalistic. He often, for instance, used the word *magla* (fog) to describe the regime's tactics of duping Serbian citizens into believing in external threats, fifth columns, and other perils that might menace the Serbian people. The previous chapter might serve as a case in point here. Other interlocutors agreed with Senad. Ekrem, for instance, stated:

I don't know, I think this area here serves the purpose of generating profit, when somebody needs it. When somebody wants to make a profit, all he needs to do is make some waves, to (*da malo zaljulja*), create some unrest, to then make a profit, here, on this territory.[59]

The reason for this, according to informants, is that Novi Pazar still serves as a channel through which goods are smuggled. Saleh explained:

The '90s still influence the present. There are a lot of consequences that influence our lives here . . . perhaps there are some . . . some people perhaps don't believe they do, but the '90s influence the present for sure. Sure, in the past couple of years, Novi Pazar is not a merchant town anymore, not the way it used to be during the '90s, and there are no longer that many people who come to shop here, to trade, and do *šverc*. But there are some other forms. . . . today, people don't smuggle coffee anymore, they don't smuggle jeans material . . . cigarettes . . . all that . . . instead . . . there are real criminals now. I don't know what sort of channels they use . . . but most of the shipments come through Novi Pazar . . . some of the goods stay here in town, others go on. . . . I mean, we are here in close proximity to Kosovo, Albania, Montenegro, and Bosnia. I mean, Serbia . . . there is this connection between Serbia, Turkey, and Bulgaria . . . it's all connected, and all those countries I mentioned are all involved in this smuggling business . . . and . . . I mean . . . this all started back in the '90s. Those people who started out back in the '90s have necessary connections to continue this job. I think this will continue forever here. Look at the history of this town. This town was not built to be lived in, it was built for trade (*on nije planiran da se živi u njemu, samo da se trguje*). It was built for people to come here, meet, and trade. . . . I am convinced that every person that grew up in this town has trading in their blood (*svi koji su porasli u ovom gradu imaju trgovinu u krvi*). Take anything, the tiniest of things, and people from here will be able to trade that thing, to make some sort of a deal. I believe this, and I was proved right many times over in my life. Myself, presently, I mean . . . I sell a few things, I trade. . . . I am a merchant, and sell merchandise. . . . I know this will always exist within the people who are from Novi Pazar. This is why, yes, the '90s influence the present, but it has always been like this in this community.[60]

Synthesis

The practice of *šverc* is highly ambiguous because, as illustrated in the previous three chapters, smuggling might be considered both inappropriate and appropriate. Inquiring about the actual practice of *šverc* draped the overarching question of how material encounters influenced the social relations in Novi Pazar with yet another layer of ambiguity as informants connected informal practices with the Milošević regime during later fieldwork stages. Material encounters, examined from the perspective of actual smuggling activities, thus brought to the fore that *šverceri* were only able to smuggle goods so long as the government profited from this trade. Merchants were, according to the data retrieved in the field, considered to be connected with the regime, however involuntary.

Examining the practice of *šverc* revealed that, because merchants were unable to trade from without the purview of the state, informal trading merge(d) with the practice of transnational organized crime in which governing forces were implicated. During the 1990s, in other words, one is no longer able to distinguish governing forces from transnational organized crime practices or informal trading that sustained ordinary citizens. *Šverc* pervaded all levels of society. It is interesting to note here that, because smuggling was widespread and indeed indispensable, trading necessitated 'interethnic' cooperation, seeing that Serbia required trading partners from neighboring countries, including Croatia and Bosnia, as well as non-adjacent states, such as Turkey. On the surface then, one might argue, Belgrade fostered an extreme-nationalist campaign for propaganda purposes. Below the surface, Belgrade depended on the continued cooperation with these very individuals and/or states it otherwise denounced and persecuted. Ordinary citizens thus perceive Milošević – and everyone connected with this regime – as criminal and consequently untrustworthy.

Ordinary citizens were suspended in midair – dependent on the affability of the state to continue with business affairs, knowing the state might at some point *criminalize* their endeavor, as demonstrated by Saleh. Empirical data suggests that locals were only able to business so long as the state permitted the trade. Between 1991 and 1994, *šverc* was a celebrated practice, seeing that smugglers managed to import the most mundane of goods, including coffee, soap, and toilet paper in addition to drugs and weapons, as illustrated by the *Večerne Novosti* paper. After 1994, the state discontinued the possibility to trade informally, though data suggests that a segment of smugglers continued to do business. As such, the assumption that informal trading is only possible if connected to the state is plausible. The line between necessity and excess, ordinary and devious, became blurred. Informal material encounters thus led to an ensuing sense of anomia in the case of Serbia. Significantly, it was the government, Belgrade, that heralded this instability that led to the absolute breakdown of social norms. As a consequence, locals (Bosniaks, Serbs, Roma, etc.) find themselves unable to trust governing institutions to this day.

Notes

1 Field notes 2015.
2 Elizabeth Shove, Mika Pantzar, and Matthew Watson, *The Dynamics of Social Practice: Everyday Life and How it Changes* (Los Angeles: Sage, 2012), 75.
3 Sanja Kljajić, "Sandžak: The Balkans Region Where Turkey Is the Big Brother," *Deutsche Welle*, October 21, 2017, http://dw.com/p/2RXJO.
4 Stephen Turner, *The Social Theory of Practices: Tradition, Tacit Knowledge and Presuppositions* (Cambridge: Polity Press, 1994).
5 Joseph Rouse, "Two Concepts of Practices," in *The Practice Turn in Contemporary Theory*, ed. R. Theodore Schatzki, Karin Knorr Cetina, and Eike Von Savigny (London: Routledge, 2001), 190.
6 Adele E. Clarke, *Situational Analysis in Practice: Mapping Research with Grounded Theory* (London: Routledge, 2016), 177.
7 Senad, interviewed in the greater Sandžak region by Sandra King-Savic, 2016.
8 Senad, interviewed in the greater Sandžak region by Sandra King-Savic, 2015.
9 Ibid.
10 Shove, Pantzar, and Watson, *The Dynamics of Social Practice: Everyday Life and How It Changes*.
11 Rouse, "Two Concepts of Practices," 190.
12 Alejandro Portes and William Haller, "The Informal Economy," in *The Handbook of Economic Sociology*, ed. Neil J. Smesler and Richard Swedberg (Princeton, NJ: Princeton University Press, 2005), 411.
13 Senad, interviewed in the greater Sandžak region by Sandra King-Savic, 2012.
14 Senad, interviewed in the greater Sandžak region by Sandra King-Savic, 2015.
15 Fieldwork 2012; see also *Serbia's Sandžak Still Forgotten*, The International Crisis Group (2005), www.files.ethz.ch/.
16 Leijla's daughter, interviewed in the greater Sandžak region by Sandra King-Savic, 2015.
17 Field notes 2015.
18 Clarke, *Situational Analysis in Practice*, 53–76, 558.
19 Karen Armstrong, "Ethnography and Audience," in *The SAGE Handbook of Social Research Methods*, ed. Pertti Alasuutari, Leonard Bickman, and Julia Brannen (London: Sage, 2008), 62.
20 Samir, interviewed in the greater Sandžak region by Sandra King-Savic, 2015.
21 Ibid.
22 Asem, interviewed in the greater Sandžak region by Sandra King-Savic, 2012.
23 Diane Vaughan, "Bourdieu and Organizations: The Empirical Challenge," *Theory and Society* 37, no. 1 (2008).
24 Ibid., 73.

25 Parliamentary Assembly, *Report on the United Nations Embargo against Serbia and Montenegro* (June 11, 1993), http://assembly.coe.int/nw/xml/XRef/X2H-Xref-ViewHTML.asp?FileID=7216&lang=EN; see also Enrico Carisch, Loraine Rickard-Martin, and Shawna R Meister, *The Evolution of UN Sanctions: From a Tool of Warfare to a Tool of Peace, Security and Human Rights* (New York: Springer, 2017), 5.
26 Senad, interviewed in the greater Sandžak region by Sandra King-Savic, 2016.
27 Samir, interviewed in the greater Sandžak region by Sandra King-Savic, 2015.
28 Dušan Bogdanović and Biljana Kovačević-Vučo, *Institutions Abused: Who Was Who in Serbia 1987–2000* (Belgrade: "Biljana Kovačević-Vučo" Fund, 2011), 128–129.
29 Wikileaks cable, "id= 07BELGRADE997_a, Djindjic Assassination Still Political Football" (April 16 and July 16, 2007), https://wikileaks.org/plusd/pdf/?df=43308.
30 Ibid.
31 Ibid.
32 Miloš Vasić, *Atentat na Zorana* (Beograd: *Politika* B92 Vreme Narodnja Knjiga, 2005).
33 Miloš Vasić, "Cane Subotić i 'duvanska mafija'," *Peščanik*, June 21, 2014, https://pescanik.net/cane-subotic-i-duvanska-mafija/.
34 See, for instance, Mirko Tepavac, "Jači od Države," *Glasilo gradjanskog samooslobodjanja – Republika Protiv stihije straha, mržnje i nasilja*, October 1–30, 2006, http://www.republika.co.rs/390-391/03.html; Aleksandar Knezević, Vojislav Tufegdžić i Radio B92, *Kriminal Koji Je Izmenio Srbiju* (Beograd: Publikum, 1995).
35 Saleh, interviewed in the greater Sandžak region by Sandra King-Savic, 2015.
36 Haller, "The Informal Economy," 405.
37 Ibid., 405–406.
38 Susan L. Woodward, *Balkan Tragedy: Chaos and Dissolution after the Cold War* (Washington, DC: Brookings Institution Press, 1995): 125.
39 King-Savic, interview.
40 Klaus von Lampe, "The Practice of Transnational Organized Crime," in *Routledge Handbook of Transnational Organized Crime*, ed. Felia Allum and Stan Gilmour (London: Taylor and Francis Group, 2015), 186–200.
41 Asem, interviewed in the greater Sandžak region by Sandra King-Savic, 2015.
42 *TIKA Continues Operation in Serbia*, Turkish Cooperation and Coordination Agency (2013), http://www.tika.gov.tr/en/news/tika_continues_operations_in_serbia-8722.
43 Thomas Faist, "Trans Nationalization in International Migration: Implications for the Study of Citizenship and Culture," *Ethnic and Racial Studies* 23, no. 2 (2000): 218.
44 Daud, interviewed in the greater Sandžak region by Sandra King-Savic, 2014.
45 Asem, interviewed in the greater Sandžak region by Sandra King-Savic, 2012.
46 Emela, interviewed in the greater Sandžak region by Sandra King-Savic, 2015.
47 Jovana Bogićević Ivana Radović, Marija Anđelković, Marijana Gligorić, Miloš Teodorović, Miša Stojiljković, Nadežda Milenković, Olivera Miloš Todorović, Olivera Otašević, Saša Leković, Svenka Savić, Tamara Vukasović, "Human Trafficking Manual for Journalists," ed. OSCE (2008), https://christusliberat.org/journal/wp-content/uploads/2017/11/MANUAL-FOR-JOURNALISTS.pdf.
48 Group of Experts on Action against Trafficking in Human Beings, *Report Concerning the Implementation of the Council of Europe Convention of Action against Trafficking in Human Beings by Serbia* (2018), https://rm.coe.int/greta-2017-37-frg-srb-en/16807809fd; see also Office to Monitor and Combat Trafficking Persons, *Trafficking in Persons Report 2017*, U.S. Department of State, https://www.state.gov/wp-content/uploads/2019/02/271339.pdf.
49 Emela, interviewed in the greater Sandžak region by Sandra King-Savic, 2015.
50 Ken Morrison, *Marx, Durkheim, Weber: Formations of Modern Social Thought* (London: Sage, 2006), 226.
51 Ekrem, interviewed in the greater Sandžak region by Sandra King-Savic, 2012.

52 Robert K. Merton, "Social Structure and Anomie," *American Sociological Review* 3, no. 5 (1938): 79, 672.

53 "Željko Ražnatović 'Arkan': IT-97-27," International Criminal Tribunal for the Former Yugoslavia, http://www.icty.org/x/cases/zeljko_raznjatovic/cis/en/cis_arkan_en.pdf.

54 See, for instance, Eric Gordy, "Sav taj folk 1–8" (April 28, 2018); Christian Axboe Nielsen, "The Goalposts of Transition: Football as a Metaphor for Serbia's Long Journey to the Rule of Law," *Nationalities Papers* 38, no. 1 (2010).

55 Senad, interviewed in the greater Sandžak region by Sandra King-Savic, 2012.

56 Ekrem, interviewed in the greater Sandžak region by Sandra King-Savic, 2012.

57 Field notes 2015.

58 Senad, interviewed in the greater Sandžak region by Sandra King-Savic, 2012.

59 Erol, interviewed in the greater Sandžak region by Sandra King-Savic in 2012.

60 Saleh, interviewed in the greater Sandžak region by Sandra King-Savic, 2015.

Conclusion

The practice of *šverc* – or material encounters across detached spaces – considerably influenced the social relations between and among Bosniaks, Serbs, and Roma in Novi Pazar. Before reflecting on my concluding remarks on how this was the case, I must iterate that *šverc* is and was practiced in all of Serbia during the wars, and indeed in all of Yugoslavia even before the Yugoslav Succession Wars started. It was, however, not my intent to analyze the continuity of prewar smuggling connections among and between supranational and adjacent states. Instead, it was my intent to learn from informants how *šverc during* the Yugoslav Succession Wars affected the everyday lives of Bosniaks within the Yugoslav rump state and how informants make sense of these connections. Based on empirical data gathered in the field, I examined the overarching question of how transnational practices affected social relations in southern Serbia through the prism of *šverc*. By adopting a grounded theory approach to my fieldwork, I learned from informants how informal trading practices influenced their everyday lives in the Sandžak region – specifically in Novi Pazar – between 1991 and 1995. Inquiring about the informal market in Novi Pazar produced two dominant narratives that I analyzed in different parts of the book.

In Part I, I considered the first narrative strand as a sense-making tool through which Bosniaks not only connected with historiographic events but also came to identify with the greater diaspora scattered in various Southeastern European states and Turkey. This narrative strand is, in other words, a mnemonic tool by which locals understand and interpret their social position within the Yugoslav rump state and Serbia, respectively, but crucially their social position within a transnational context.

Narrative memory transmission is a significant aspect within this first narrative strand because elders serve as vehicular units by which younger generations learn about a past they did not experience. Crucial is that younger generations identified with the past as told by their grandparents as opposed to their parents. Because history turned operational again, present circumstances as experienced by younger generations mirrored those of elders who experienced and/or served as a link to the bygone Ottoman Empire – a link that served as a strong symbolic anchor for informants in the region. Connections with the émigré community in Turkey represent a crucial and a very tangible connection with this past.

Transnational networks between the local and the émigré Bosniak community in Turkey, in other words, carried the unofficial (non-state-sanctioned) history of the Ottoman Empire into the public sphere, even in the absence of any given individual's lack of concrete connections with the Bosniak émigré community in Turkey. The aspect of a non-state-sanctioned history is couched into the architectural Ottoman remnants in Novi Pazar, whose dilapidating state serves as a very public reminder of the social marginalization of the Bosniak/Muslim community in Southern Serbia; this is especially the case during the Yugoslav Succession Wars. Political entrepreneurs of all backgrounds used historic landmarks to ensure and conjure legitimate claims over Southern Serbia. A case in point is Stanko Ravić, a public historian who claimed the capital city of ancient Ras was built on top of Novi Pazar, for instance. Locals, therefore, view the state-sanctioned history with cynicism, which endows narrative memory transmission by elders with additional weight.

The salience of transnational material encounters across detached borders can only be understood against the backdrop of historical circumstances as understood by locals in – and to some extent since – the 1990s. Trading with and/or receiving aid from the émigré community in Turkey heralded a time-space continuum, a chronological continuity that imbued locals with a sense of *communitas* with fellow Bosniaks and/or Muslims wherever they lived. The practice of *šverc* was thus, seen from the perspective of the first narrative, not only a necessary means of survival and security. *Šverc* was an appropriate tool by which locals endured the economic downturn in Serbia that also served as a centripetal force for the ongoing memory construction and reconstruction among Bosniaks in Novi Pazar.

In Part II, I considered the second narrative strand that consisted of the actual doing of *šverc*: the practice of smuggling. Probing into the actual *practice* of smuggling goods brought to the surface that *šverc* cut(s) across ethnic, religious, and political boundaries and was practiced in all of Serbia. A recontextualization of smuggling practices based on the *Večernje Novosti* newspaper revealed that smuggling was not a deviant act but an ordinary way to earn a living. More than that, it was necessary due to the exceedingly unpredictable economic situation in Serbia, especially during the first half of the 1990s. As a consequence, the paper reported freely and amicably about the practice of *šverc*, individual *šverceri*, and where one could find the best markets for the acquisition of goods and black-market exchange rates.

The paper proved to be a highly fruitful source by which to triangulate data obtained in the field. Especially intriguing is the inconsistent depiction of Bosniaks and/or Muslims in Novi Pazar compared to other residents in Serbia. According to the paper, Serbs did not partake in this trade in Novi Pazar, seeing that Serbs had no existing connections with individuals in Turkey. And yet, the paper regularly reported about the breakup of smuggling channels by which Bosniaks and Serbs cooperated, according to the paper, to the detriment to either the Republic of Serbia, Republika Srpska, or both. The paper, meanwhile, depicted Bosniaks as a fifth column and collaborator of Turkey, which regularly attacked the Serbian state. Most glaring is the contradiction relating to the accusation that

Bosniaks deprived the state of critical revenue by withholding taxes, seeing that *šverc* occurred in all of Serbia. Overall, one might consider Serbia as a strong-weak hybrid state. Belgrade – which was increasingly undistinguishable from the criminal netherworld – was unable to provide citizens with basic goods such as toilet paper and soap, though it supported paramilitary and military offensives in Croatia and Bosnia. Consequently, *šverc* is highly ambiguous, depending on the angle from which one examines the practice.

Repeated inquiry about *šverc* increasingly stripped the practice of its sense-making property. Instead of highlighting transnational connections as a symbolic anchor, the way interlocutors did during initial interviews, transnational connections increasingly appeared as transactional networks during later interview and fieldwork stages. Informants, moreover, progressively connected informal practices with the Milošević regime, and the regime itself as a criminal enterprise. It is here where one sees most clearly that ethnic categories fade away. Citizens who live in a corrupted system may find themselves compelled to make a living by informal means as well as by way of involuntary cooperation with regimes they otherwise despise.

Among the most inveterate unintended consequences is the sense of anomia that permeates all levels of society in Serbia, including Novi Pazar. Because Belgrade relied on smuggling activities and criminal networks during the 1990s, locals no longer trust the sociopolitical and economic process in Serbia. Distrust of governing institutions cuts across ethnic and theistic boundaries.

Theoretical implications address an encouragement of combining two (and more) seemingly incompatible theoretical approaches to study a phenomenon encountered in the field. To be sure, the practice turn in social sciences – examining the sayings and doings of agents in the field – might stand in seeming contradiction to a mnemonics approach, a method that purports to look inside the heads of interlocutors to glean relevant information. Combining the two paradigms, however, yielded remarkable insight. Not only was I able to study local attitudes toward *šverc* by doing so, but I also learned how individuals use narratives to make sense of their situation and how to compare insight gleaned from open-ended, semi-structured interviews to results garnered from a practice-oriented approach.

Observing collective attitudes toward sociopolitical and economic events based on mnemonics is fruitful because one can learn to understand experiences from the point of view of interlocutors. Examining the same phenomena from the perspective of practice, meanwhile, might have prevented a skewed data set, seeing that informants narrate a self to resist another. As argued earlier, for instance, locals shied away from disclosing their own involvement in *šverc* though readily highlighted the significance of transnational connections with the Bosniak émigré community in Turkey. It took somewhere between three and four years, in other words, to learn about those narratives informants sought to resist at first.

In summary, transnational networks are seen as a solidarity chain that enabled locals to make a living but also as a system of connections within which to cohere the transmutation of their existence in the former Yugoslav Republic. And herein lies the irony: though Belgrade waged an extremely bloody war in Croatia and Bosnia, the internationally imposed sanctions affected all citizens of Serbia, including the Bosniak minority population that also experienced persecution by Belgrade. In turn, the market benefited all of Novi Pazar – Albanian, Bosniak, Serbian, and Roma alike – even the Milošević regime. At the most obvious level, the present study illustrates that international sanctions harm the most vulnerable people, in addition to the average citizen who may or may not support the actions of the ruling regime. International actors – specifically the five permanent, plus rotating members of the United Nations Security Council – thus not only impose but enforce an otherwise inexistent, and artificial, homogeneity upon the 'nation-state' to rid the 'international community' of a rogue leader. One may argue the international community replicates the very nationalism it opposes by way of economic warfare. In due course, those affected by the sanctions experience isolation and seek 'aid' elsewhere. Internationally imposed sanctions bear a maximum of unintended consequences, one of which is the creation of informal markets one is unable to contain long after the violence subsided.

Appendix – questionnaire

Osnovne Informacije

1. Državljanstvo
   Citizenship
2. Nacionalna pripadnost
   Nationality
3. Godište
   Age
4. Pol
   Sex
5. Mesto rođenja
   Place of birth
6. Grad u kojem trenutno živite
   The city in which you currently live
7. Koliko dugo već živite u tom gradu
   How long have you been living in that city
8. Koji je Vaš maternji jezik
   What is your native language
9. Državljanstvo Vašeg oca
   Your father's citizenship
10. Nacionalna pripadnost Vašeg oca
    Your father's nationality
11. Maternji jezik Vašeg oca
    Your father's native language
12. Državljanstvo Vaše majke
    Your mother's citizenship
13. Nacionalna pripadnost Vaše majke
    Your mother's nationality
14. Maternji jezik Vaše majke
    Your mother's native language
15. Verska pripadnost
    Religious affiliation

16. Obrazovanje: a) Osnovna škola b) Srednja škola c) Viša škola d) Univerzitetske studije
(MOLIM VAS DA ZAOKRUŽITE)
Education: a) Elementary school b) High school c) Higher education d) University
(Please circle relevant answer)
17. Da li ste zaposleni? nezaposleni, ili penzioner (MOLIM VAS DA ZAOKRUŽITE)
Are you employed? Unemployed, or are you retired (Please circle relevant answer)

Ocenite u kojoj meri se slažete, odnosno ne slažete sa sledećim tvrdnjama? (4) Potpuno
se slažem (3) Delimično se slažem (2) Delimično se neslažem (1) Uopšte se ne slažem|
Please evaluate to what extent you agree or disagree with the following statements
(4) I completely agree (3) I partially agree (2) I partially disagree (1) I disagree

Ljudi su nagrađeni za svoji rad *People are rewarded for their work*	1	2	3	4
U ovoj regiji, ljudi su cjenjene zbog svoje inteligencije i sposobnosti *In this region, people are appreciated for their intelligence and ability*	1	2	3	4
Ako dolazim iz bogate porodice, sva vrata su mi otvorena *If I come from a wealthy family, all doors are open to me*	1	2	3	4
Napredovanje u karijeri u mojoj zemlji zavisi od toga koga znam *Career progression in my country depends on who I know*	1	2	3	4
U mestu u kojem živim imam jednake šanse za napredovanje kao i ljudi u drugim delovima moje zemlje *In the place where I live, I have the same chance of advancement as people in other parts of my country*	1	2	3	4

(Continued)

Vlada je odgovorna za neravnomeran razvoj regiona *The government is responsible for the uneven development of the region*	1	2	3	4
Vlada čini dovoljno da bi svi regioni bili jednako razvijeni *The government is doing enough to ensure that all regions are equally developed*	1	2	3	4

Ocenite u kojoj meri se slažete, odnosno ne slažete sa sledećim tvrdnjama? (4) Potpuno se slažem (3) Delimično se slažem (2) Delimično se neslažem (1) Uopšte se ne slažem| *Please evaluate to what extent you agree or disagree with the following statements (4) I completely agree (3) I partially agree (2) I partially disagree (1) I disagree*

Zarađujem dovoljno novca da izdržavam sebe/porodicu *I earn enough money to support myself/my family*	1	2	3	4
Treba dva ili više radnih mesta da bih sebe/svoju porodicu finansijski izdržavao *It takes two or more jobs to support myself/my family*	1	2	3	4
Obično dobijam platu preko bankovnog računa *I usually receive my paycheck via bank deposit*	1	2	3	4
Obično dobijam platu u gotovini *I usually get paid in cash*	1	2	3	4

Ocenite u kojoj meri se slažete, odnosno ne slažete sa sledećim tvrdnjama? (4) Potpuno se slažem (3) Delimično se slažem (2) Delimično se neslažem (1) Uopšte se ne slažem|
Please evaluate to what extent you agree or disagree with the following statements (4) I completely agree (3) I partially agree (2) I partially disagree (1) I disagree

Život u Vašem gradu i/ ili regiji *Life in your city and/or region*	1	2	3	4
Život u Sandžaku *Life in Sandžak*	1	2	3	4
Život u Srbiji *Life in Serbia*	1	2	3	4
Potencijalno evropsko članstvo *Potential European Union membership*	1	2	3	4
Vaša nacionalna pripadnost *Your nationality*	1	2	3	4
Vaš materni jezik *Your mother tongue*	1	2	3	4
Vaša verska pripadnost *Your religious affiliation*	1	2	3	4

Ocenite u kojoj meri se slažete, odnosno ne slažete sa sledećim tvrdnjama? (4) Potpuno se slažem (3) Delimično se slažem (2) Delimično se neslažem (1) Uopšte se ne slažem|
Please evaluate to what extent you agree or disagree with the following statements (4) I completely agree (3) I partially agree (2) I partially disagree (1) I disagree

Trgovina na buvljak/ pijaci u Novom Pazaru je snabdevala Novog Pazara sa robom tokom 1990-ih godina *The flea market/the market supplied Novi Pazar with goods during the 1990s*	1	2	3	4
Trgovina na buvljak/ pijaci u Novom Pazaru je snabdevala Srbiju sa robom tokom 1990-ih godina *The flea market/the market supplied Serbia with goods during the 1990s*				

Ocenite u kojoj meri se slažete, odnosno ne slažete sa sledećim tvrdnjama? (4) Potpuno se slažem (3) Delimično se slažem (2) Delimično se neslažem (1) Uopšte se ne slažem| *Please evaluate to what extent you agree or disagree with the following statements (4) I completely agree (3) I partially agree (2) I partially disagree (1) I disagree*

Trgovina na buvljak/ pijaci u Novom Pazaru je snabdevala Crnu Goru sa robom tokom 1990-ih godina *The flea market/the market supplied Montenegro with goods during the 1990s*	1	2	3	4
Znam nekoga ko je radio na buvljak/pijaci kao trgovac tokom 1990-ih godina *I know someone who worked on the flea market/the market as a trader during the 1990s*	1	2	3	4
Ja sam radio/radila na buvljak/pijaci kao trgovac tokom 1990-ih godina *I worked as a trader on the flea market/ the market as a trader during the 1990s*	1	2	3	4
Još uvek radim na buvljak/pijaci kao trgovac u Novom Pazaru *I still work as a trader on the flea market/ the market as a trader during the 1990s*	1	2	3	4
Većina robe koja je bila prodata/koja se proda u Novom Pazaru dolazi iz Bugarske *Most of the goods that were sold/are sold in Novi Pazar come from Bulgaria*	1	2	3	4

Većina robe koja je bila prodata/koja se proda u Novom Pazaru dolazi iz Mađarske *Most of the goods that were sold/are sold in Novi Pazar come from Hungary*	1	2	3	4
Većina robe koja je bila prodata/koja se proda u Novom Pazaru dolazi iz Turske *Most of the goods that were sold/are sold in Novi Pazar come from Turkey*	1	2	3	4

Sledeće izjave su tačno ili netačno (označite odgovarajuće sa X) *The following statements are true or false (mark corresponding answer with an X)*	**Tačno**	**Netačno**
Znam nekoga ko dovozi robu iz Bugarske *I know someone who brings in goods from Bulgaria*		
Znam nekoga ko dovozi robu iz Mađarske *I know someone who brings in goods from Hungary*		
Znam nekoga ko dovozirobu iz Turske *I know someone who brings in goods from Turkey*		
Ja sam dovozio/dovozim robu iz Bugarske *I bring in goods from Bulgaria*		
Ja sam dovozio/dovozim robu iz Mađarske *I bring in goods from Hungary*		
Ja sam dovozio/dovozim robu iz Turske *I bring in goods from Turkey*		
Dovozio /la sam robu uz pomoć jednog člana porodice/prijatelja koji živi u Bugarskoj *I brought the goods with the help of a family member/a friend who lives in Bulgaria*		
Dovozio/la sam robu uz pomoć jednog člana porodice/prijatelja koji živi u Mađarskoj *I brought the goods with the help of a family member/a friend who lives in Hungary*		
Dovozio /la sam robu uz pomoć jednog člana porodice/prijatelja koji živi u Turskoj *I brought the goods with the help of a family member/a friend who lives in Turkey*		

Ocenite u kojoj meri se slažete, odnosno ne slažete sa sledećim tvrdnjama? (4) Potpuno se slažem (3) Delimično se slažem (2) Delimično se neslažem (1) Uopšte se ne slažem| *Please evaluate to what extent you agree or disagree with the following statements (4) I completely agree (3) I partially agree (2) I partially disagree (1) I disagree*

Verska pripadnost utiče na nivo mog poverenja u potencijalne poslovne partnere *Religious affiliation affects my level of trust in potential business partners*	1	2	3	4
Znanje jezika utica na nivo mog povjerenja u potencijalne poslovne partnere *Linguistic skills affect my level of trust in potential business partners*	1	2	3	4
Nacionalnu pripadnost/ nacionalno opredeljenje utica na nivo mog povjerenja u potencijalne poslovne partnere *National affiliation affects my level of trust in potential business partners*	1	2	3	4

Ocenite u kojoj meri se slažete, odnosno ne slažete sa sledećim tvrdnjama? (4) Potpuno se slažem (3) Delimično se slažem (2) Delimično se neslažem (1) Uopšte se ne slažem| *Please evaluate to what extent you agree or disagree with the following statements (4) I completely agree (3) I partially agree (2) I partially disagree (1) I disagree*

Ljudi Vaše nacionalnosti koji žive u vašem gradu ili regiji *People of your nationality who live in your city or region*	1	2	3	4

Ljudi druge nacionalnosti koji žive u Vašem gradu ili regiji *People of another nationality who live in your city or region*	1	2	3	4
Ljudi Vaše nacionalnosti koji žive u Srbiji *People of your nationality who live in Serbia*	1	2	3	4
Ljudi druge nacionalnosti koji žive u Srbiji *People of another nationality who live in Serbia*	1	2	3	4
Ljudi Vaše nacionalnosti koji žive bilo gde u bivšoj Jugoslaviji *People of your nationality who live anywhere in former Yugoslavia*	1	2	3	4
Ljudi druge nacionalnosti koji žive bilo gde u bivšoj Jugoslaviji *People of another nationality who live anywhere in former Yugoslavia*	1	2	3	4
Ljudi vaše nacionalnosti koji žive bilo gde u svetu *People of your nationality who live anywhere in the world*	1	2	3	4
Ljudi druge nacionalnosti koji žive bilo gde u svetu *People of another nationality who live anywhere in the world*	1	2	3	4

Sledeće izjave su tačno ili netačno (označite odgovarajuće sa X) *The following statements are true or false (mark corresponding answer with an X)*	Tačno	Netačno
Imam članove porodice koji su napustili ovu regiju, i emigrirali u Tursku nakon 1918 *I have family members who left the region and emigrated to Turkey after 1918*		
Znam potomke tih članova porodice koji su napustili ovaj region da žive u Turskoj *I know the descendants of those family members who left this region to live in Turkey*		
Imam redovne kontakte sa članovima porodice koji žive u Turskoj *I have regular contact with family members who live in Turkey*		
Imam članove u mojoj široj porodici koji su napustili ovu regiju, i emigrirali u Tursku nakon 1918 *I have members in my extended family who left the region and emigrated to Turkey after 1918*		
Znam potomke tih članova šire porodice koji su napustili ovaj regijon da žive u Turskoj *I know the descendants of those members of the extended family who left this region to live in Turkey*		
Imam redovne kontakte sa članovima šire porodice koja živi u Turskoj *I have regular contacts with members of my extended family who live in Turkey*		
Znam ljudi koji su napustili ovaj region da žive u Turskoj nakon 1918 *I know people who left this region to live in Turkey after 1918*		
Imam prijatelje u Turskoj *I have friends in Turkey*		

Ocenite u kojoj meri se slažete, odnosno ne slažete sa sledećim tvrdnjama? (4) Potpuno se slažem (3) Delimično se slažem (2) Delimično se neslažem (1) Uopšte se ne slažem| *Please evaluate to what extent you agree or disagree with the following statements (4) I completely agree (3) I partially agree (2) I partially disagree (1) I disagree*

Prva Jugoslavija (1918–1941) *First Yugoslavia (1918–1941)*	1	2	3	4
Bivša Jugoslavija *Former Yugoslavia*	1	2	3	4
Sovjetski Savez *The Soviet Union*	1	2	3	4
Austro-Ugarska *The Austro-Hungarian Empire*	1	2	3	4

Ocenite u kojoj meri se slažete, odnosno ne slažete sa sledećim tvrdnjama? (4) Potpuno se slažem (3) Delimično se slažem (2) Delimično se neslažem (1) Uopšte se ne slažem|
Please evaluate to what extent you agree or disagree with the following statements (4) I completely agree (3) I partially agree (2) I partially disagree (1) I disagree

Osmansko Carstvo	1	2	3	4
The Ottoman Empire				
Potencijalno članstvo u EU	1	2	3	4
Potential EU membership				
Drugo (molim Vas,	1	2	3	4
napišite):				
Other statements (please				
indicate here):				

_____)

U prostoru ispod, molim Vas da nacrtate svoju domovinu i označite tri mesta koja smatrate najvažnijim. Ako ne želite da crtate, molim Vas da napišete imena lokaliteta, zemalja, ulica, ili šta god, koja Vi smatrate kao najvažnijim
In the space below, please draw your homeland and mark the three places you consider most important. If you do not want to draw, please write the localities, countries, streets, or whatever you consider to be the most important.

Bibliography

A/N. (2010). "Novopazarski ribnjak 'Vojin Popović' ponovo u funkciji." In *Sandžakpress*. Novi Pazar, Serbia. http://sandzakpress.net/novopazarski-ribnjak-vojin-popovic-ponovo-u-funkciji.

Aasland, A., et al. (2012). "Trust and Informal Practice among Elites in East Central Europe, South East Europe and the West Balkans." *Europe-Asia Studies* 64(1): 115–143.

Agar, M. H. (2008). *The Professional Stranger: An Informal Introduction to Ethnography*. London, Emerald.

Alba, R. D., et al. (2003). *Germans or Foreigners? Attitudes toward Ethnic Minorities in Post-reunification Germany*. Basingstoke, Palgrave Macmillan.

Allum, F. and S. Gilmour (2015). "Introduction." In *Routledge Handbook of Transnational Organized Crime*, edited by F. Allum and S. Gilmour. London, Routledge: 10.

Altman, Y. (1983, June). *A Reconstruction, Using Anthropological Methods, of the Second Economy of Soviet Georgia*. PhD dissertation, Centre of Occupational and Community Research, Middlesex Polytechnic.

Andreas, P. (2004). "Criminalized Legacies of War: The Clandestine Political Economy of the Western Balkans." *Problems of Post-Communism* 51(3): 3–9.

Andreas, P. (2008). *Blue Helmets and Black Markets: The Business of Survival in the Siege of Sarajevo*. Ithaca, NY, Cornell University Press.

Andrejevich, M. (1997). "The Sandžak: A Perspective of Serb-Muslim Relations." In *Muslim Identity and the Balkan State*, edited by H. Poulton. London, Hurst in association with the Islamic Council.

Archer, R. and K. Rácz (2012). *Šverc and the Šinobus: Small-Scale Smuggling in Vojvodina*. Subverting Borders, Springer Fachmedien Wiesbaden GmbH: 59–83.

Armstrong, K. (2008). "Ethnography and Audience." In *The SAGE Handbook of Social Research Methods*, edited by P. Alasuutari, L. Bickman, and J. Brannen. London, Sage: 62.

Banac, I. (1994). *The National Question in Yugoslavia – Origins, History, Politics*. Ithaca, NY, Cornell University Press.

Bandžović, S. (2006). *Iseljavanje Bošnjaka u Tursku*. Sarajevo, Institut za istraživanje zločina protiv čovječnosti I medjunarodnog prava.

Baser, B. and A. E. Öztürk (2017). *Authoritarian Politics in Turkey: Elections, Resistance and the AKP*. London, New York, I.B. Tauris.

Bauböck, R., et al. (2009). "Citizenship Policies in the New Europe: (Expanded and Updated Edition)." IMISCOE Research Series, Amsterdam, Amsterdam University Press.

Bechev, D. (2017). *Rival Power: Russia's Influence in Southeast Europe.* New Haven, CT, Yale University Press.

Bideleux, R. and I. Jeffries (2007). *The Balkans: A Post-communist History.* New York, Routledge.

Bieber, F. and N. Tzifakis (2019). *The Western Balkans in the World: Linkages and Relations with Non-western Countries.* London, Routledge.

Blumer, H. (1986). *Symbolic Interactionism: Perspective and Method.* Berkeley, University of California Press.

Bogdanović, D. and B. Kovačević-Vučo (2011). *Institutions Abused: Who Was Who in Serbia 1987–2000.* Belgrade, "Biljana Kovačević-Vučo" Fund.

Bonomi, M. and M. Uvalić (2019). "The Economic Development of the Western Balkans, the Importance of Non-EU Actors." In *The Western Balkans in the World: Linkages and Relations with Non-western Countries,* edited by F. Bieber and N. Tzifakis. Milton Park, Routledge.

Böröcz, J. (2000). "Informality Rules." *East European Politics and Societies* 14(2): 348–380.

Bourdieu, P. (1993). *The Field of Cultural Production.* New York City, Columbia University Press.

Bourdieu, P. (2003). *Picturing Algeria.* New York, Columbia University Press.

Bourdieu, P. and R. Nice (1977). *Outline of a Theory of Practice.* Cambridge, Cambridge University Press.

Brkić, M. (2001). "Pipci i konci svemoćnog gazde." *Vreme.*

Brubaker, R. (2002). "Ethnicity without Groups." *European Journal of Sociology* 43(2): 163–189.

Brubaker, R. (2005). "The 'Diaspora' Diaspora." *Ethnic and Racial Studies* 28(1): 5.

Brubaker, R. and F. Cooper (2000). "Beyond 'Identity'." *Theory and Society* 29(1): 1–47.

Bulut, E. (2006). " 'Friends, Balkans, Statesmen Lend Us Your Ears': The Trans-state and State in Links between Turkey and the Balkans." *Ethnopolitics* 5(3): 309–326.

Burger, T. (1987). *Max Weber's Theory of Concept Formation: History, Laws, and Ideal Types.* Durham, NC, Duke University Press.

Carisch, E., et al. (2017). *The Evolution of UN Sanctions: From a Tool of Warfare to a Tool of Peace, Security and Human Rights.* Switzerland, Springer.

Ćirić-Bogetić, L. and M. Djordjević (1980). *Iz Političke Istorije Jugoslovenskih Naroda – XIX i XX vek.* Beograd, Privredni Pregled Beograd.

Clarke, A. E. (2016). *Situational Analysis in Practice: Mapping Research with Grounded Theory.* London, Routledge.

Communication Service of the ICTY. "(IT-97-27) Željko Ražnatović 'Arkan'." United Nations International Criminal Tribunal for the Former Yugoslavia. Accessed April 28, 2018. https://www.icty.org/x/cases/zeljko_raznjatovic/cis/en/cis_arkan_en.pdf.

Coser, L.A. (1992). *Maurice Halbwachs: On Collective Memory.* Chicago, University of Chicago Press.

Costa, A. M. (2008). *Crime and its Impact on the Balkans.* Vienna, Austria, United Nations Office on Drugs and Crime.

Cressey, D.R. (2008). *Theft of the Nation: The Structure and Operations of Organized Crime in America.* New Brunswick, NJ, Transaction.

Danielsson, A. (2016). "Reforming and Performing the Informal Economy: Constitutive Effects of the World Bank's Anti-informality Practices in Kosovo." *Journal of Intervention and Statebuilding* 10(2): 241–260.

Davutoğlu, A. (2008). "Turkey's Foreign Policy Vision: An Assessment of 2007." *Insight Turkey* 10(1): 29.

Denny, F. M. (2006). *An Introduction to Islam*. New Jersey, Pearson.

Dervišević, A. (2006). *Bošnjaci u Dijaspori – Historijat, Problemi, Analize i Perspektive*. Sarajevo, Wuppertal.

Dinkić, M. (1996). *Ekonomija Destrukcije: Velika Pljačka Naroda*. Beograd, Stubovi Kulture.

Durkheim, É. (1965). *The Division of Labor in Society*, translated by George Simpson. New York, Free Press.

Dyker, D. A. "Economic Overview: Serbia." *Europaworld*. Accessed March 8, 2012. http://www.europaworld.com/entry/rs.ec.

Džokić, A., Marc Neelen and Emil Jurcan (2012). *Sta je u Pazaru zajedničko/What Pazar has in Common(s)?* Novi Sad, Serbia, Daniel Print.

Edvin, P. (2013). *Zwangsmigration in Friedenszeiten? Jugoslawische Migrationspolitik und Die Auswanderung von Muslimen in die Türkei (1918–1966)*. Berlin: De Gruyter.

Erjavec, K. and Z. Volčič (2009). "Rehabilitating Milošević: Posthumous Coverage of the Milošević Regime in Serbian Newspapers." *Social Semiotics* 19(2): 125–147.

Faist, T. (2000). "Trans Nationalization in International Migration: Implications for the Study of Citizenship and Culture." *Ethnic and Racial Studies* 23(2): 218.

Faist, T. (2010). "Diaspora and Transnationalism: What Kind of Dance Partners?" In *Diaspora and Transnationalism – Concepts, Theories and Methods*, edited by R. Bauböck and T. Faist. Amsterdam, Amsterdam University Press: 11.

Faist, T. (2013). "Transnationalization and Development." In *Migration, Development, And Transnationalization: A Critical Stance*, edited by N. G. Schiller and T. Faist. New York, Berghahn Books.

Feinstein, A. (2011). *The Shadow World: Inside the Global Arms Trade*. New York, Farrar, Straus and Giroux.

Freie, J. F. (1998). *Counterfeit Community – The Exploitation of Our Longings for Connectedness*. Lanham, Rowman & Littlefield.

Geertz, C. (1974). "From the Native's Point of View: On the Nature of Anthropological Understanding." *Bulletin of the American Academy of Arts and Sciences* 28(1).

Geertz, C. (1998). "Deep Hanging Out." *New York Review of Books* 45(16): 69–72.

Geertz, C. (2017). *The Interpretation of Cultures*, 3rd edition. New York, Basic Books. Reprinted with permission of Johns Hopkins University Press.

Gillani, S.Y.M., et al. (2009). "Unemployment, Poverty, Inflation and Crime Nexus: Cointegration and Causality Analysis of Pakistan." *Pakistan Economic and Social Review*, 79–98.

Ginio, E. (2005). "Mobilizing the Ottoman Nation during the Balkan Wars (1912–1913): Awakening from the Ottoman Dream." *War in History* 12(2): 156–177.

Glaser, B. G. and A. L. Strauss (2008). *The Discovery of Grounded Theory: Strategies for Qualitative Research*. New Brunswick, NJ, Transaction.

Glenny, M. (2009). *McMafia: Seriously Organised Crime*. London, Vintage.

Glick-Schiller, N. (2010). "A Global Perspective on Transnational Migration: Theorizing Migration without Methodological Nationalism." In *Diaspora and Transnationalism – Concepts, Theories and Methods*, edited by R. Bauböck and T. Faist. Amsterdam, Amsterdam University Press: 111.

Goldstein, D. M. (2016). *Owners of the Sidewalk: Security and Survival in the Informal City*. Durham, NC, Duke University Press.

Gordy, E. D. (1999). *The Culture of Power in Serbia: Nationalism and the Destruction of Alternatives*. University Park, Pennsylvania State University Press.

Grandits, H. (2008). *Herrschaft und Loyalität in der spätosmanischen Gesellschaft – Das Beispiel der multikonfessionellen Herzegowina*. Wien, Boehlau Verlag.

Granovetter, M. (1985). "Economic Action and Social Structure: The Problem of Embeddedness." *American Journal of Sociology* 91(3): 481–510.

Group of Experts on Action against Trafficking in Human Beings (2018). *Report Concerning the Implementation of the Council of Europe Convention of Action against Trafficking in Human Beings by Serbia*. Strasbourg, Council of Europe.

Grubač, M. (2009). "Organizovani kriminal u Srbiji." *Zbornik radova Pravnog fakulteta u Splitu* 46(4): 701–709.

Guha-Khasnobis, B. and R. Kanbur (2006). *Linking the Formal and Informal Economy: Concepts and Policies*. Oxford, Oxford University Press.

Hajdinjak, M. (2002). *Smuggling in Southeast Europe. The Yugoslav Wars and the Development of Regional Criminal Networks in the Balkans*. Bulgaria, Center for the Study of Democracy.

Halbwachs, M. and L.A. Coser (1992). *On Collective Memory*. Chicago, University of Chicago Press.

Hall, R.C. (2011). "Balkan Wars (1912–1913)." In *The Encyclopedia of War*. Oxford, Wiley-Blackwell.

Hall, T. (2001). "The Geography of Transnational Organized Crime." In *The Geography of Transnational Organized Crime – Spaces Networks and Flows. Routledge Handbook of Transnational Organized Crime,* edited by F. Allum and S. Gilmour. New York, Routledge.

Hayden, R.M. (1996). "Reply." *Slavic Review* 55(1): 727.

Hersant, J. and A. Toumarkine (2005). "Hometown Organisations in Turkey: An Overview." *European Journal of Turkish Studies. Social Sciences on Contemporary Turkey* 2.

Höck, L. (2014). "Organizing and Interpreting Your Data." In *Doing Anthropological Research: A Practical Guide,* edited by N. Konopinski. London, Routledge: 105.

Hockenos, P. (2003). *Homeland Calling: Exile Patriotism and the Balkan Wars*. Ithaca, NY, Cornell University Press.

Hodžić, Š. (1958). "Migracije muslimanskog stanovništva iz Srbije u sjevernoistočnu Bosnu izmedju 1788–1862 godine." In *Članci i gradja za kulturnu istoriju istočne Bosne*. knj II, Tuzla: 65–143.

Höpken, W. (1997). " 'Blockierte Zivilisierung'? Staatsbildung, Modernisierung und ethnische Gewalt auf dem Balkan (19./20. Jahrhundert)." *Leviathan* 25(4): 518–538.

Hyvärinen, M. (2008). "Analyzing Narratives and Story-Telling." In *The Sage Handbook of Social Research Methods,* edited by P. Alasuutari, L. Bickman, and J. Brannen. Los Angeles, Sage: 452.

Ilcan, S. and I. Ebrary (2002). *Longing in Belonging: The Cultural Politics of Settlement*. Westport, CT, Praeger.

Imamović, M. (1998). *Historija Bošnjaka*. Bošnjačka Zajednica Kulture Sarajevo, Preporod.

Inalcik, H. (1952). "Od Stefana Dušana do Osmanskog carstva." *Orijentalni Institut u Sarajevu* (3–4): 23–54.

Inalcik, H. (1973). *The Ottoman Empire the Classical Age 1300–1600*. London, Phoenix Press.

Inalcik, H. (1993). *The Middle East and the Balkans under the Ottoman Empire*. Bloomington, Indiana University Press.

International Crisis Group (2005). "Serbia's Sandžak Still Forgotten." Europe Report No. 162–8, April.

Jeffrey, L. and N. Konopinski (2014). "Planning Your Research Project." In *Doing Anthropological Research: A Practical Guide*, edited by N. Konopinski. New York, Routledge: 33.

Jovanovic, P. and D. Sukovic (2002). "A Decade under Sanctions." *Transparency Serbia Documents*. http://www.transparentnost.org.rs.

Jovanović, S. (1932–1940). *Sabrana Dela, prvi deo*. Belgrade, Geca Kon.

Jovanović, V. (2007). "Iseljavanje Muslimana iz Vardarske Banovine – Izmedju Stijihe I Drzavne Akcije." In *Pisati Istoriju Jugoslavije – Vidjenje Srpskog Faktora*. Belgrade, Altera: 81.

Jovanović, V. (2013). *Iz FNRJ u Tursku*. Beograd, Peščanik.net.

Jovanović, V. (2015). "Land Reform and Serbian Colonization: Belgrade's Problems in Interwar Kosovo and Macedonia." *East Central Europe* 42(1): 87–103.

Kamberović, H. (2017). *Bošnjaci, Hrvati i Srbi u Bosni I Hercegovini i u Jugoslaviji – U Stalnom Procepu. Jugoslavija u Istorijskoj Perspektivi*. Beograd, Helsinški odbor za ljudska prava u Srbiji: 64–65.

Kennan, G. F. and International Commission to Inquire into the Causes and Conduct of the Balkan Wars (1993). *The Other Balkan Wars: A 1913 Carnegie Endowment Inquiry in Retrospect*. Washington, DC, Brookings Institution Press.

King-Savic, S. (2017). "Serbia's Sandžak: Caught Between Two Islamic Communities." In *Islam in Central Asia and Southeastern Europe*. University St. Gallen, Euxeinos.

Kirişci, K. (1995a). "New Patterns of Turkish Foreign Policy Behavior." In *Turkey – Political, Social, and Economic Challenges in the 1990s*. Leiden, E. J. Brill.

Kirişci, K. (1995b). "Post Second World War Immigration from Balkan Countries to Turkey." *New Perspectives on Turkey* 12: 61–77.

Kirk, J. and M. L. Miller (1986). *Reliability and Validity in Qualitative Research. Qualitative Research Methods Volume 1*. Newbury Park, CA, Sage: 38.

Kleemans, E. R. and H. G. van de Bunt (2002). "The Social Embeddedness of Organized Crime." *Transnational Organized Crime* 5(1): 19–36.

Kljajić, S. (2017). "Sandžak: The Balkans Region Where Turkey Is the Big Brother." *Deutsche Welle*. https://www.dw.com/en/sandzak-the-balkans-region-where-turkey-is-the-big-brother/a-36115582.

Knezević, A. and V. Tufegdžić (1995). *Kriminal Koji Je Izmenio Srbiju*. Beograd, B92.

Kornai, J. (1980). *Economics of Shortage*. Amsterdam, North-Holland.

Kostovicova, D. (2003). "Fake Levis, Real Threat." *Balkan Reconstruction Report* (08/18).

Крстић, Г.; Б. Стојановић анализа формалног и неформалног трзиста рада у србији, у прилози за јавну расправу о Институционалним реформама у Србији. Б. С. и. др, Београд: Центар за либерално-Демократске Студије: 31–33.

Kulturni Centar Novi Pazar. "Turski Kulturni Centar." Accessed February 5, 2017. http://www.kcnovipazar.com/prostori/turski-kulturni-centar/.

Law, J. (2010). *After Method: Mess in Social Science Research*. London, Routledge.

Ledeneva, A. V. (2018). *The Global Encyclopaedia of Informality*. Volume I. London, UCL Press.

Luhmann, N. (1994). *Die Wirtschaft der Gesellschaft*. Berlin, Suhrkamp.

Lyon, J. (2008). "Serbia's Sandžak under Milošević: Identity, Nationalism and Survival." *Human Rights Review* 9: 71–92.

Marković, S. (2001). *Country Report – Yugoslavia*. The APC European Internet Rights Project.

Marsden, M. (2016). *Trading Worlds – Afghan Merchants across Modern Frontiers*. London, Hurst.

McDevitt, A. (2016). *Fighting Corruption in the Western Balkans and Turkey: Priorities for Reform*, Transparency International – the Global Coalition against Corruption. https://images.transparencycdn.org/images/NISWBT_EN.pdf.

Merton, R. K. (1938). "Social Structure and Anomie." *American Sociological Review* 3(5): 672–682.

Milošević, M. (2000). "The Media Wars." In *Burn This House: The Making and Unmaking of Yugoslavia*, edited by J. Udovicki and J. Ridgeway. Durham, NC, Duke University Press: 109–130.

Morrison, K. (2006). *Marx, Durkheim, Weber: Formations of Modern Social Thought*. London, Sage.

Morrison, K. and E. Roberts (2013). *The Sandzak: A History*. London, Hurst.

Naylor, R. T. (1999a). *Economic Warfare – Sanctions, Embargo Busting, and their Human Cost*. Boston, Northeastern University Press.

Naylor, R. T. (1999b). *Patriots and Profiteers: On Economic Warfare, Embargo Busting, and State-Sponsored Crime*. Toronto, M&S.

Nielsen, C. A. (2010). "The Goalposts of Transition: Football as a Metaphor for Serbia's Long Journey to the Rule of Law." *Nationalities Papers* 38(1): 87–103.

Nielsen, C. A. (2016). "The State Security Service of the Republic of Serbia and Its Interaction with Ministries of Internal Affairs in Serb-Controlled Entities, 1990–1995." Research Report Prepared for the Case of Stanišić and Simatović (IT-03-69).

Ochs, E. et al. (2002). *Living Narrative: Creating Lives in Everyday Storytelling*. Cambridge, MA, Harvard University Press.

Office to Monitor and Combat Trafficking Persons (2017). *Trafficking in Persons Report*. U.S. Department of State.

Öktem, K. (2012). "Global Diyanet and Multiple Networks: Turkey's New Presence in the Balkans." *Journal of Muslims in Europe* 1(1): 27–58.

Oldenburg, R. (1989). *The Great Good Place*. New York, Paragon House.

Oldenburg, R. and D. Brissett (1982). "The Third Place." *Qualitative Sociology* 5(4): 265–284.

Østergaard-Nielsen, E. (2003). "The Politics of Migrants' Transnational Political Practices." *International Migration Review* 37(3).

Öztürk, A. E. (2016). "Turkey's Diyanet under AKP Rule: From Protector to Imposer of State Ideology?" *Southeast European and Black Sea Studies* 16(4): 619–635.

Öztürk, A. E. and S. Akgönül (2019). "Turkey-Forced Marriage or Marriage of Convenience with the Western Balkans." In *The Western Balkans in the World: Linkages and Relations with Non-western Countries*, edited by F. Bieber and N. Tzifakis. Milton Park, Routledge.

Ozyurek, E. (2007). *The Politics of Public Memory in Turkey: Modern Intellectual & Political History of the Middle East*. New York, Syracuse University Press.

Pačaric, S. (2016). *The Migration of Bosniaks – The Case of Sandžak*. Sarajevo, Center for Advanced Studies.

Pantic, D. (1997). "Internet in Serbia: From Dark Side of the Moon to the Internet Revolution." *First Monday* 2(4).

Parliamentary Assembly (1993). "Report on the United Nations Embargo against Serbia and Montenegro." http://assembly.coe.int/nw/xml/XRef/X2H-Xref-ViewHTML.asp?FileID=7216&lang=EN.

Pešić, V. (2012). *Divlje društvo-kako smo stigli dovde*. Beograd, Peščanik.

Petrović, V. (2013). "Uloga medija u učvršćenju vlasti Slobodana Miloševića." *Istorija 20. veka* (2): 183–204.

Pezo, E. (2012). "Komparativna analiza jugoslovensko-turske Konvencije iz 1938. i 'džentelmenskog sporazuma' iz 1953. Pregovori oko iseljavanja muslimana iz Jugoslavije." *Tokovi Istorije* 2: 114.

Pfeifer, C. and B. Šećeragić (2009). *Percepcija privatnog biznis sektora Sandžaka o političkom i ekonomskom ambijentu.* Evropski Pokret U Srbiji, Novi Pazar, Forum ZDF.

Polese, A., et al. (2019). *Governance beyond the Law: The Immoral, the Illegal, the Criminal.* Basingstoke, Palgrave Macmillan.

Portes, A. and W. Haller (2005). "The Informal Economy." In *The Handbook of Economic Sociology*, edited by N. J. Smesler and R. Swedberg. Princeton, NJ, Princeton University Press: 403–425.

Radniz, S. (2011). "Informal Politics and the State." *Comparative Politics* 43(3).

Radović, I., et al. (2008). "Human Trafficking Manual for Journalists." *OSCE* 21.

Ramet, S. P. (2002). *Balkan Babel: The Disintegration of Yugoslavia from the Death of Tito to the Fall of Milosevic.* London, Hachette.

Ramet, S. P. (2006). *The Three Yugoslavias State-building and Legitimation, 1918–2005.* Washington, DC, Woodrow Wilson Center Press; Bloomington, Indiana University Press.

Reeves, M. (2007). "18. Travels in the Margins of the State: Everyday Geography in the Ferghana Valley Borderlands." *Everyday Life in Central Asia: Past and Present*, 281–297.

Reeves, M. (2014). *Border Work – Spatial Lives of the State in Rural Central Asia.* Ithaca, NY, Cornell University Press.

Reisigl, M. and R. Wodak (2009). "The Discourse Historical Approach." In *Methods of Critical Discourse Analysis*, edited by R. Wodak and M. Meyer. Los Angeles, Sage.

Републички завод за статистику (2011). "Попис у Србији 2011, Преузимање пописних књига. Књига 1: Национална припадност." Accessed July 26, 2017. http://popis2011.stat.rs/?page_id=1103.

Ricoeur, P. (1990). *Time and Narrative.* Volume 3. Chicago, University of Chicago Press.

Ricoeur, P. (2004). *Memory, History, Forgetting.* Translated by Kathleen Blamey and David Pellauer. Chicago, University of Chicago Press.

Roitman, J. (2005). *Fiscal Disobedience: An Anthropology of Economic Regulation in Central Africa.* Princeton, NJ, Princeton University Press.

Ron, J. (2000). "Boundaries and Violence: Repertoires of State Action along the Bosnia/ Yugoslavia Divide." *Theory and Society* 29(5): 609–649.

Rossman, P. (1995). "Scooping the Dictator; Serbia's Last Independent Newspaper Fights for Its Life." *The Washington Post.*

Rouse, J. (2001). "Two Concepts of Practices." In *The Practice Turn in Contemporary Theory*, edited by R. T. Schatzki, K. Knorr Cetina, and E. Von Savigny. London, Routledge: 190–198.

Rouse, J. (2007). "Practice Theory. Division 1 Faculty Publications 43." http://wesscholar.wesleyan.edu/div1facpubs/43.

RUDAR 7 (2014). Vuk Drašković, speech at St. Peter's Church.

Saffron, I. (1993). "In Serbia, the News Is an Art Form." *The Philadelphia Inquirer.*

Safran, W. (1991). "Diasporas in Modern Societies: Myths of Homeland and Return." *Diaspora: A Journal of Transnational Studies* 1(1): 83.

Schad, T. (2015). "The Rediscovery of the Balkans? A Bosniak-Turkish Figuration in the Third Space between Istanbul and Sarajevo." Istanbul Bilgi University, Istanbul.

Shove, E., et al. (2012). *The Dynamics of Social Practice: Everyday Life and How It Changes.* Los Angeles, Sage.

Sik, E. and C. Wallace (1999). "The Development of Open-air Markets in East-Central Europe." *International Journal of Urban and Regional Research* 23(4): 697–714.

Smith, A. L. (2004). "Heteroglossia, 'Common Sense', and Social Memory." *American Ethnologist* 31(2): 251–269.

Sörensen, J. S. (2006). "The Shadow Economy, War and State Building: Social Transformation and Re-stratification in an Illiberal Economy (Serbia and Kosovo)." *Journal of Contemporary European Studies* 14(3): 317–351.

Squire, C. (2004). "Narrative Genres." In *Qualitative Research Practice*, edited by C. Seale, G. Gobo, J. F. Gubrium, and D. Silverman. London, Sage: 116.

Sredl, K. C., et al. (2017). "The Arizona Market: A Marketing Systems Perspective on Pre- and Post-war Developments in Bosnia, with Implications for Sustainable Peace and Prosperity." *Journal of Macromarketing* 37(3): 300–316.

Statistical Office of the Republic of Serbia. *Labor Force Survey.* Belgrade. https://www. stat.gov.rs.

Sugar, P. (2006). *Southeastern Europe under Ottoman Rule, 1354–1804.* Seattle, University of Washington Press.

танасковић, д. (2010). *неоосманизам – повратак турске на балкан.* Београ, службени гласник републике србије: 105.

Tanner, M. (1993). "Belgrade Sacks Anti-Milosevic Journalists." *Independent.* London.

Tepavac, M. (2006). "Jači od Države. Glasilo gradjanskog samooslobodjanja – Republika Protiv stihije straha, mržnje i nasilja." http://www.republika.co.rs/390-391/03.html.

Thieme, T. (2017). "The Hustle Economy: Informality, Uncertainty and the Geographies of Getting By." *Progress in Human Geography* 42(4): 529–548.

TIKA (2013). *TIKA Continues Operation in Serbia.* Turkish Cooperation and Coordination Agency. http://www.tika.gov.tr/en/news/tika_continues_operations_in_serbia-8722.

Türköz, M. (2010). "The Social Life of the State's Fantasy: Turkish Family Names in 1934." Middle East Studies Association Meeting, San Francisco.

Turner, S. (1994). *The Social Theory of Practices: Tradition, Tacit Knowledge and Presuppositions.* Cambridge, Polity Press.

Turner, V. (1969). "Liminality and Communitas." *The Ritual Process: Structure and Anti-structure* 94: 130.

UCL SEES. "The Global Informality Project." http://www.in-formality.com/wiki/index.php?title=Global_Informality_Project.

UCL SEES. "In/Form: 'Exploring Tactical Maneuvering between Formal and Informal Institutions in Balkan Societies'." https://www.ucl.ac.uk/ssees/research/funded-research-projects/inform/home.html.

Valtchinova, G. (2006). "Kinship and Transborder Exchange at the Bulgarian-Serbian Border in the Second Half of the 20th Century." *European Journal of Turkish Studies. Social Sciences on Contemporary Turkey* (4).

Van Maanen, J. (1988). *Tales of the Field: On Writing Ethnography.* Chicago, University of Chicago Press.

Vasić, M. (2005). *Atentat na Zorana.* Beograd, Politika B92 Vreme Narodna Knjiga.

Vasić, M. (2014). "Cane Subotić i 'duvanska mafija'." *Peščanik.* https://pescanik.net/cane-subotic-i-duvanska-mafija/.

Vaughan, D. (2008). "Bourdieu and Organizations: The Empirical Challenge." *Theory and Society* 37(1): 65–81.

Vijeću, O. "Bošnjačko nacionalno vijeće." Accessed October 31, 2017. http://www.bnv.org.rs/o-nama/.

Voloder, L. (2013). "Secular Citizenship and Muslim Belonging in Turkey: Migrant Perspectives." *Ethnic and Racial Studies* 36(5): 838–856.

Voltaire (François Marie Arouet) and T. Besterman (2005). *Miracles and Idolatry*. London, Penguin Books.

Von Lampe, K. (2015). "The Practice of Transnational Organized Crime." In *Routledge Handbook of Transnational Organized Crime*, edited by F. Allum and S. Gilmour. London, Taylor and Francis Group: 187.

Vreme, N. P. and B92 (2013). "Jedinica – Film o Crvenim beretkama ili kako je ubijen Djindjić 1–3." https://www.youtube.com/watch?v=n-UO7lm_5S4.

Vuković, S. (2000). "Ekonomska Struktura Društva I Kontinuitet Vlasti U Srbiji." *Sociološki pregled* 1–2: 9.

Walker, J. W. (2012). "Shadows of Empire: How Post-Imperial Successor States Shape Memories." PhD dissertation, Public and International Affairs Department, Princeton University.

Watmough, S. P. and A. E. Öztürk (2018). "From 'Diaspora by Design' to Transnational Political Exile: The Gülen Movement in Transition." *Politics, Religion & Ideology* 19(1): 33–52.

Weiss, T. G. (2007). *The United Nations and Changing World Politics*. Boulder, CO, Westview Press.

Welzer, H. (2017). *Wir sind die Mehrheit: für eine offene Gesellschaft*. Frankfurt am Main, Fischer Taschenbuch.

White, H. (1982). "The Politics of Historical Interpretation: Discipline and De-sublimation." *Critical Inquiry* 9(1): 113–137.

Wikileaks Cable (2007). "id= 07BELGRADE997_a, Djindjic Assassination Still Political Football." https://wikileaks.org/plusd/pdf/?df=43308.

Wodak, R. and M. Meyer (2009). "Critical Discourse Analysis: History, Agenda, Theory and Methodology." In *Methods of Critical Discourse Analysis*, edited by R. Wodak and M. Meyer. London, Sage: 2.

Woodward, S. L. (1995). *Balkan Tragedy: Chaos and Dissolution after the Cold War*. Washington, DC, Brookings Institution Press.

YUNUS EMRE ENSTİTÜSÜ. https://turkce.yee.org.tr.

Zdravkovski, A. (2017). *Politics, Religion and the Autonomy Movement in Sandžak (1990–2014)*. PhD dissertation, Institute for Sociology and Statistics, Norwegian University of Science and Technology.

Articles cited

Aksić, M. (1994). "Нема наивне дроге." *Novosti*.

Dinkić, V. (1994a). "Trka za Markama." *Novosti*.

Dinkić, V. (1994b). "подземље пере руке." *Novosti*.

E.B.H. (1993). "нема шта нема." *Novosti*.

J. C. (1993). "Нови прелаз риђица." *Novosti*.

Milić, M. (1994). "из цезве кипи цена." *Novosti*.

M. M. (1993). "нема робног промета." *Novosti*.

N/A. (1994a). "Снови о великој Турској." *Novosti*.

N/A. (1994b). "одмотава се српско-муслиманско трговачко клупко на Теслићком ратишту – Рworkови пуним- шверца." *Novosti*.

N/A. (1994c). "дрога за шанком. дрога за шанком." *Novosti*.

Nedeljković, D. (1993). "Динар брише нуле Вечјерне." *Novosti.*
Nedeljković, D. (1994). "Београд постаје највеће тржиште дроге на балкану – Хероин из – Немачке." *Novosti.*
Nićivorović, M. (1994). "Статус или – Батине/статус или новац." *Novosti.*
P. M. (1994). "Нема ништа од Санџака." *Novosti.*
Pasić, S. (1993). "Кроз Руке – Милион Марака." *Novosti.*
Pavlović, P. (1994). "Стари Рас Нови Пазар." *Novosti.*
Sekulović, M. (1994). "побуну плаћали турци." *Novosti.*
Stevanović, M. (1994). "дроги – дупла рампа." *Novosti.*
Z.V.L. (1994). "шверц у излогу, порез у – џепу." *Novosti.*

UN resolutions

United Nations. (1992a). Resolution 713: Socialist Federal Rep. of Yugoslavia (September 25).
United Nations. (1992b). Resolution 721: Socialist Federal Rep. of Yugoslavia (November 27).
United Nations. (1992c). Resolution 724: Socialist Federal Rep. of Yugoslavia (December 15).
United Nations. (1992d). United Nations Resolution 757 (November 27).
United Nations. (1995). A/50/60-S/1995/1, Supplement to an Agenda for Peace: Position Paper of the Secretary-General on the Occasion of the Fiftieth Anniversary of the United Nations, para. 70.
United Nations Security Council. (1992). United Nations Security Council Resolution 757.

Index

Page numbers followed by 'n' indicate a note on the corresponding page.

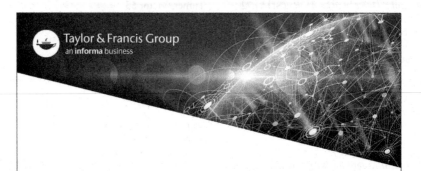

Printed in the United States
by Baker & Taylor Publisher Services